LAW, HEALTH AND MEDICAL REGULATION

Acknowledgements

Never let it be said that compiling and editing a collection of essays is easy. We owe a great deal to the people who have assisted us. In particular, many thanks to Amanda Godfrey and Carole Fox who gave very generously of their time over Christmas 1991; without them it could not have been produced. Thanks also to those who were subjected to our difficulties in meeting the deadline: Jo Shaw, Danielle Go and others.
We gratefully acknowledge the Howard League and Blackwell for permission to reproduce McHale and Young's essay on *Rights, Policy amd the Dilemmas of the HIV Prisoner*, in which they hold the copyright.

Law, Health and Medical Regulation

Edited by

Sally Wheeler

and

Shaun McVeigh

Dartmouth

Aldershot • Brookfield USA • Hong Kong • Singapore • Sydney

Published by
Dartmouth Publishing Company Ltd
Gower House
Croft Road
Aldershot
Hants GU11 3HR
England

Dartmouth Publishing Company Ltd
Distributed in the United States by
Ashgate Publishing Company
Old Post Road
Brookfield
Vermont 05036
USA

A CIP catalogue record for this book is available from the British Library and the US Library of Congress

ISBN 1 85521 283 8

Printed and bound in Great Britain by
Billing and Sons Ltd, Worcester

Contents

Introduction

Perhaps there was a time when introducing a collection of essays entitled *Law, Health and Medical Regulation*, that the work contained therein would respond to a unifying theme. In a period dominated by the possibility of changing regimes of regulation, and health, it might be thought that the rewards would be high for anybody capable of encapsulating the multiplicity of issues in health and medical regulation under one title. Few, however, would trust the purposes of such an enterprise, let alone its results.

We begin this introduction, and thus end the book, with the suspicion that the title will have to betray its promise of moving from law to medical regulation by simply passing through health. There is no satisfactory way of organising the words in the title, let alone the events they are called on to explain. Yet, with any work that seeks to address law and medical regulation there is always the belated recognition of the struggle to understand what it is that is being regulated. In so far as the essays collected here can be said to share an emphasis, it is in the way that law and medical regulation shape the experience of health, not just as an institutionally located service but as part of 'our' shared subjectivities. This is where we make our beginning.

While lawyers might find it gratifying to have their suspicions confirmed, that law must be at the centre of any discussion of responsibility in regulation. Few others could be convinced that law has anything other than a peripheral role to play in the regulation of medicine and health. The real framing of regulatory issues of health and medicine is taking place elsewhere by the medical and biological scientists and technicians who are constantly recreating the potentialities and threats of health care; by the accountants, economists and health care workers who are disputing the ways of organising and the evaluating health; and amongst the politicians, patients and others who have reason to engage with the institutions and practices of health. Indeed it would be a little surprising if the situation were otherwise. As a dominant language of social organisation, law has been of declining importance since the eighteenth century. Yet law and legal concepts still have a powerful ordering role in almost all regulation, sometimes as a distinct enterprise bringing thought and action to judgment before its tribunal; at other times, law, itself, is frequently indistinguishable from other practices of regulation accounting daily life. Of necessity, all the work presented here reflects both aspects of this relation.

Jonathon Montgomery's essay *Doctors' Handmaidens*, provides a powerful example of the way general principles of law continue to create and structure what otherwise might be seen to be an inevitable or even natural relationship between doctors as clinical experts and nurses as subordinate providers of care. By concentrating on this narrow aspect of the many legal relations available, Montgomery is able to show how general legal principles have been used to support entrenched hierarchies within the profession in the name of clinical autonomy. For Montgomery, current legal regulation clearly favours the continued emphasis on the technologically based practices of doctors at the expence of other health care workers and their caring practices. This is achieved through the distressingly simple process of attributing legal responsibility only to doctors. At a more general level Robert Lee's essay, *Doctors as Allocators*, points to the ways in which such attributions of responsibility and autonomy necessarily result in a failure of accountability over many resource allocations at their point of delivery.

Lee's essay serves to highlight many of the differences between legal and regulatory thought without simply severing the relation between the two. For if he makes a strong plea for increased accountability, he also points to the ways in which law is increasingly led to render an account, as judicial activity (often belatedly and inaccurately) incorporates policy issues as the calculus of its decisions.

If legal thought takes precedence in this collection for institutional reasons, then the essays presented on medical regulation serve to show the extent to which it has already adopted regulatory thinking. Crispin Jenkinson and Brian Wilkinson's analysis of the use of subjective quality of life questionnaires both exposes the critical limitations and assumptions concerning the evaluation of pain and suffering in negligence law, as well as pointing the way to reform. The question of accounting for the suffering of others is taken up at a more general level in Anne McBride's critical interrogation of the Medical Audit. By concentrating on the twin aspects of procedures for account and peer review, McBride emphasises the potential for the Audit both to restructure relations of accountability through the normalising capabilities of standardised peer review, and to connect to the rhetoric and economics of competition and the politics of health.

Buttressed between law and medical regulation, health appears as something of an absent referent. Sometimes it appears as nothing more than the procedural endpoint of regulation, at others it is presented as a fundamental moral good. Yet over the last twenty five years feminists and feminist analyses have persistently emphasised the ways in which legal and regulatory practices have participated in the construction of relations of health, sexuality and the family, along with more general relations of gender, race and class. Josephine Shaw's essay, *Regulating Sexuality*, carries out a comparative analysis of the regulatory regimes for non-consensual sterilisation in Germany and the UK. Through a discussion of the detailed workings of the two jurisdictions, she shows how the German legislation both establishes a more procedurally accountable regulatory practice and continues to occlude the subject matter of its regulation, female sexuality and reproductive rights. This is very much the theme of Jean McHale and Alison Young's work on HIV positive prisoners and Derek Morgan and Linda Nielsen's comparative analysis of the regulation of embryo and infertility research in Denmark and the UK.

Much of the critical resistance of these essays lies not in the promotion of oppositional rhetorics, but in the response to the meticulous detail of regulation and the tracing of its effects in the social body and gendered relations. In outlining the problem of the 'Europeanisation' of ethics as part of wider systems of moral regulation, Morgan and Nielson raise the possibility of an ethics that thinks health and regulation otherwise. At this point the law is returned to in its relation with ethics. The opening essays of this collection seek to elaborate this relation, not as part of a despairing attempt to establish an ethics capable of founding social action, but to rework the body (lived or otherwise) into the discourses of law, health and medical regulation. In responding to the tragic body inscribed in relations and theories of (Kantian) autonomy, Costas Douzinas and Shaun McVeigh, seek to counter the dispersal of the experience of the pain and suffering of ill-health in the technologies of health and law, by recognising an ethics of alterity. Calliope Farsides on the other hand, explores the other founding concept of modern ethics and law, that of self-ownership as a (Lockean) property right. Together they offer a reminder of the ethical body against which law, health and medical regulation comes to be thought.

The Tragic Body: The Inscription of Autonomy in Medical Ethics and Law.

Costas Douzinas* and Shaun McVeigh**

Introduction

It is hardly possible to think of any ethico-legal discourse concerning medical practice that does not, at some stage, come to be thought of in terms of autonomy. In general terms the modern conception of autonomy is taken to be the privileged site of the encounter between pathos and logos; between the singularity of the demand to alleviate the suffering in the other, and the requirements, of law and justice, for a judgment in the name of a general and universal reason (ethical and legal). At a more particular level, autonomy acts as a conduit through which access to the core of the ethical, legal and the medical discourse can be sought, if not grasped, as the law of self-rule. And yet the term 'autonomy' occupies a far from unequivocal position in such thought, not the least problem is its status as a self-referential law that has no determinate place within the legal order itself. It is at once both the title of a particular medico-ethico-legal discourse and its key term of organisation. It regulates the minutiae of every ethico-legal encounter in medical practice and yet occupies a position of utmost philosophical generality. Indeed it is in many ways the exemplary term of modern social thought.

This essay sets out to investigate how this allegiance of autonomy to what we understand as ethico-legal thought, both in itself and as a medical matter, has come about; and to ask who decides the conditions under which pathos and logos are deemed to meet (as pathology). Our purpose here is not to answer either of these questions directly, but to instigate a genealogy of autonomy, a tracing of its coming to be. To do so we return the question of autonomy to the present, as part of the problem of the Kantian tribunal of reason and the law of the law (the categorical imperative). In short, autonomy, is reintroduced as a metaphysic of the self which, as we will argue, will bring with it, not only versions of the freewilled body of autonomy, but also the memory of a tragic body in law. It is this haunting of memory to which we address ourselves. The pragmatic argument of this essay is that unless autonomy, as the embodiment of pathos and logos, is understood in relation to the inescapable force of the law, current concerns with patient subjectivity, the 'lived body' and the government of the self, will miss their bodily targets. Or, rather, they will hit them with such force that they will intensify the subjection and regulation they seek to resist.

The autonomous self

The modern conception of will and its psychological corollary, free will, find one of their most complete elaborations in the work of Kant, who produced a formulation of great significance for the realm of practical judgment, both as law and as morality. The move, in ontology, ethics and concepts of art and imagination, from their pre-modern understanding to their modern version is long, tortuous, and cannot be summarised here.[1] However, it is broadly true to say following a felicitous presentation of the move from the ancients to the moderns that modern man is no longer conceived as a mirror of some superior and external reality but as a lamp, a source and centre of light illuminating the world.

Modern ontology does not understand Being as a product of a divine first cause nor reality as a copy of a pre-existing original. Being is now seen as productive and man becomes the centre, creator and cause of actions and things, and the bestower of meaning upon a profane reality. Imagination and its produce, art, are no longer conceived as resemblances of a transcendent reality of forms, nor the artist as a craftsman who imitates the *demiourge*. On the contrary, the model of the modern artist is that of the inventor whose imagination, in its ability to coordinate the faculties, becomes itself transcendental (Derrida, 1989a). Finally in the realm of praxis the concept of agency becomes central. The subject is enthroned as the free agent, as the immediate source of activity and

2

the cause of actions that emanate from it. The modern self fulfils itself in what it[2] does, our actions and our work express our true existence and as a result we take responsibility for the consequences of our activities.

The modern Will is always directed towards an outside. Action projects the sovereign self onto the world both in its orientation towards others and in its work that bestows value and mastery on nature. The self as agent recognises himself as the centre of decision making with a power that springs neither from emotions nor from pure intelligence. The power of will is a unique type of power which Descartes describes as the same in us as it is in God. Power of will knows no theoretical, only empirical limits; it is the power of choice, of choice between yes and no, an indivisible sovereignty of the self. This power finds its perfect manifestation in decision.

In making a decision self becomes an agent, an autonomous and responsible subject, the sign of whom is to be found in those external manifestations, in actions that can be imputed to him. If there is no self without free will, similarly there is not action without its agent. 'There can be no agent without this power that links the action to the subject who decides upon it and thereby assumes full responsibility for it' (Vernant and Vidal-Naquet, 1990, p.50).

These statements appear to be commonsensical descriptions of how we understand our own place in the world but also not inaccurate representations of the law's attitude towards causation and the attribution of responsibility. Acts are natural extensions of the human self and responsibility, moral or legal, follows on from the 'irrefutable fact' that man is free to cause to happen in the external world what he wills.

It is the self evidence of some of those truisms about the character of will, causation and responsibility that has come under increasing strain in the field of medical law and ethics. We would want to argue that natural model was right from before its inception a myth, one which is constantly involved in the forceful re-inscription of relations of self and other. Recent debates in medical ethics and law can help us bring to the surface the ambiguous character of will and autonomy, and the tragic nature of the body

3

as the site of medical intervention, and help us move towards an ethics open to the call of the suffering other. We trace this through the sites of the social thought of modernity: the white mythology of rationality, the technologies of bodily regulation, and (redemptive) capacities of practical reason.

The social thought of modernity

Modern social theory can be traced back to the Cartesian meditations and their inward turn. Descartes recognised that knowledge is shrouded in universal doubt, and that the only certainty is the doubting self. The phenomenal world of reality is external to the subject, but it can be approached on the analogy of the subject's understanding of himself. Behind every *cogito* (I know) there is an *ego* (I), 'the apodictically certain and last basis of judgment upon which all radical philosophy must be grounded' (Husserl, 1964,p.7).

After Descartes, philosophy becomes a meditation on the subject and its relationship with its opposite, the object. This co-ordinated split and the aspiration to transcend the apparent opposition have been at the heart of modern thought and philosophy ever since. The critical philosophy of Kant was the first to bring together subject and object under the reign of reason.

Kant's *Critique of Practical Reason* (1788, 1956a) is the foundation stone of modern jurisprudence. In it Kant sets out to deduce the (moral) law in the same way that he deduces knowledge in the *Critique of Pure Reason* (1781, 1964). Kant's starting point was the experience of personal, social and intellectual fragmentation of early modernity. His interest was both philosophical and political. He wanted to show how freedom and reason were inseparable in their common concern to enlighten man and release him from his self-incurred tutelage, his 'inability to make use of his understanding without direction from another' (Kant, 1965, p.3). Reason, accordingly, has two forms. In the theoretical domain the subject acquires knowledge by using a priori forms of intuition (space and time) and categories of understanding (identity/difference, cause/effect, necessity/contingency, substance/accident) to construct the manifold data of experience as coherent and unified.

Practical reason on the other hand helps unite the personality by subjecting conflicting inclinations and desires to the a priori moral law. Reason acts as the principle that unites the subject and the world. When Kant turns to the law, he asks it by what right is it the law? From where does its authority derive? Why should people follow it? The law, like reason, is subjected to a tribunal which tries to derive its legitimacy through the same procedure. Here, however, Kant notices a fundamental asymmetry. In the case of theoretical reason, the critical meta-language that deduces the principles of knowledge (mainly causality) is homologous to the language of its object (the operations of a scientist extracting axioms from his experience and experiments). With law, this is impossible. Moral law does not follow causality. Morality is itself a cause of acts; nor can the principle of law be deduced from the recitation or examination of any particular laws.

Kant now reverses his procedure. If the 'You must' cannot be derived, it is itself a 'fact of reason' and not of experience and its principle helps deduce freedom. The law prescribes through an inscrutable power, freedom, which is the practical aspect of reason. But free and rational will acts according to the law as posited in the categorical imperative: '[a]ct in such a way that the maxim of your will can always be valid as the principle of universal legislation' (Kant, 1956a, p.142), and again 'act so that you treat humanity, whether in your person or in that of an other, always as an end' (Kant, 1956b, p.47). The moral law acts as if it is a 'universal law of nature'.

This law is rather strange; it is imperative, a rule (act in such a way...), but its commandment upon the will is to follow a pure form, the form of legality (the principle of the action will always be valid, in the form of a universal norm). While it forces and obligates the will, it also emanates from it. Kantian autonomy makes modern man the subject *of* the law in a double sense, he is the legislator (the subject that makes the law) and the legal subject (who obeys the law on condition that it has participated in its legislation). And again as a quasi-law of nature, the moral law appears as both regularity, the universal interconnection of things, and as a purposeful order in the tradition of natural law. All the concepts, conceptual oppositions and strategies of modern jurisprudence can be traced to this 'foundational' text: form and substance, validity and value, regularity and law, sovereign and subject, legality and morality.

Gillian Rose in the *Dialectics of Nihilism* (1984) argues that all metaphysical thought after Kant has become a jurisprudence. The Kantian critical enterprise itself is a legal procedure. Reason is arraigned before a tribunal in which it itself is the judge and is asked to justify its possessions and title. The judgment of the tribunal follows the categories of Roman law and introduces its logic at the heart of reason. Rationality, while presented as an absolute end, is a reworking of the Justinian distinction of law into persons, things and actions.

The Kantian move launches the 'antinomy of law', the dual implication of rule and regularity, in the corpus of postKantian thought and demarcates its horizon and strategies. Philosophy as jurisprudence is set to veer between an exploration of form and validity (positivism) or of substance and value (hermeneutics) and maybe dreams of the reconciliation of the two in a totality of spirit or a future becoming. Jurisprudence, on the other hand, becomes an uninteresting metaphysics.

Hegel is the main representative of the third approach. He shares with Kant the aspiration to reconcile the personal, social and intellectual fragmentation ushered in by modernity but he believes that Kant has failed in all three critiques to mediate the opposites. The aim of speculative philosophy is to establish the 'union' of union and nonunion and the 'identity' of identity and difference.

> The sole interest of reason is to sublate...rigid opposites. But this does not mean that reason is altogether opposed to opposition and limitation. For the necessary dichotomy is *one* factor of life... What reason opposes, rather, is just the absolute fixity that the understanding gives to the dichotomy; and it does so all the more if the absolute opposites themselves originated in reason (Hegel, 1977, pp.90-91).

In *The Science of Logic* (1969), Hegel carefully analyses identity and difference, the basic categories behind all the Kantian

6

oppositions, and concludes that each contains in itself its opposite and both are united in a dialectical structure which is present in everything that exists. The knowledge of this structure emerges gradually as all aspects of subjectivity and objectivity are progressively reconciled. Objectivity is only a moment in the development and self-realisation of a universal subject. This absolute subject, the spirit, is the entire history of the West understood as an evolving totality.

Thus, Hegel and after him Marx historicised the conflict of law by transporting it from philosophy to the constitution of civil society and of the legal subject. The modern legal form of property and right gives rise to the separation of state from society, public from private law, a realm of politics, the common good and citizenship from that of needs, individual egotism and economic life; finally it leads to the constitution of formally equal legal subjects, bearers of rights, and to their separation from individuals as subjected, as 'commodities', part of the labour force. It is this juridical opposition of free subjects and subjected things which characterise the core of the speculative thinking of modernity.

In Hegel, the splits and confrontations come finally to rest as rational consciousness recognises itself in the becoming of the spirit. Reality is declared ideal and as the *telos* of history. Reason, the spirit of the western world recognises the history of metaphysics as the slow journey towards its own self-consciousness. It has turned full circle from its pre-modern beginnings and has declared its own triumph. In Marx, on the other hand, the reconciliation of state and society, and necessity and freedom, is promised in the future unfolding of history.

After Hegel's dialectic, which claims to bring the drama of the law to an end, the move from the philosophy of history to sociology repeats the legal antinomy in the concept of society. Rose (1984) argues that the epigones of Nietzsche and Heidegger can do no more than dream the world as a legalism without law, their writings nothing but self-defeating legislation. We are condemned to repeat the same moves and the same mistakes, we can escape neither law nor metaphysics. All the categories of the postmetaphysical thought, structure in Saussure, power in Foucault, repetition in Deleuze, differance in Derrida reveal 'a speculative jurisprudence: a story of the identity and non-identity of law and metaphysics' (Rose, 1984, p.208). The Kantian discovery, that the form of reason and the form of law imply each other, cannot be overcome. The method and the antinomies set up in this foundational move are lurking behind all these attempts to think after the end of metaphysics.

It would seem the Kantian tribunal and the Hegelian system, in their overwhelming all-inclusiveness, appear to have preempted any rebellion against them, and to have laid down the law with some finality. Indeed if there is something new to be said about the alliance between metaphysics and jurisprudence, that dates from the morning that Kant's critical tribunal opened its proceedings in *re reason*, it is only the belated acknowledgement of this situation.

The Kantian tribunal can be the starting point in addressing the question of law from an ethical perspective. But the questioning will focus on certain absences that characterise the critical process and its outcome. Three factors, however, determine our elliptic encounter with this tribunal. The categorical command is the law that stands behind both moral and positive law and makes them law; it is the law of the law. And yet this essence of the law is simply asserted. It can neither be derived nor deduced (Lyotard, 1988, pp.118-127).

Secondly, being categorical this law of law has no history and no origin. The categorical is the formal presentation of the absolute. As such, the law of the law exists even behind those distinctions of Roman law that Rose thinks lead to its discovery. Finally, the law cannot be known as such. It can be approximated, one can act *as if* he knew it, *as if* the law was a universalisable maxim. Of course we are involved with laws all the time, we follow 'Thou shall' and 'Thou shall not'. But in so doing we act 'as if the law had no history or at any rate no longer depended on its historical presentation' (Derrida, 1989, p.134). We are tempted to write the history of this non-history. For we know that we can have access only to the simulations of law, we can know it only by analogy in its narratives and fictions.

Critiques of will and autonomy

Let us have another look at the Kantian tribunal and its distinctions between the faculties of pure and practical reason. According to the *Critique of Pure Reason* (Kant, 1964), the data of experience and the metalanguage of scientific principles are homologous making the passage from observation to theory unproblematic. But in ethics the object language of prescription ('You must ..') and the metalanguage of the realm of moral norms are not isomorphic. The Good is not given and cannot be apprehended in experience nor are moral judgments the affective reactions of moral agents to empirical properties. The knowledge of a state of affairs cannot be the basis of moral knowledge and action. In a move that resembles the operations of the aesthetic in the *Critique of Judgement*, Kant (1973) tries to deduce the ethical command by analogy, as if it were a fact of nature amenable to reason. '[T]he "you must" of obligation is assimilated, via what Kant calls the "type" (i.e. the form of conformity to the law in general) to the "I know" of knowledge and the "I can" of freedom' (Bennington, 1988, p.16).

The categorical imperative asks me to act as if the maxim of any will may become a principle of universal legislation. The recognition of will's involvement in action is a typically modern move which distinguishes practical from pure reason. But, the injunction to universalise the maxim of the will presents the world as a totality. To act on principles that would be acceptable and willed to govern the actions of all rational people is to assume that self's desires and actions are compatible and coherent with those of all others. The radical first step of the Kantian moral philosophy comes to an end in the assertion that we live in a totalisable community of reason. Furthermore, the categorical imperative installs self as both legislator and subject, sender of the law and its addressee. This is the modern conception of autonomy or self-determination, the other side of will's enthronement. Within the legal system, laws from now on will be considered as just if they are prescribed by those who will have to obey them.

A white mythology

The Kantian conception of autonomy then depends upon a universalisable and rational community which both legislates the law and is subjected to it. We are autonomous in the strong sense that we follow the law we give ourselves. This move must necessarily be repeated in the text of the law, as a metaleptic act of self-foundation, that is as a (rhetorical) reversal of cause and effect (Rousseau, 1953, p.32), in which what comes after (the legislator) is presented as the source of his law (de Man, 1979; Goodrich, 1990; Douzinas and Warrington, 1991b; Bennington, 1990; Seuss 1957, p.11). In this sense, as de Man's (1979) analysis of Rousseau's *Social Contract* has shown, from the very moment of its institution the (constitutional) structures of autonomy are fictional (although none the less effective for that). That what is established as pure will (the contract) has at its core a performative narrative creating the participants in the agreement.

The foundation of meaning has been removed from the realm of transcendance and placed in society; similarly the principle of will and action has been transferred from the divine and the mechanical to the sovereign self. But at the same time the first signs a disenchantment with the world can be felt. The legislator/subject of the law of freedom is an imposter, a trickster put on stage by the operations of rhetoric. What concerns us here is another type of deceit, one that the assumed 'we' of the rational community introduces. The 'we' implied by the categorical norm can never be coextensive with the 'we' of the prescriptive statements of law of an actual nation-state. Nation-states are demarcated through territorial boundaries, and through that, automatically exclude other states and people from the role of the legislator. The 'we', the rational community to which the autonomous subject must refer in order to formulate the law, becomes a mirage, once any of the empirical characteristics of the historical legislator and subject are added to it. The principle of autonomy is created in the moulding together (in the letter of the law) of the split self and the split community that modernity introduces against the horizon of an alleged universal community. But all empirical law is bound by sovereignty and territory and therefore excludes from the 'we' of its legislator, everyone who does not fall within its borders.

The two most far-ranging attempts of modernity to make the 'we' of the universal rational community and of the empirical nation-state coincide, can be found in the discourse of human rights and the law of imperialism. The subject of human rights as exemplified by Art 1 of the *Universal Declaration of Human Rights*, which only repeats the universalistic claims of the *Declaration de Droits de L'Homme de Citoyen* states that all 'men are born equal in rights and in dignity'. Human nature is totally abstract and universal and is being parcelled out in equal shares that belong to everyone, to all people in all eternity. Once the slightest introduction of empirical and historical material is made upon this abstract human nature, equally shared and equally free for all, once we move from the legal subject to the embodied person, universal human nature retreats. In other words, when we move from the abstract legal subject of the Kantian discourse and the declarations of human rights to the concrete human being in the world, the discourse of human rights is seen for what it is: an indeterminate discourse of legitimation, or of rebellion. The community of human rights is universal but imaginary. While the draughtsmen of the Universal Declaration, with a certain loss of philosophical understanding or historical sensitivity that accompanies the twentieth century, may have believed that they were acting on behalf of the whole human kind, the French revolutionaries were much more aware of the philosophical necessities. It was they, as representatives of the French nation, that were enunciating the discourse of universality. Nations owe their existence and uniqueness to narratives, emblems and symbols. There has never been a nationalism in the world that has successfully based its claim to nationhood and independence on abstract claims of right and universality, nor following our analysis, could there be. Nations owe their existence to the repeated narrations of their origins, continuity and tradition.[3]

The French National Assembly of 1789 acted as a typical Kantian Legislator. It split itself in two parts: the philosophical part legislated for the whole world, the historical and empirical part for the only terrritory and people they could, France and its dependents. In so doing, it attempted to make the discourse of universal right part of the foundation myth of modern France. As Lyotard puts it, from that point onwards it remains unknown whether the law is French or pan-human (Lyotard, 1988, p.147). A similar analysis could apply to the American revolutionaries and their Declaration of Independence (Derrida, 1986).

A second possibility suggests itself in the French and American revolutionary moves. The Kantian notion of autonomy is premised upon the power of the national legislature to impose its law upon the universe, the alien, the colonial, the third (world) in the name of the community of reason. All wars from that point onwards are in a certain sense imperial wars, they are civil wars in the cause of uniting the national legislator with the universal human subject. The purpose of the empire is to expand the community of citizens subjected to the law of nation and make it coextensive with the whole world. To be sure, those thirds subjected to imperial law are not and can never become its legislators, they can never be autonomous in a Kantian sense. In short, a white mythology is enacted (Derrida, 1982; Spivak, 1987; Young, 1990). The other side of the universal legal subject, of equality and autonomy, of law's formalism and imperative (categorical command) is the necessary inequality and the lack of autonomy of the other of nation.

In the turn from political philosophy of nations towards the ethics and the law of medical professions, many of the problems of the nation-state as legislator/subject find themselves reworked within the boundaries of a professional community, split between carer/patient.[4] In this context two readings of the Kantian problem would seem appropriate. The first relates to the possibility and kinds of inequality and subjugation contained within the categorical abstraction (the liberal/marxist reading). The second, points out the necessary gap between the nouomenal and phenomenal worlds, which will be replicated in the move from the general to the particular, and the universal to the historical. Both find their location, with the usual reservations as to finding any secure relations between discourses, in medical ethics and law, in the question of consent in general, and the doctrine of informed consent in particular.

Within the Common law, at least, consent functions both as a necessary part of the legal regulation of relations between health care institutions and the patient, and of relations between law and ethics. It does so in the name of autonomy. In terms of legal liability, consent to touching can negative a civil or criminal charge of battery. Consent, traditionally, has not formed a major part of a civil action for negligence. For it to be actionable, the plaintiff must show, first, that lack of consent was the (objective) cause of the injury, in the sense that the plaintiff would not have given consent to the treatment and so would not have had the operation at all and, second, that the defendant had a duty to disclose such information.[5]

The doctrine of informed consent, turns what are essentially conceptual elements designed to negative specific 'situation liabilities' into positive values (or rights) (Faden and Childress, 1986 pp.116-125). Whilst, the status of informed consent in the UK is somewhat tentative, in Lord Scarman's view,[6] at least, the question of whether the patient had consented to the particular medical insult she received, should be phrased in terms of the patient's right to know of the risks involved in her medical treatment (Silverman, 1989; Gillett, 1989). It becomes a way of protecting the patient's autonomy against the threatened paternalism of the medical expert by imposing a duty on the doctor to disclose medical risks. Along with a 'right to know', for (informed) consent, there must also be the appropriate 'capacity to consent' and in the absence of this, the courts (when approached) will act in 'the best interests of the patient'. As such, whatever its particular legal genealogy, these concepts operate as a sufficiently flexible concept to encompass both Kantian, deontological, and Millian, utilitarian arguments for an autonomous agency (Faden and Beauchamp, 1986; Gillon, 1985).

Consent then can provide a model in the Kantian engagement between the carer and the patient in the community of reason. Informed consent enables the isomorphy required between legislator and self to be established. Through it, the patient becomes able to legislate for her own recovery. But as many have pointed out, the choice is somewhat limited. The decision in *Sidaway* has firmly tied the question of informed consent to the *Bolam* principle,[7] and declared that disclosure should be governed by the appropriate professional standards and not the patient (Lee, 1987). The choice which the patient has to make is either one identical with that of carer/legislator or of stepping outside the system altogether.

It does not take much imagination to point out the extent to which the abstract notion of consent is being used to mask more 'real' power relations based on systematic inequalities concealed in the process of justifying subordination to the medical profession. Nor indeed to suggest that this can be tied in generally with the requirement within capitalism to express social relations in abstract terms (Edelman, 1979). Both of these arguments, however, still make the presumption of a potential identity and equality of power relations between the carer/patient on which to base their analysis of difference. At best, however, the patient enters into the medical encounter precisely because of the differences of knowledge and expertise. To analyse this encounter in terms of a potential reconciliation in terms of equality would miss the point of the appeal to consent. The wound that it is required to heal is more than an accidental product of external inequality. Consent, it would seem, is being invoked to cure a more fundamental disremption.

Let us follow the workings of the white mythology further in the law in the (im)possibility of the Kantian move from the noumenal essence of the ethical to the empirical. At any point where the patient threatens to fall below the capacity of the 'autonomous' moral/legal person, the court must act to reinstate it. To do so it invokes a variety of 'substituted judgments' premised on an idea of restoring the capacity to consent and thus autonomy. The language and scope of these judgments are diverse, but one example can be given. The most forceful (and fictional) is the use of 'subjective test' where the court will make a decision on the basis of what the patient would have 'wanted' had they been autonomous.

In Re J (a minor)(wardship: medical treatment)[8] the Court of Appeal issued a ruling that in the event of baby J requiring resuscitation, it would not prevent the medical authorities from not so doing. Baby J was born prematurely and had suffered severe brain damage, and medical experts were of the opinion too that he would develop quadraplegia. In delivering his judgment Lord Donaldson approved Mr Justice MacKenzie's dictum that

> the decison can only be made in the context of the disabled person viewing the worthwhileness or otherwise of his life in its own context as a disabled person - and in that context he would not compare his life with a person enjoying normal advantages. He would know nothing of a normal person's life

having never experienced it.[9]

Bearing in mind the insistence by the courts that it did not have 'the right to impose death' and that it respected the 'sanctity of life' of the patient, this statement is a startling assertion of autonomy.

However, the courts did not grant full autonomy, baby J was to be treated as if he had the autonomy of a disabled person. If this is not to be taken as a rather oblique pointer to the amount of pain and suffering that baby J could be taken to endure, the question of the disabled point of view, or of disabled autonomy, ought to alert us to a number of things. With regard to questions of Kantian autonomy, it is not just the ease with which the autonomous view point of the medical profession comes to be affirmed. To be disabled within this scheme is still to be firmly held in the medical frame. If baby J was outside this frame, no categorical imperative would be needed, the legal commandment of autonomy would be unnecessary. Of most importance is the character of the exchange between the patient and the carer, and the impropriety of the 'substituted judgment'.

In the medical exchange, the patient is prompted to demand the alleviation of suffering in its most extreme form. At a quite literal level the Kantian moral injunction to treat your neighbour as yourself is interpreted as 'put yourself in my place'. The answer comes back 'if I was in your place I would be a morally autonomous human (or at least a disabled one) and would not struggle to survive because I have no chance of ever achieving moral autonomy'. Baby J can only momentarily gain entry to the autonomous world on condition that he vacate it as soon as it is decently proper to do so. The presence of disablement marks the point of difficulty thrown up by the 'white mythology'. Far from healing the disremption between the noumenal and phenomenal, consent can act only by invoking another, prior, reason, as the condition of coming before the law. Within the Court's reasoning the scandal lies, not with baby J's poor prognosis, or with any covert eugenics, but with the fact that the courts have been excluded, disabled, from treating baby J properly as an object of human knowledge and judgment. What disqualifies the court from putting themselves in baby J's place is that baby J has revealed his lack of rationality. He must be made to be rational, as near as possible, in the eyes of the courts.

However, in coming to judgment, the court itself does in one sense get put in baby J's place by having its own ability to pass judgment put to question. It has to answer an impossible demand. In so doing it reaches the limits of its 'universal' rationality and is joined with the medical profession in not being able to alleviate the suffering demand of the other. Baby J is excluded because he has sought alleviation of his suffering in the wrong place, or by showing that there is no such alleviation. The impropriety of the Court lies in insisting on relating to baby J as a subject, at the same time as marking the conditions of legal subjectivity and autonomy as belonging to another (elsewhere). No basis is given for reponding as moral agents other than as rational sentinent beings.[10]

Much the same argument can be made for the problems with breach of confidence, patients and doctors who lie (Brown, 1986), and the uncooperative patient who refuses to follow treatment, or conducts 'high risk' activities that endanger the lives of others - mothers and their foetus's, HIV positive people and their fluid contacts. So too with those patients who seek voluntarily assisted euthanasia, whose interests are made to conform to the state/carer split by asserting a desire to conform to the prohibitions of laws of homicide.

As has already been intimated, the move being traced in instituting Kant's (autonomous) thought is aporetic, there is no passage, through which judgment can come to pass. This is not to say that judgment is not made, it must be, but that there can be no simple assertion that such a decision is just or curable by consent. The white mythology finds its congruence in the forceful bringing together of two different orders in law, the noumenal form of proper ethical conduct and phenomenal subjectivity of individual beings. The problems highlighted in the attempts to produce autonomous consent within the rational community of carers lead in two related directions. The first raises matters of propriety. Kantian autonomy would appear to be engaged not just in a process of ethical judgment predicated on a universal will, it also demands a number of autonomous attributes, to enable the possibility of consent (capacity etc). Indeed with the relatively limited requirements for autonomy proposed it opens the way for the development of moral technologies for creation of the rational self. The other direction in which the problem of the white mythology leads us is to the presence of the Other.

The difficulty lies with the insistence of the law in defining the other/patient in terms of a (fictional) congnitive understanding of the needs of the coloniser. Not only is the patient forbidden from relating the experience of the colonised, but their will (free or otherwise), which is meant to form the basis of autonomy is rendered an utterly contingent mark of the presence of the other. Only that willing patient, who already conforms to reason (and who is thus already inside the law) is autonomously admitted to the law. The split 'we' of legislator/subject cannot become the horizon of the autonomous ethico-legal relationship without more.

As Levinas (1986) has written, if the Other is to be responded to as Other, 'we' must accept the demand, 'Be Just' or 'Ease My Suffering' as arising prior to and being constitutive of the carer. For Levinas, the other is completely Other and unknowable. Being ethical does not consist in making the rational, autonomous, but in the equitable honouring of faces, the recognition of being 'heteronomic to others that govern me, whose infinity I cannot thematise and, whose hostage I remain' (Derrida, 1990, p.959). The Other cannot, without violence, be turned into an integrated part of an autonomous whole or into a monad of an empirical consensus.[11] It raises the possibility that the Other can not be treated ethically within a purely cognitive order. Yet the demands of the Other are multiple and must be ranked and met. This necessitates a move from the singular response to the ranking and calculating of claims according to a more universal justice (and law). It is with this double need for universality, calculation, rule, repitition and symmetry in law, and the singular, individual, irreplacable and asymetrical demand of the Other, that ethics and law (as justice) must impossibly engage (Derrida, 1990, p.949). Without the safe anchorage of a concept and without law, ethics is left only with responsibility. Indeed with a responsibility for the responsibility created by the suffering face of my neighbour, one, however, which will inevitably be met again by law and the technologies of the self.

Technologies of dispersal and remembrance.

Far from being an extrinsic feature of the creation of autonomy, the technologies of self and the relation to the other would appear to be essential supplements that must be maintained to create autonomy. Here we trace through language and the technologies for the care the body (medicine), some of the ways in which autonomous technological self comes into being.

In ethics and in law it is possible to rephrase the split subjectivity that Kant introduces in terms of a new regime of signification which is characteristic of modernity. The pre-modern subject is a mirror image of the face of the sovereign. The God or King at the centre of the Universe delegates the attributes of subjectivity in a series of imitative concentric circles that always return and are stabilised on the king's head and the sovereign body (Goodrich, 1990, Ch.3).

The modern subject on the other hand replaces the centre of sovereignty. According to Deleuze and Guattari (1988), self becomes subject in a process of doubling up evidenced in discourse. This process starts with a myriad of points of subjectification which serve as the focus of delirious fixation. In responding to them the subject emerges as both a speaking subject and as the subject of speech, both the mental reality of the *Cogito* and the specific existence of the *ergo sum* come into existence. In linguistic terms the split is evident in the dual function of the subject of enunciation (the speaking subject behind a statement 'I am now writing') and the subject of the statement (the 'I' within the statement). The subject becomes the cause of statements in which it itself, is an actor in another form.

Such processes are not static, in so far as they are to be related to the creation of the autonomous Kantian legislator/subject, they exist as a continuous process of self creation at each point creating a new autonomous subject. The modern subject as desiring-machine is in continuous production, emerging here as a dispersed body, a third-world body, split into administrative, health, medical and other units (Donzelot, 1979; Minson, 1985). Faced with this proliferation, a new priesthood and bureaucracy takes form whose task is self subjection.

The genealogies of the twin processes and techniques of subjectification and objectification, in health, medicine and the 'psy-subjects' are well known. They receive attention here only in so far as they relate to the presence of the Kantian autonomous subject in ethico-legal aspects of medical regulation.

As object of study the body has been individuated, tabulated, palpitated and prompted into modern existence by the exacting discipline of the hospital and the clinical gaze. At the level of the general population the epidemics and the quarantines of the eighteenth century created the possibility of the public documentation and regulation of populations under the watchful architechtonics of eyeless panopticon. At the level of the individual body, the clinical gaze, which took as its model the painstaking dissections of the cadavers of the poor, the criminal, the mad and the foreign, began the formal dismemberment of the body at the very moment that it began to emerge into visibility (Foucault, 1977; Richardson, 1988). By the end of the eighteenth century the fate of illness was no longer to be understood as a legible but pathological visitation carried by ill-winds, it had become an internalised malfunction needing medical investigation and decipherment (Foucault, 1963).

The twentieth century intensifications of the techniques of surveillance in medicine have contributed not just to the observation of the symptoms within the individual body, but also to the measuring of spaces and relations between them. Whereas the panoptic vision fixed on the irregularities of the individual body, the dispensary, through the distribution of health technologies such as drugs and education and by working with the products of the statistical survey, charted and regulated, the incidence of illness, both regular and irregular, within the (statistical) community (Armstrong, 1983). With the dispensary gaze the body comes to be investigated and understood in juxtaposition to others.

It is with the development of the (morbidity) survey that the idea of health becomes calculable and the health of the nation a probability. The monitoring of the ill, the insane and the criminal, gradually comes to cover all who have health of any kind. If we add to the postwar development of the specialisms of obstetrics, paediatrics and geriatrics, the more recent proliferation of preventative health care regimes, the potential for the normalising capabilities of health care technologies is there to cover the entire population over space and time. This is particularly so as this regulatory regime is extended to cover the regulation of hygiene and sexuality, as well as birth, death and what comes between (Weeks, 1981; Watney, 1985).

A universal medical object then is in the making, but one no longer concentrated in a three dimensional body but dispersed in a multitude of relations over space and time. Within the hospital it is possible to note the different departments, staff, regulatory practices etc, through which the patient must be distributed, held together by nothing more than (the confidential truth) of the medical record. Outside of the hospital, regimes of preventative health care have become common from the control of stress to the regulation of sexual contact. Given the stronger claims made in the name of the holistic patient, perhaps even the institutions which are currently required to sustain the dispensary gaze can become both fully dispersed and self-regulating (Coward, 1989). Along with the privatisation of hygiene and welfare in the family comes health and self (Rose, 1989). Relations of illness-health have become traceable throughout the social body. The metaphors of the body politic beloved of the pre-modern philosophy have been literalised and the psychopathology of self and society comes again into discourse (Levin, 1987). This time, however, the body of society is more clearly acephalous.

Such minute individuations between bodily relations have also produced changes in the understanding of the role of the patient. Far from being a docile, or merely inaccurate reporter of her symptoms, under the dispensary regime the patient is required to speak herself, to explain her relations with the world (sexual, familial, social, business etc). If the interstices of health relations are to be measured, they need to be filled. Of this only the patient can know - the medical object becomes the speaking subject, the orator of the personal experience or relation of health. It is here that the doctor-patient relationship is born (Armstrong, 1986).

If the figure of the patient was initially created by the objectifying gaze of the medico-scientific profession, it is appropriate that the patients' ability to consent to treatment is also determined by it. Yet with the emergent subjecthood of the patient required by the dispensary gaze, and the enthronement of personal experience as the source of health care information, the patient begins to take on a life of her own. The ambivalence of judicial attitudes to theories of informed consent perhaps reflects the position of this new subject without subjectivity (self) (Shelley, 1985; Keller, 1990).

All the while this re-positioning of the patient/subject is being carried on, the internal reordering of the patient is also being conducted. From the techniques of micro-surgery to the mapping of the genetic body in the Genum Project, the body is being broken down into smaller and more heterogenous parts, each participating in its own medico-scientific existence and in the 'whole' body. It is already a commonplace that embryos should have an 'existence' independent from the womb, that body organs (less significant than the brain) can be transferred at will. The cyborg body and the coupling of humans and machines have been present since before our hospital births (Treichler, 1990). The patenting of mutant cancer strains, the replacement of old body parts etc, establishes a law of the industrial technology of organs without body.

Faced with this increasingly apocalyptic and technophiliac (Doanne, 1990) dispersal of organs and body through networks of medical technology and the detritus of social relations, the presence of the freewilling subject would both be vital to sustain any vision of agency and appear to have little chance of existence, except as the contingent product of the failure of such a 'rationalising' project. The body exists as little more than the subject of administrative agency, remembered only in the records of treatment and as a permeable skin stretched to mark its passing. Yet the technologies of freedom and care continue to constitute the self as autonomous subject.

Within law, the process of subjectification and objectification is met through a variety of devices. Some like, patents and copyright law, simply accept the commodification of the body, others like criminal law and the civil laws of tort, take control through concepts like consent and self ownership (Farsides, infra). Still more, however, simply declare the matter one that should not be before the law at all and set up a regulatory framework to limit the form of legal scrutiny. All, however, require the possibility of enfolding and controlling the technological body by the use of the split Cartesian will. The technological body is still bounded in the (im)possible language of the Kantian subject.

One reading of Foucault finds a location for such a subject in the generalisation of the model of the confession developed from the disciplines of western christianity and the ethics of self. Whilst the former, especially when related to confessing pain and sexuality, can be witnessed as yet one more elaboration of the technologies of power and their relations to knowledge, they also allow for the presence of the latter. Yet they open the way not just to the disciplinary regime of subjugation and inscription, but also to the practices of autonomy (Foucault, 1988). What emerges from this move most clearly in the context of medical technologies is that the reformulations of individual subjectivities can not simply be achieved by side-stepping the Kantian tribunal. The process of inscription will continue. In attempting to remember the body, Foucault makes an appeal to the practices of care as a form of practical reason. It is to practical reason in law and ethics that we now turn.

Legality and ethics

The Kantian categorical imperative is the law of law of modernity. It lies behind both aspects of practical judgment and action, both legality and morality. A new split, then, is opened up within the domain of practical activity. Kant, however, offers a second formulation of the categorical imperative directly borrowed from christian ethics: people should be treated as ends and not as means.

There appears to be a correlation between the two distinct facets of the imperative and the two domains of practical reason. The legal sphere is imbued with the formalism (the categorical character) of the Kantian injunction. The christian ethic of treating thy neighbour as thyself on the other hand, appears to be the substantive content of morality within the Kantian moment.

If the universality of the form (generality and validity) is the main characteristic and value of the modern *rechstaat* (rule of law), we can understand why our inability to ever know the substance of the law is a consistent theme of modern philosophy (Derrida, 1989b; Freud, 1913; Kafka, 1976a, 1976b; Lyotard, 1988b). The law prescribes acts and at the same time it prescribes itself. We can never have access to the essence of the law like the man from the country in Kafka's story whose attempts to enter law's door are continually deferred and frustrated until his death (Kafka, 1971; Douzinas and Warrington, 1991c). We are in the law if we act according to a universal form. Within the law we only know the sentence of the law as it is inscribed on the body. The formalism of the law appears unbounded (Cornell, 1989).

Could then morality be used as a horizon or a limitation upon the declared autonomy of the modern will which only knows the law in its form and validity rather than in its substance or value? From the side of law's consciousness, jurisprudence, the answer seems to be negative. There is no need here to repeat the arguments of the various positivisms that establish the specificity of the legal enterprise by excluding programmatically from the domain of the law all question of value and substance. We can only note in passing here that in criminal law, which is routinely distinguished from civil law as being the protector and guarantor of the fabric and mores of society, the element of intention has been turned into a requirement of forseeability, of prognosis and acceptance of the consequences of one's acts. Doctrine seems to exclude all reference to motive or the realm of value and the Good. This has been achieved by the simple gesture of reducing all such issues either to ones of capacity or by posing, and so losing, them within the formal question of whether the accused acted with the intention of bringing about the consequences of her action (Duff, 1990). Motives, desire and the Good get treated only at the level of responsibility. The criminal subject is one who autonomously, wills, knows, calculates and causes (or at least fails to prevent) those acts for which he takes responsibility (Hart, 1968). The subject in criminal law has no moral existence; in that he is the model for the legal subject tout court and for modernity.

We now turn to the other side of the split realm of practical reason, morality. It is true to say that although jurisprudence (especially of positivism) excludes morality from law, we can not avoid the feeling that some of form of morality remains included as the other within the law.[12] To be sure the moral philosophy of modernity has its own extensive history and theory which however shadows that of jurisprudence; they both owe their specifically modern existence to the contest of faculties and their joint appearance before the Kantian tribunal of reason. To try to tease out therefore the (non-)place of morality in law, we have to turn to moral philosophy and the elaborate and diverse critiques of ethics as moral philosophy.

Pre-modern western ethics has appealed since Plato to the concept of the Good. An action is moral if it promotes what counts as good according to the theory. For the moralists and deontologists of modernity on the other hand, both of the Kantian and Hegelian type, the moral act applies and respects some stipulated conception of rightness in itself. Utilitarians by contrast adjudge the morality of an act in accordance with its consequences.

A large part of recent moral philosophy accepts that while moral beliefs and judgments are linked with cognitive discourses they often fail to trigger off moral acts. In other words, moral theory does not seem to be either an indispensable or necessary component of moral action. People may be persuaded by arguments about the superiority of a particular conception of the good but then fail to pursue any particular course of action as a result (MacIntyre, 1981, p.141). If ethics is the field of moral action towards other people, the failure to translate ethical judgments into action is of great concern to moral philosophers. Both MacIntyre (1981) and Nagel (1970) have pointed out that there is no assurance that moral action will necessarily follow even a perfect moral theory. Indeed, Nagel starts his attempt at refashioning moral philosophy from this very recognition.[13] How could a critical theory account for this extraordinary state of affairs?

As constitutively other-orientated *action*, ethics must be distinguished clearly from all types of cognition. According to Michel de Certeau

> ethics is articulated through effective operations, and it defines a distance between what is and what ought to be. This distance designates a space where we have something to do.

On the other hand dogmatism is authorised by a reality that it claims to represent and in the name of this reality it imposes laws (de Certeau, 1986, p.199).

In this definition the space of ethics is suspended between - cognitive and moral - theory and the call to action. The moment of moral action the 'something' we have to do is not coextensive with 'what is' (cognition) and does not simply follow 'what ought to be' (moral philosophy). In this sense the pragmatic critique of McIntyre and Nagel is only a starting point.

Theory of all type is a form of representation of reality, a reflection of present or past contents that claims for itself truth and coherence. Theory is a description of the existent, a re-presentation of presence. As such it can never fully occupy the space of ethics. Moral action on the other hand is a response to an ethical stimulus; it is always still to come. Furthermore, as Heidegger's ontological critique of the modern technological Being has shown, theory is involved in an endless pursuit of control (Heidegger, 1976). The identification of truth with logic in modern technological reason turns the 'real' into a system of causal links, infinitely calculable and manipulable. People too are treated as 'homogeneous units that lend themselves to abstraction and formulaic manipulation based on the principle of parsimony' (Wyschogrod, 1990, p.135).

Moral philosophy is not innocent of Heidegger's indictment. Even those theories that emphasise practice, like Nagel's, cannot avoid the ontological condition of modernity steeped in the dream of total control. Both the means/ends distinction in Kantian ethics and the calculus of happiness, utility and equitable distribution in utilitarianism and Rawls belong to the modern horizon of manipulable Being. The metaphysical identification of Being with the Good since Plato and the 'idea of the Good [as] the basic determination of all order, of all that belongs together' (Heidegger, 1984, p.116) finds its most disturbing expression in the transformation of the Good into an aspiration of control over Being. Boxed between theory-as-logic that can represent but cannot act and a praxis that can only act as technique, calculation and control, ethics seems to veer violently between an incapacitating subjectivism of will and a cynical objectivism of value. It is for this reason that the role of the regulatory bodies and ethical committees is of advantage for both legality and ethics alike. It allows for, and covers, their necessary but impossible separation before the law.

We can conclude from this analysis that while jurisprudence excludes morality from the field of legal judgment, moral philosophy (particularly in its analytical form) seems to shadow the law and legality by presenting ethical action as the response to an abstract juridical code of value and principle.

The tragic body

The claim of this essay so far has been that at the threshold of modernity Kant in a series of brilliantly executed moves, resituated the foundation of the social bond from a realm beyond society into society itself. He achieved this through a number of concentric doubling up operations in which the body (politic) was both split into two and reunited. In the realm practical judgment this operation took the form of a differentiation between legality and morality and re-integration through the principle of juridical formalism that was launched both in law and in ethics.

The Kantian elevation of will and autonomy took place both at a specific historical moment and as a gesture of self-ordained presence necessary to philosophy (Derrida, 1978). As such it comes to be understood differentially. On the one hand it emerges as time bound, alterable, historical moment (dead, and forgetful of its origins), whose claims of inevitability are capable of historical and anthropological scrutiny. On the other hand it participates in an (aporetic) institution of meaning that makes the thought of time, history, law, ethics etc. possible (Derrida, 1990). As such its self engendered effects are traceable in the results of this (non-)event. If we turn to an earlier period that has repeatedly been compared with early modernity, that of fifth centruy BC Athenian democracy, as presented in tragedy. We can compare the classical concept of will with that of modernity.

One key to the understanding of the great tragedies is a creative tension between destiny and choice (freewill) in which the tragic hero finds himself. For example the myth of the Atreides as represented by Aeschylus in his *Iphigenia in Aulis* and *Agamemnon*. Agamemnon, the King of the Greeks, is being told by the divine Chalcas that in order to raise the wind necessary to sail the fleet to Troy, he must sacrifice his daughter, Iphigenia, on the order of the goddess Artemis. Agamemnon can not avoid or escape this fatal and vile crime. Zeus demands that the Greek alliance destroys Troy and Artemis makes clear that for the expedition to start the maiden must be sacrificed. Agamemnon acts under a double divine constraint (*ananke*, necessity) and he can not be adjudged culpable for the act. But at the same time, the King accepts his role in the unfolding of destiny and fervently desires the murder of his daughter, if that is what will fill the sails of his ships. 'If this sacrifice, this virginal blood, is what binds the winds, it is permitted to desire it fervently, most fervently', Agamemnon repeats three times (Aeschylus, Agamemnon, v.214-218). The chorus faced with this desired but involuntary crime, proclaims that the King 'made himself the accomplice of a capricious destiny' (Aeschylus, Agamemnon, v.186-188).

Could we not argue then, that there is a doubling up in the tragic hero which precedes the Kantian move. On the one hand his actions seem predetermined and in this sense he can not be seen to be an agent. On the other hand, he desires (*boulesis*) the outcome of his action and deliberates (*bouleusis*) as to the best means to bring about the desired outcome. In this he is not far removed from the legal subject in modern criminal law whose responsibility depends on mens rea, forseeability, calculation of the result, and acceptance (or recognition) of the consequences. But in choosing and in acting, the tragic actor, also places himself in the hands of unknown, unshareable, and uninterpretable forces which involve his actions in a fatal plot. They invest them with a meaning that will remain opaque to him until destiny has completed its course. The actor is autonomous and willing his acts, but at the same time he belongs to a higher register at work at the very heart of his decisions. He is both of human nature and part of a divine scheme that gives him his ends. The two parts of his role make him both culpable and a plaything in the hands of the Gods. Human and divine nature, means and ends, are totally opposed to each other but are inseperable and intermingled. It is within the tension thus created that the actor becomes both the author and the victim of his own actions.

Oedipus too is an example of this ambiguous logic between freewill and imposed destiny. In killing his father and marrying his mother, unknowingly and unwillingly, he becomes the puppet in the hands of an evil daemon, which makes of Oedipus's life an unwitting transgression of the key taboos of family and society. His blood and lineage (*genos*) is cursed, he defiles everything he touches, and he condemns his *genos* to extinction. But on the other hand, he willingly accepts his responsibility; he gouges out his eyes, abandons Thebes as a scapegoat (*pharmakos*). Eventually, he becomes a semi-divine whose grave will later bestow blessing upon Athens when it welcomed him from his wandering.

Again what animates the action is the tension between action and pathos, freewill and predetermination, autonomy and the tragic body. The actor obsessively pursues his inquiry as to the identity of Laios's killer and willingly moves towards the final revelation and judgment. Yet throughout the action the basis of this judgment lies elsewhere, in the original transgression of his progenitor Labdakos, and in the defilement of the bodies of his parents. His final success in his quest, is at the same time, the recognition that he himself is the paricide, and husband to his mother. That *hamartema* (sin, transgression) has been inscribed in Oedipus's own body and in that of his sons and brothers, and daughters and sisters. In the divine order, the body will be reintegrated in the mutilation of Oedipus and in the destruction of all his descendents.

Within the order of tragedy, then, action can never be viewed as operating on the single register of the freewilled event. It will always involve the choice of means and the imposition of ends. As such this whole scheme of destiny is inscribed, with blood, on the body of the protagonists. The tragic double reading insists on the presence of a body that is both integral as embodied action and inscribed within lineage, genealogy and tradition. This connection, in tragedy, enables the actor to bear the physical responsibility of his transgressions as ethical. It produces the ethical body. Perhaps, then, it is no surprise that it is with Oedipus, the most transgressive and ethical of the figures of tragedy, that the meaning of destiny in the modern body has come to be joined.

The tragic modern body

Let us return to modernity for the last time. Following the formal organisation of the tragic dualism, the Kantian doubling of the self is, on the surface, the total antithesis of the tragic tension. Destiny, the divine imposition of value and aim, is resituated within the limits of society. Man is finally declared free from tradition and fate; free to choose, to will and to act - to be fully responsible.

Yet predetermination, the heterological disposition of ends is still as much a part of the modern conception of the actor. Destiny may have become social context; pathos may have changed into the pathology of the psyche; divine violence may have turned to the social causes of crime; the defilement of the body may have been transformed into disease; mutilation and sacrifice, the accomplices of destiny, may have been translated into surgery as the dismembering and reintegration of the body into the social order. Finally the seers and divines may have turned into experts, psychiatrists and sociologists. But the tension between free will and the dark origins of personality or the inaccessible forces of society is as much present today as it was in the classical period.

What remains is a break up of the body into its various components that are to be treated as displaced atoms according to medical technologies of care that in their legal formulation will concern themselves with the calculation of economic cost, bureaucratic convenience and administrative rationality. Danger and the incalculable, what escapes expectation has become risk and cost management, the planning for the untoward event.[14]

For the tragic actor every action involved a double reading; what he freely chose could turn out to be the unwilled plan of fate and could transform him from actor to victim. For the modern subject in law on the other hand, free willed choice and determined destiny are both absolute and distinct, arranged on a spatial and temporal continuum, and disseminated through the medico-legal body and text. From the point of view of criminal responsibility the actor does not have the option of guilt or innocence. He is either guilty or not guilty, as if destiny does not count (or can only be counted elsewhere).[15]

From the point of view of medico-scientific expertise the illness or health of the actor is distributed not just within the body but in the spaces between bodies. Destiny has been changed from the incalculable into the calculation of a statistical relation. In this, individual decisions on (of) health and illness can not be made without reference to another. The expert will pass clinical judgment on a patient, but he will base it on his construction of the differential relation between the individual and the unknown others included in the statistical medical calculation. Individual fate can not be met or judged other than in a detour through the fates of an infinite number of others. As we have seen, the reconciliation of such a dispersal of bodies and fates can not be achieved with autonomy. It can not succeed because such a reconciliation is always deferred both to some other time of judgment and because the prospect of autonomy has become totally other referring.

It is the possibility or guarantee of the non-arrival of the ethical that keeps open - with the violence that the double binding of destiny and will brings with it- the grounds of ethicity. To proceed through the critique of autonomy in modernity is not to anticipate or celebrate the loss of autonomy, but to present what the invisibility of autonomy brings with it. Beneath the statistical others of medical and legal calculation, the spectre of the Other has remained within the unconscious of law and ethics.

Even when treating the medicalised body as the target of technology and subject of calculation, the law assumes that judgment has to be passed upon a person who comes before the law, endowed with a name and a life history. More specifically when judgment is to be passed upon those liminal conditions of existence, the staple diet of medical ethics and law, upon birth and death, or the line that connects the two, a story of destiny, usually in the christian narrative of fall and redemption, will be gleaned behind the judgment. Medical ethics and law too seem to be engaged in a double reading: they both disperse the body through the medical encounter and re-arranges its parts under the ethico-legal fiction of autonomy. They are haunted by the appeal of the embodied other in pain and suffering.

Rather than a rational community of form (Habermas, 1984),

judgment demands an ethical community of hostages to the other as Levinas (1986) calls it. This community can never be either a community of universality or one that excludes the alien and the third. Its very existence is being tested in each moment in which the other comes to it and asks to be welcomed. Only in that moment can we have an ethical community. It can never be universal and it cannot be based exclusively on reason. It creates itself when it answers the call of suffering in the face of the other. The law of the law in that community can not be one that dismembers and calculates, but must circulate in the space between calculation and the incalculable (Derrida, 1990). It is this incalculable; the need to respond to the indivisible pain and suffering the face of the other that brings in the ethical community, it is the ghost which exists hidden in the body of medical ethics and law.

In his *Critique of Violence*, Benjamin (1986) writes that there is something rotten in the law. In our interpretation of the law of the ethical community, a law that is always still to come in response to the request of the other, what is rotting is the tragic body. The inscribed body, whose existence the law has always to deny, even as it cuts in order to be able to dismember and calculate it, is the haunting underground presence that returns to remind the law of its foundation.

*Costas Douzinas, Lecturer in Law, Lancaster University.
**Shaun McVeigh, Lecturer in Law, Keele University.

1. Clearly the post/modern reading of Kant must now proceed through Heidegger (1962). For synoptic overviews see Douzinas, Warrington, McVeigh (1991) and MacIntyre (1988).

2. We accept the 'modern self' as being necessarily gendered as male, with the effects on the understanding of autonomy that this brings. However, for certain necessary effects, some gender neutral terms will be used.

3. This is so despite declarations to the contrary, and the metaleptic effect of the *coup de force* that institutes the new legal order. This *coup de force* is a disremption of the 'fabric' of history, but it still must be joined with it - the question is how (Bhabha, 1990; Derrida, 1990).

4. Put this way, the question of the construction and the administration of the 'autonomy' of the medical profession is ignored, but its self-evidence is not assumed (Montgomery, 1992). Jacobs (1988) suggests a limited scope for the place of a Kantian understanding of the health care professions, but makes extensive use of a sociological tradition that does.

5. Along with establishing the specific requirements of a claim in negligence, legal doctrine is also involved in constructing competing understandings of the body in pain, both within and without, the medical and legal professions (Gibson, 1989).

6. [1985] 2 WLR 480.

7. [1957] All ER 118. A doctor is not negligent if he acts in accordance with a practice accepted at the time as proper by a responsible body of medical opinion.

8. [1990] 3 All ER 930.

9. [1990] 3 All ER 930 at 936, quoting MacKenzie J. in *Re Superintendent of Family and Child Services and Dawson* (1983) 145 DLR (3d) 610, 620-621.

10. On the significance of J names see Bloom (1991) where J figures are traced, as oppositionalists and the disenchanted, from biblical sources to the present.

11. The view presented here differs from the phenomenological approach of Pellegrino and Thomasma (1981) in that they, with Satre, presuppose a prior social existence that constitutes the other. For Levinas the suffering face of the Other is both pre-linguistic and pre-ontological. Nor do they take into account any question of law or multiplicity (Cornell, 1989; Derrida, 1990; Douzinas, Warrington, 1991c).

12. The contorted but impossible attempts of Lord Bridge in *R v Moloney* [1985] 1 A.C. 905, to avoid any definition of intention and exclude all mention of desire and motive are well known. (This is indeed quite understandable given the distinctly Oedipal (Freudian) character of the encounter between Moloney and his stepfather.) Even Lord Bridge, however, was impelled to invoke some notion of motive and desire in his attempts to maintain a distinction between forseeability and intention.

13. Nagel distinguishes between epistemological scepticism (the rejection of arguments or evidence offered to ground belief) from moral scepticism (the rejection of moral reasons intented to induce action). He accepts that cognitive beliefs can not motivate altruistic action and proposes instead a non-cognitive theory of moral judgment. This theory depends on 'our' ability to adopt an impersonal standpoint in moral arguments and accepts that moral action is subject to formal conditions of objectivity. To accept these conditions, however, would amount to a reimposition of cognitive considerations and return it to the Kantian tribunal (Nagal, 1970, Wyschogrod, 1990, pp.39-41).

14. For example cancer quite regularly gets encoded as a calculable medical expense within research and treatment programmes; as an identifiable, probable, consequence of certain 'at risk' activities; as well as that which refuses to respond ('here is a cell that does not hear the command'). It is this last as the incalculable derangement before the law that prevents it from being accountable, that refuses

the law as pure calculability (Blanchot, 1986, p.86).

15. Vestigal elements of this struggle can be found in attempts to define notions of necessity and duress in terms other than a loss of will akin to automatism.

Body Ownership

Introduction

Feminist writers have rarely underestimated the complex relationship between our experience of ourselves as bodies, and the creation of our selves as moral and political agents. In 1855 the suffragette Lucy Stone observed that '[i]t is very little to me to have the right to vote, to own property, etcetera, if I may not keep my body and its uses, in my absolute right' (Dworkin, 1984, p.11). In this essay I wish to begin by exploring the idea of women as bodies before going on to suggest a way in which women can claim to own their bodies and the products thereof.

Women cannot ignore the patterns that their bodies impose upon their lives - menstruation, pregnancy (and the avoidance thereof), childbirth and menopause all demand an acknowledgement by the woman of her functioning as a physical body. Nature and culture then combine to confront women with taboos and rituals which mark them, control them, and limit them, dependent upon their bodily state.

Yet at the same time many women experience these bodily processes as separate from the self, and the language, metaphors and imagery employed demonstrate this. In her extensive interviews with women Emily Martin (Martin, 1989) noted that a central image frequently emerged along with a number of corollaries.

Women offered the following account. Your self is something separate from your body, and so the body is something which needs to be controlled by the self, and which can go out of control with devastating consequences for the self. Your body sends you signals to which you have to respond, and forces you to go through stages

35

when different things happen to you because your body dictates it. At these stages - menstruation, birth, menopause - you experience physical symptoms as separate from the self, they 'come on', you 'get them', you don't 'do them'.

Frequently women spoke of a conflict, separation and fragmentation, and many presented their bodies as something which was outside their control, indeed as something which was controlling them. Luckily this was not the whole story, and although society reinforces much of the negative imagery and destructive metaphor associated with the female body and bodily functions, more positive moves are afoot.

The body in feminist discourse

Feminist discourse has paid close attention to the body, its form, functions and representations, and gradually women are benefiting from the new insights gained. The second wave of feminism that began as a trickle in the fifties but became a torrent in the seventies demanded that the previously private sphere be open to scrutiny, and that the personal aspects of women's lives be acknowledged as politically important.[1] Part of the process of consciousness raising was to make women comfortable with their bodies and particularly their new found sexual freedom. *Our Bodies Ourselves*, the practical manual of seventies feminism, sought to demystify the biological, and thereby empower a generation of women newly comfortable with the cycles of life, and work in this vein continues with for example Germaine Greer's recent study of menopause.

Women are learning to oppose the imposition of male-dominated medical models upon their bodily experiences, and have begun to question the dominant reality presented to them. New imagery is being created, and women have fought hard to control their own fertility and to manage childbirth. They have fought the political battle over abortion on both sides, ensuring that it can no longer be left to church or government to decide. They have demanded that the effects of pre-menstrual tension and post-natal depression be recognised, but at the same time have required that they be de-mystified. They have objected to the traditional paternalism within medicine that for too long made them the uninvolved victims of clinical decision making. They have begun to see menopause not as a medical condition which 'happens to them', but as a life experience which represents much more than physiological and hormonal change.

These advances are examples of the way in which women are trying to establish ownership over their own bodies, and control over their bodily functions; first by creating their own metaphors and placing their own meaning and interpretation on bodily experiences, and then by seeking to exert control over the reality of their bodily experiences and the processes of production in which they are engaged.

Questions of ownership

Although the idea of owning one's body is suggestive of Cartesian dualism it need not be read in this way. At a moral level ownership gives one certain rights and allows one to make certain claims, whether or not they are supported in law. Where the law does intervene it regulates the exercise of these moral rights, and protects the property owner from abuse.

The Oxford English Dictionary defines the verb to own as to 'have as property, possess' (OED, p.733) which is singularly unhelpful given that property is defined as 'being owned' (OED, p. 825). Property lawyers and philosophers need a fuller definition than this, but as Tawney observed '[p]roperty is the most ambiguous of categories' (Tawney, 1921 ch. 5).

As Lucas points out, many definitions are too simple; '..ownership is not a simple relation of attachment but a complicated bundle of rights' (Lucas, 1985, p.184). One cannot infer from ownership the existence of one essential right nor can one universalise claims of what it means to own something over the entire range of objects. Although certain rights appear central to most definitions of ownership, the most obvious being the right to alienate by gift or sale, even these can be explained away in particular circumstances. Nevertheless, most definitions of property choose to emphasis the notion of a right to exclusive use and control. Private property is thus presented as a legal privilege of using and disposing of some good, together with a security against other people using or disposing of it (Lucas, 1985, p.183).

The simplest model of private property is that of individual proprietorship where exclusive rights of control vest in natural persons. On this pattern the owner of an object is clearly entitled, to the exclusion of other private persons, to decide what should be done with it 'except as he is limited by law, or by voluntary agreement' (Benn & Peters, 1975, p.158).

Allowing for the intervention of law and contract ensures that the rights of ownership depend upon both the nature of the thing owned and the circumstances within which the relationship is defined. 'Rights of property are not and never have been absolutely absolute. Always they have been fettered by various legal obligations' (Lucas, 1985, p.186).

The context of the body in law

In the sense used here to own one's body demands an expansion of the usual concept. It is to have the right to exclusive use and control, with the notion of control extending to include control over the *interpretations* placed upon the body and the *meanings* attached to bodily functions. In this sense it combines possessing the material object with controlling the way in which it is represented, and the rights attached to ownership include the right not to be treated in a discriminatory or derogatory manner.

When you examine the treatment of bodies in law the complexity of the situation becomes clear. For example, I have certain rights for my body not to be interfered with without my agreement, thus affirming the traditional right of exclusion. In a medical context this leads to the requirement for informed consent and the possible charges of battery or assault where it is not acquired. However, this negative right not to be assaulted is not extended into a positive right to exercise complete control over my own body.

Even without including cases where my individual control is restricted in order to prevent harm to others (infectious diseases, childbirth) we can see that an implicit assumption of body ownership does not necessarily guarantee exclusivity of use and control over my body, or the products of its labour. The law states quite different things concerning ownership and control in respect to different types of product and or labour/activity.

The laws on prostitution permit me to sell/hire my body for sex as long as I do not solicit business, and as long as I am legally entitled to have sex, that is, if I have reached the legal age of consent. However, even if I am a consenting adult, the law may seek to control my private sexual activities if they are considered depraved. This became an issue recently when a group of homosexual men were imprisoned for engaging in sado-masochistic sexual acts, albeit privately and willingly. As the law stands at present I may end my own life (suicide), but I may not engage others to assist me in doing so (euthanasia); thus my control in this respect is dependent upon my ability to act for myself.

In terms of the products my body brings forth increasingly the laws of copyright and patent seek to leave control over intellectual products with the producer, and clearly mark as her own the results of her creative or innovative labour, at least within the period of the copyright. The laws of libel and slander could be said to operate on the assumption that I own my good reputation, although the extent to which my privacy may be invaded without a law being broken makes control in this area difficult to exercise. The laws governing inheritance and transfer of wealth allow me control over my land, money, and chattels within certain specified circumstances, even after my death. My property in the narrow sense of my goods and chattels is mine in the fullest sense available, and the products of my labour, be it manual or cerebral are fairly easy to mark as my own. The law makes many distinctions, but in important respects the law can be seen as irrelevant either because it does not afford women the appropriate rights over their own bodies, or because women lack the control and power necessary to ensure exclusivity of use, whatever the law says.

The battle for control

Because of the way in which women themselves, and society at large, tends to identify a woman very closely with her body it is important not to ignore the implications of this fact. The battle for ownership must proceed on two fronts; first women need to gain power and control over their own bodies, thus asserting self ownership in a moral sense, and second they need to acquire legal rights to exercise that power and control.

The first battle must ensue at the level of culture, the focus being language, interpretation and representation. Women must be afforded control over their own bodies by being allowed to control the interpretation of the bodily functions which punctuate their lives. Women must claim their bodies as parts of their selves, and understand their bodily experiences as something which they control rather than something which controls them. This is obviously an issue within the medical realm, particularly within reproductive medicine, but having power and control over interpretations of the body is also important in the much wider arena.

In our culture the demands of 'normal' femininity still set highly specific standards of bodily attainment ensuring that fat is indeed a feminist issue, and that physical beauty is both a route to power and a compensation for powerlessness. It is on these issues that new battles need to be fought. Women need to seize control of the imagery of self that is presented to them by society.

In her extremely successful book *The Beauty Myth* Naomi Wolf argues that women who successfully carried through the Second Wave of feminism in the 1970s are faced with a new threat (Wolf, 1990). The backlash against female success has come in the form of the beauty myth, 'the last remaining feminine ideology' which according to Wolf has 'taken over the work of social coercion that myths about motherhood, domesticity, chastity, and passivity, no longer can manage. It is seeking currently to undo psychologically and covertly all the good things that feminism did for women materially and overtly' (Wolf, 1990, p.11).

Wolf quotes Barthes who defines a myth in the following terms '[i]t transforms history into nature....Myth has the task of giving an historical intention a natural justification, and making contingency appear eternal' (Barthes, 1972, p.129). Although she rarely refers to his work directly the particular myth that Wolf relates owes a great deal to orthodox Freudian pronouncements upon femininity, and the myth of Oedipus.

In his 1933 lecture *Femininity* Freud presented an account of women's biological destiny, and most importantly, charted the route for the development of normal femininity (Freud, 1986). Women, due to their peculiar experience of the Oedipus complex, emerge from adolescence with certain 'marks'. One of these is physical vanity 'since they are bound to value their charms more highly as a late compensation for their original sexual inferiority', others are narcissism - preferring to be loved to than to love -, and shame because of their physical mutilation (the lack of a penis).

Feminists have succeeded to a certain extent in rehabilitating Freud and would argue that his representation of normality with respect to femininity is structurally determined as opposed to biologically determined.[2]   Thus a generous reading of Freud's account would interpret it as description and critique rather than prescription. The beauty myth as presented by Wolf feeds on the Freudian myth of normal femininity, and complements it by tyrannising even those who reject normal femininity as described by Freud in favour of a masculinity complex - even the conventionally successful working woman is oppressed by the heroines of the myth.

The greatest danger lies in the fact of this being a 'covert psychological' operation, thus making it more difficult to control, but it also has its overt signs. For example, the woman's body is still under attack from the surgeon's knife, but now the boom industry is cosmetic as opposed to gynaecological. Similarly, the 'weight control cult' has replaced organised religion as the opiate of the female masses.

The problem is one of the way in which women are made to see themselves, and how they cope with what they see. To borrow Rousseau's terms, amour de soi has been completely supplanted by amour propre (Rousseau, 1968). Women see themselves only in relation to others, and the most visible others are the 'ideal' types presented to them by the dominant culture. The problem is that these ideal types are unrealistic and even dangerous.

Wolf calls upon women as 'tenants of their bodies' to decide for themselves what they see when they look in the mirror - only then will they have the power to enjoy the fruits of previous feminist battles, and go forward to claim more victories. At present we judge our bodies against an impossibly high standard set for us by society - hence we always fail, and there is always more we could and should do in order to succeed. The myth has the power to bankrupt us economically, divert attention from more worthwhile projects, and most worryingly of all it can make us ill.

Dismantling the beauty myth is possibly the hardest battle that women will face, and it is a battle in which the law can offer them little assistance. Short of censoring the pages of womens' magazines and controlling other purveyors of popular culture little can be done to protect women from the battery of images that keep her in her place. Women will only come to own and control the interpretation of their bodies through their own efforts, through a new way of seeing, and a new social representation of beauty.

Rosalind Coward believes that many women have found a new arena for involvement with their bodies in alternative health (Coward, 1989). Women have worked with the age old idea that they are closer to nature than men, and so when medicine moved back to more natural means they saw themselves as better equipped to be healers. Alongside this involvement there has been a reinterpretation of history and the emergence of a new mythical woman. Ostensibly at least she is more acceptable than the emaciated beauty queen of Wolf's account; 'part goddess, part mother, part witch, part ancient healer, this woman is the symbol of creative and healing nature itself' (Coward, 1989, p.154). The problem is that once again she is a symbol and 'when any group (whether it be sexual or ethnic) becomes a symbol, the individuals in that group will be defined from outside and suffer from that identity' (Coward, 1989, p.175).

Women are once again over-identified as, and with, themselves as bodies this time primarily 'geared up for reproduction'. A valuable opportunity has been lost because instead of engaging in a political battle for control as healers, women have diverted their energies to developing what Coward calls 'a philosophy of nature and feminine values' (Coward, 1989, p.176). Within this philosophy the imagery evoked and the symbolism developed allows all too easily for women to be classed once again as a minority, and to be marginalised by the dominant ideology. In fact the ideology itself has constructed the two main features of the symbolic representation of earth mother so prevalent in this discourse - nature and femininity.

Women have chosen an unfortunate image with which to identify because it takes the fight out of them. There is no place for anger and aggression in the new image of the woman at one with nature dancing under the light of the moon, her emotions tied up with her body, and her body devoted to reproduction and healing. Nor should the risk of personal failure be underestimated, just as the woman suffers because of expectations attached to the beauty myth, she can also fail to fulfil the expectations set by the myth of alternative health; 'natural' childbirth being a classic example.

Women cannot win the battle for control over their own bodies simply through supplanting traditional images with ones of their own making because they do not have the power to create an image impervious to distortion or marginalisation. Myth is not a useful weapon in the political struggle for control, indeed it should be an early focus of attack.

Law as an adjunct to control

I would now like to consider whether the law can assist women in establishing ownership rights at a different level particularly in the area of reproductive medicine which has always provided stark examples of the way in which society seeks to control women by controlling bodily experiences such as childbirth, and the fundamental choices concerning contraception and abortion. It is worth acknowledging at this stage that if one makes something the subject of legal discussion, this in itself can pose problems in terms of controlling the images created and utilised. For example, in discussing the crime of rape two distinct personalities have emerged - the angel and the whore - the latter has done no more than admit to a sexual past and a certain degree of substantive independence, the former is the true innocent. If the foetus were to become a character in case law, a step so far avoided in Britain, (Gibson,

1990), emotively he would be cast by most as the innocent.

Although women have experienced a significant degree of success in de-medicalising and re-claiming childbirth, recent technological advances have created new issues which need to be addressed. Advances in pre-natal screening and the ability to see the foetus in utero have contributed to the increasingly common representation of 'foetus as patient.' Naturally we welcome any opportunity to relieve suffering and reduce mortality but it should be recognised that the heightened profile of the foetus poses new threats to the woman's control over her pregnancy, and in the extreme reduces her role to a mere carrier - a womb.

This creates a new potential for conflict of interest in which the woman may be at an emotive disadvantage. The pressure placed on a woman to 'behave properly' is not restricted to situations requiring medical intervention. Even perfectly healthy women carrying healthy foetuses feel the tyranny of social pressure which focuses upon them once their bodies announce their pregnancy to the world. This pressure is increased by the more general move towards holistic explanations within medicine, and the prevailing metaphor of 'wholeness' bequeathed by alternative health therapy. Given the growing evidence of the way in which the life style of a pregnant woman influences the well-being of the foetus, society increasingly demands that women restrict their activities to those which society considers 'safe'. In the US the social pressure has been reinforced by legal sanction and the wishes of the woman are viewed in the context of potential litigation by dissatisfied off-spring.

The question then arises as to what a woman may be required to do in the interests of her foetus, and the extent to which she should be held responsible for the consequences of her choices and actions. Since the Wolfenden Report of 1957 English law has enthusiastically employed the Millian notion that one of the clearest justifications for the fact that something is the law's business is that it causes harm to others. What we now have to ask is whether the fact that a woman's actions may harm her foetus is a justification for legally enforcing the woman to act or refrain from acting in particular ways. We are free to ask this question because we see that the existence of a harm is not in itself sufficient to ensure the involvement of the law eg. adultery.

The law may well be decisive in setting limits of acceptable harm or in establishing specific circumstances within which harms are permitted; so, for example the Abortion Act specifies when and for what reasons a foetus may be aborted. However, the law is not the only agent of social control; social opinion and popular moral climate also make demands on the individual and often influence actions far more directly. It has also been claimed that 'resource management' has been employed as an easy unaccountable means of restricting abortion choice in Britain (Gibson, 1990, p.183).

Society is free to set higher standards than the law requires, and this has already begun to happen in relation to smoking during pregnancy. For as long as the pressures are social, as opposed to legal, individual women retain control, albeit limited, over their own experience of pregnancy. If the law spoke on behalf of her foetus, and that foetus was afforded significant status and rights in law the status of a pregnant woman is potentially diminished and until safe delivery is ensured she may find her entire existence controlled by others in the interests of another. The pregnancy and the pregnant woman's body would be owned by the foetus and the woman would lose control of all important areas of her life for the period of 'confinement'. This fact was recently acknowledged within the courts when a judge refused to prevent a young woman from having an abortion against her partner's wishes - to do so he said would be to tantamount to enslaving the woman. (Gibson, 1990, p.182)

Issues of ownership have also arisen as a result of advances in reproductive technology and the emergence of surrogacy. The Warnock Committee consciously avoided discussions in terms of property rights (Warnock, 1984) but this has not prevented property disputes arising. There have been cases in the US where frozen embryos have become an issue in divorce settlements. There have been cases in which surrogate mothers have refused to hand babies over to their natural fathers, and there may yet be a case in which the donor of egg or sperm claims some right to the resulting offspring, or alternatively where the offspring makes demands upon the donor.

A theory of property rights

These examples all raise interesting issues and suggest that as well as a clear definition of property or ownership we need a theory which explains when and how property rights are created. Many such theories exist but one seems particularly useful in this context - this is the theory developed by the eighteenth century philosopher John Locke in his work the *Second Treatise of Government* (Locke, 1963).

Locke used the term property in a number of different ways and incorporated both narrow notions of money, land etc. and broader notions of well being. His theory was straightforward and began with the assumption that every man has property in his own body - in Locke's opinion this is given to him by God - he also has property in his labour. 'Property right arises out of a combination of the right of preservation and the fact that each is master of himself and proprietor of his person' (Grant, 1987, p.97).

However, Locke has a very specific explanation of how one creates a property right in a particular object, say land. Locke believes that God bequeathed the Earth to all men in common, but prudence and simple economics suggests that it should not be held in common, therefore it has to be divided up. He further believed that land as such is of little or no value, rather '[l]abour...puts the difference of value on everything' (Locke, 1963, p.40). By working on the land man puts value into the land which was not previously there, and makes it his own as his labour is now mixed in with the land. That which is his own can be removed from the common stock and may be used by him as long as he does not allow it to spoil and as long as he leaves as much and as good for others. What becomes his private property may only then be removed from him with his consent.

Locke's property theory and the law

There are a number of interesting ideas that can be utilised here, in the first instance in the area of egg, embryo, and sperm donation.

It is now relatively easy to implant a donated egg into a woman who cannot produce viable eggs, and artificial insemination by donor sperm has never been problematic. In the case of egg donation we accept that the genetic material belonged to another woman because we ask for her consent before collecting her spare eggs and donating them. But if we follow Locke's reasoning, once an egg is placed in the host woman she mixes her labour with it and ownership is transferred in two senses. First, because the donor has consented to the transfer either directly or through participating in a donation programme, and secondly because the recipient has made it her own by mixing her labour with it and ensuring it becomes a valuable form of life.

Locke's principles might also be applied within the context of surrogacy arrangements. In the case of broken surrogacy contracts, although a man donates his sperm, the surrogate usually supplies the egg and always mixes her labour with it to create the embryo, and then nurture the foetus. Without the efforts of the surrogate the sperm would be of no value. She creates a right of ownership which she can choose to transfer back to the natural father, but she may also choose to claim the child as her own. If her claim goes against a legal commitment to hand the child over there will be a conflict between moral claims and legal obligations. Given Locke's theory she would appear to have a strong moral claim to ownership and one which means that contracts of surrogacy could not be enforced once the surrogate withdraws her consent to the transfer of ownership.

In cases where the fate of frozen embryos depends on the outcome of a dispute between parents, the situation is immediately more complex. We could still argue that without the labour of gestation the embryos are not going to become a valuable form of human life. However, it is open to the father, or indeed the mother, to find a surrogate. This introduces further complexities. The surrogate would appear to have less claim in this case because the genetic material and the egg are owned by another woman. Ownership is not transferred by contract, rather to use another of Locke's terms, the donor 'entrusts' her own egg to the surrogate.

If embryos are to be stored it seems important to establish clear rights of ownership and control so as to accommodate the incidence of separation or bereavement. There are a number of arrangements couples may choose to make including disposal or donation of the embryos if they, as a couple, choose not to use them together. It is also possible that the storing facility may lay some claim to the embryos if they were artificially created by them. Having said this, it would be preferable for the specific couples involved to make a contract and lodge it with the storing facility, rather than for the law to make a blanket recommendation. A pre-fertilisation as opposed to pre-nuptial agreement may be an answer.

Locke's theory also has a bearing on the question of abortion and the use of aborted foetuses. It would appear from Locke's argument that the woman has the right to decide whether or not to have an abortion, but having decided to do so, her right to determine the fate of the foetus diminishes. Unless some labour is again mixed with the foetus, in terms of experimentation or medical application, it will in Locke's terms be 'wasted.' Ownership may therefore transfer to those who can make use of the material, with control over their activities being exerted by someone other than the woman. Mary Warnock would find this approach unpalatable, feeling as she does that the woman's views should be taken into account even if she can provide no rational reason for denying use of the aborted foetus (Warnock, 1984).

A rather different example suggests how Locke's theory might prove useful outside the realm of reproductive medicine. Recently in the United States a case occurred in which an individual claimed a share of the financial rewards attached to the development of a new drug, because the drug had been developed using a part of his body which had been removed following disease. To test his claim it is necessary to ask whether there was any value in the organ before the scientists mixed their labour with it. The answer to this is surely no, and the courts implicitly followed Locke's reasoning. The patient had to consent to the organ being removed, but the next question is whether he has to be asked for his permission for it to be used for scientific purposes? It would appear that the answer is no with two important provisos. First, consent must be acquired if the bodily material is going to contribute to the formation of new human life, and second in the case of experimentation or therapy the practices proposed must have been approved by the appropriate regulatory bodies.

The first proviso may need some further explanation. If I require a new lung, medical evidence suggests that it is easier to give me a new heart and lung, so I then have a spare heart which can be donated to someone else. If the operation is a success the result is that a person who already exists is kept alive. If I donate an egg or embryo and the procedure is successful, the result is the creation of a sentient being which would not otherwise have existed. I have helped to create a life, and I am in some sense causally responsible for what happens from there on. This is true in a limited sense in the earlier example, because there I have caused the person to remain alive, and therefore have had a part in allowing whatever they do or experience. The difference is that the person chose life, whilst in the second example I created a life independent of the will of the person created. For this I must take some responsibility and an acknowledgement of this responsibility will be demonstrated through my willing consent.

The second proviso is surely difficult to argue with. No procedure experimental or otherwise should be free from ethical scrutiny. If appropriate bodies and processes exist then individuals may be sure that the morality of the practices involved has been assessed. However, one might wish to accept that those with strong moral views which oppose the prevailing morality on the issue should be free to act on those views. One way of allowing this is to have an acknowledged general policy of utilising removed organs without specific consent, and require that those who object on conscientious grounds opt out.

This general policy would dictate that once an individual has consented to the removal of a part of her body, or an unwanted foetus, it is as if these return to the common stock. It is then open to other individuals, in practice doctors or scientists, to remove them once again and put value into them on behalf of their patients or society as a whole (as long as the practices involved meet ethical approval).

One final point takes the discussion even further. Do I, according to Locke's theory, still own my body when I am dead, or does the fact that it will be 'wasted' unless utilised diminish my property rights in it? Given that there is not 'enough and as good' to go round do I have the right to deny the use of my organs after death? As English law stands the ownership of a body passes to the relatives after death, and they have the power to decide what happens to it, but is this right? If by mixing labour with it the doctors can place value back into parts of a dead body, and transfer its organs to another would we not benefit from regarding dead bodies as something else which goes back in to the 'common stock'? These latter thoughts are as yet undeveloped, but I offer them for consideration.

Conclusion

This essay has fallen into several parts, but it should also come together as a coherent whole. The thesis is this. We need to establish ownership over our own bodies, but to do so we must first make our bodies a real part of our selves - this is particularly difficult for women operating within a patriarchal framework. On the one hand, women identify very powerfully with themselves as bodies, but on the other hand, the images they identify with and the myths surrounding that identification are not conducive to successful ownership in terms of exclusive use and control.

In order to seize control of the way in which this aspect of their selves is represented by popular culture women need to attack the destructive myths and ideal types imposed upon them. The law can be of little direct assistance here, unless we get into wider discussions of censorship and antidiscriminatory legislation. However, we can look to the role of law in clarifying relationships of ownership, and look for a theoretical basis upon which to decide what body ownership actually means in more mainstream terms. It has been my suggestion that Locke's theory allows us to apply a principled response in the instance of conflict.

Although I have chosen to speak mainly of women and women's bodies this is no longer a subject over which men can afford to be complacent. Advancements in genetic screening make each of our bodies vulnerable in a new and quite frightening way. It is even possible that we might have to unearth the old law which stated that a man owned his hair clippings, but we would do so for reasons that the originators of the law would have found impossible to comprehend. By using DNA 'finger printing' an untrained individual with the appropriate kit can test a strand of hair for a range of genetic markers, which in term provide highly sensitive information about an individual's health. In such cases Locke's theory would provide little help and so we may need to think further on this issue, and quickly.

* Lecturer in Philosophy and Medical Ethics, Keele University.

1. Debate still rages as to whether there have been two, and now maybe three distinct waves of British feminism. However, it is generally accepted that the early 1970s saw a change in the focus of feminist attention onto matters previously considered personal as opposed to political, private as opposed to public.

2. See for example Juliet Mitchell's *Psychoanalysis and Feminism*, 1975, Harmondsworth, Penguin.

Dangerous Liaisons?

Law, Technology, Reproduction and European Ethics

Derek Morgan* and Linda Nielsen**

... we lack a perspective for judgement of transformations that go so deep ... Everything around us is new and different - our concerns, our working habits, our relations with one another. Our very psychology has been shaken to its foundations, to its most secret recesses. Our notions of separation, absence, distance, return, are reflections of a new set of realities, though the words themselves remain unchanged. To grasp the meaning of the world of today we use a language created to express the world of yesterday (de Saint Exupery, 1939).

Rosalind Petchesky has argued that

despite their benefits for individual women, [reproductive technologies] also have the effect of carving out more and more space/time for obstetrical 'management' of pregnancy ... they divert social resources from epidemiological research into the causes of foetal damage. But the presumption of foetal 'autonomy' ('patienthood' if not 'personhood') is not an inevitable requirement of the technologies. Rather, the technologies take on the meanings and uses they do because of the cultural climate of foetal images and the politics of hostility towards pregnant women and abortion (Petchesky, 1987).

The development of reproductive technology presents contradictory choices, especially for women. Technically, some of the developments have increased the capacity of women to take control of their own bodies; with some versions of cloning and parthenogenesis it has even been argued that the notion that reproduction belongs to women would take on a new dynamic with the ability to reproduce without the need for the patriarchal genetic. AID and even IVF have brought about the possibility of reproduction without most of the family structures which have for long been associated with it. These 'liberating' capacities and possibilities are, however, being offered at the potential price of making those same bodies available for and accessible to medical technocrats, giving greater power to it to exercise over women's lives. As Gena Corea foreshadows, '[when] reproductive engineers have developed an artificial womb, they might place the cultured embryo directly into the mother machine' (Corea 1985). The categories of language and thought which we use descriptively are strained by the pace and propulsion of change. Technological 'medicine' has developed in such a way in the past decades that it is possible to envisage and soon to create concepts of birth, parenthood and family faster than vocabulary can be brought to the aid of understanding. When and how much people are disturbed by things anomalous to their systems of classification is not, of course, susceptible to easy evaluation; the 'normal' and the 'pathological' are cultural and historical specificites (Canguilhem, 1949).

Technology has hastened our notion of self conception to the brink of an evolutionary surge; the notions of value and worth which we attach to individuals and social groups, the nature and meaning of fertility, and the concept of the family are all implicated. The ensuing debate cuts into fundamental values and increasingly the very institutions of maternity, paternity, motherhood and fatherhood are subject to examination and re-evaluation. New demons and chimeras and spirits are conjured to haunt the new families which technological and personal upheavals have introduced. The 'reproduction revolution' brings in its wake many new and difficult choices. This gives rise to the dilema that 'for every complex problem there is a solution that is neat, plausible and wrong' (Borrie, 1991).

Developments and choices

Human fertilisation is often said to be remarkably inefficient, although the concept of efficiency which is prayed in aid here is often unspecified. The use of reproductive technologies is based on the wish to become parent(s). Clinicians are thus encouraged to provide services within the ambit of medical competence. Between one in seven and one in ten couples in the reproductive population seek help in their efforts to conceive. Amongst these couples are those whose infertility remains unexplained after all the standard diagnostic tests. Despite this, most women who attempt to conceive do so within one year, although women and men may experience great distress when they confront difficulties and may be recommended to consider assisted conception.

The plight of the 'infertile' is seen as legitimating the time, technology and resources spent upon it, such that the announcement by the United Kingdom government in late 1991 that they would fund the new regulatory authority HFEA to only 50 per cent of its total operating costs led to renewed charges that 'the infertile' are being unfairly, even unlawfully, discriminated against, and that charges raised for private infertility treatments amount to a 'tax upon the infertile'.[1] This stands in contrast with the position in Denmark, where although there is a roughly similar level of GDP provided in respect of health care, it is seen as axiomatic that if there is to be provision for infertility treatments then this, as with other aspects of health care, should usually be undertaken at public expense. The existence of a few specialist clinics has, however, revealed a global market for assisted conception services. The techniques and trappings of assisted conception, AID, IVF, GIFT, cryopreservation of gametes, eggs and embryos, gamete and embryo donation, surrogacy, and other developments in assisted conception also challenge our traditional views of procreation and parenthood. This challenge has legal as well as ethical implications.

In each country of Europe, including Eastern Europe, similar questions arise with respect to law, medicine and bioethics. But there are differences of a philosophical, economic, social, political and even geographical nature which are not easily (even if desirably) bridged. The parallel between explosive political change within and across Europe and the rapid developments in bioethical sciences and their impacts on the fields of law, ethics and human rights give rise to challenges on at least three levels;[2]

1. Human rights; what is the meaning, for example, of a 'fundamental right to human life', and in what way(s) is this question metamorphosed by biotechnology? What is meant by the European Convention on Human Rights' guarantee (in Article 12) of the right to 'marry and found a family' and how do substantive and procedural barriers to access to biotechnology impinge on that 'right'?

Reconciliation of advances in medicine and science with values expressed through human rights is necessary to preserve the bioethical balance; to ensure that the risks to patients, providers and the subjects of biotechnology are minimised. Laws, administrative regulations and professional codes of conduct must be carefully scrutinised to elaborate the effects they set out to achieve, whether they achieve those and only those ends, and whether there are other, unintended, unforeseen or unforeseeable effects (Griffiths, 1979).

2. Democracy and public choice; how should these difficult issues be mediated; towards consensus, a toleration of moral pluralism, or within the dictates of one dominant philosophical approach? What is the fulcrum of the bioethical balance? What institutional structures are used, proposed or necessary to articulate and effect these determinations of public choice? Is there a difference between, and are there advantages to, standing national ethics councils charged with parliamentary accountability (such as the Danish Council on Ethics), compared with either the voluntary committee such as recently instituted in the United Kingdom under the auspices of the Nuffield Foundation or the voluntary Interim Licensing Authority and its statutory regulatory successor; the Human Fertilisation and Embryology Authority?

3. The rule of law: a fundamental question which arises for any jurisdiction is whether there is any existing law which regulates biomedical practice, research and development and

whether it is satisfactory in assisting our responses to ethical dilemmas posed by biotechnology; is it too accommodating or too hostile? Examples of very different responses are well illustrated in an Anglo-Danish comparison.

For example, in 1990 the United Kingdom Parliament passed the Human Fertilisation and Embryology Act which is a highly 'permissive' statute. In contrast,the Danish Parliament enacted in 1987 a piece of 'restrictive', holding legislation[3] while debate was reviewed by the contemporaneously constituted statutory Council of Ethics, which has no direct counterpart in the United Kingdom. That review has now been completed and the proposed Danish legislation, which has been debated in 1991-92 is expected to be enacted and come into force on 1 October 1992. Here we provide a cursory overview of each legislative framework as an introduction to the comparative exercise which we later want to establish.

The Human Fertilisation & Embryology Act 1990

The legislation has several purposes (Morgan & Lee, 1990). The first is to regulate certain infertility treatments which involve keeping or using human gametes and to regulate the keeping of human embryos outside the human body. The Act deals with only four of the treatments currently in use; artificial insemination using donated gametes: AID, egg donation, embryo donation, and in vitro fertilisation: IVF.

The second purpose is the statutory regulation of embryo research, which is now permitted until the appearance of the 'primitive streak'; for the purposes of the legislation that 'is to be taken to have appeared in the embryo not later than the end of the period of 14 days beginning with the day when the gametes are mixed', excluding any period of cryopreservation.

Thirdly, there is a prohibition on the creation of hybrids using human gametes, the cloning of embryos by nucleus substitution to produce genetically identical individuals, and genetic engineering to change the structure of an embryo. The fourth purpose is to effect changes to the Abortion Act 1967.

The main vehicle for conveying these changes is the Human Fertilisation & Embryology Authority, which came into being on 7 November 1990. The Human Fertilisation & Embryology Authority is a statutory agency charged with a wider range of responsibilities than its voluntary predecessor, the Voluntary, later Interim Licensing Authority, established following the publication of the *Warnock Committee* report by the Royal College of Obstetricians & Gynaecologists and the Medical Research Council. HFEA is primarily a licensing body concerned with three main areas of activity; the storage of gametes and embryos, research on human embryos, and any infertility treatment which involves the use of either donated gametes or embryos created outside the human body.

Different parts of the Act apply to the collection, storage and usage of such gametes. Where a clinic performs AID using gametes from the couple alone, or where it undertakes a procedure such as GIFT - gamete intrafallopian transfer - using the couples own gametes, then the licensing conditions of the legislation do not apply. There are some provisions of the Act to be attended to, but not the full blown licensing scheme.

In addition, HFEA is charged with maintaining a register of information concerning donors, treatment services and children born following licensed services, publicising services which centres and HFEA itself provides, producing advice and information to centres and publishing a code of practice to which centres should adhere or aspire and providing information to donors, to potential patients and to children born following regulated services. The Code of Practice contains provisions which deal with the confidentiality of records kept in pursuance of the Act, specify arrangements necessary for securing compliance with the 'consents' requirements of sch.3, establish screening procedures for donors of egg and sperm, provide guidance on the numbers of eggs, or preembryos, which should be transferred to the uterus and detail appropriate laboratory standards and qualifications and experience of staff employed at licensed centres.

Jonathan Montgomery has summarised these provisions in a characteristically perceptive fashion. The Act, he writes provides the first attempt in English law to provide a comprehensive framework for making medical science democratically accountable. Its interest therefore arises both from the solutions it adopts for particular issues and from the model of regulation on which it builds (Montgomery, 1991).

The Danish legislation of 1987 and 1992

In April 1984 the Danish Minister of the Interior established a committee to investigate the ethical problems connected with genetic engineering, in vitro fertilisation, artificial insemination and prenatal diagnosis. The Committee's report, *The Price of Progress*, was presented six months later. In it, the establishment of a central ethics council for the health system was recommended. Following the Danish Parliament's consideration of the report the Council of Ethics' work was initiated in January 1988. The legislation provided that a number of specific matters should be reviewed and that legislative proposals should be laid before the Parliament in the session 1989-90 at the latest. The Ethics Council produced background and briefing papers, held public meetings and published a book of the proceedings in order to inform and stimulate public debate. Specific interest groups and public and private institutions were asked to comment before the Council presented its report *The Danish Council of Ethics Second Annnual Report 1989; Protection of Human Gametes, Fertilized Ova, Embryos and Fetuses*, in 1990. This 'interim' approach to regulation is in itself worthy of comment. When issues of reproductive technology came initially to be discussed in Denmark, the view was taken that the issues at stake were of such importance that a legal vacuum or hiatus was quite inappropriate, and the law of 1987 was enacted to provide what in effect amounted to a moratorium on embryo research and a restriction on the uses of assisted conception until the contemporaneously established Ethics Committee had had the opportunity to address the social, legal and ethical questions which it believed that these developments disclosed. The draft Danish bill was originally published on 17 April 1991 and in an amended form after initial debate on 23 October 1991. It is expected that the resulting legislation will be enacted to come into force in October

1992, with a statutory obligation to undertake review and revision if necessary by 1995-96.

The Council was charged by the 1987 legislation to proceed on the basis that human life begins at the time of conception. The intention of this provision was later interpreted by the Minister of the Interior, in responding to a question from the Parliamentary Committee responsible for the Ethics Council, as not to give a definition of human life and its inception, but 'to establish that the Council of Ethics ought to work from the basis that it is not ethically or legally an argument for unlimited freedom of action toward the human ovum that this is not human life. In other words from the moment of conception onwards, a situation exists where it is ethically and legally necessary to consider and perhaps introduce particular limitations in the freedom of action'.[4]

This is not the place to dissect or debate the philosophical, ethical or scientific assumptions underlying this formulation. It is sufficient to observe that the 'protection' given by the 1987 Act did not prevent a majority of the Ethics Council sanctioning very limited forms of experimentation, nor the draft legislation before Parliament approving of embryo research up to 14 days after fertilisation. The proviso is that the object of the research, sanctioned by a regional as well as the central committee, must be the improvement of techniques of in vitro fertilisation with a view to promoting pregnancy. Removing and fertilising eggs or embryos for any other purpose is however prohibited.[5] The legal motives (explanatory memorandum) appended to the Bill make it clear that the main reason for accepting research but restricting it in this way is that IVF is a recognised treatment and that research is accepted internationally as an integrated part of the development of treatment; prohibiting all research would mean consciously offering less optimal treatment than possible.

Chapter 2 section 5 of the legislation provides that any biomedical research project which includes research on living human individuals, human gametes which are intended for use in fertilisation, fertilised human eggs and pre-embryos or embryos should be reported to regional ethical committees. There are presently seven such committees, established according local government boundaries, and they comprise 9 or 11 members, three of whom are nominated by the state authorised scientific committee. The Constitutional position of the Ethical Council is parallelled by committees charged to oversee narcotics, alcohol, traffic safety, consumer questions, and the independent economic council.

The central and regional committees are charged to supervise and where appropriate to approve research, although the Bill nowhere contains a definition of that term. Section 9 provides that fertilised eggs may only be kept outside the woman's womb for 14 days from conception, excluding any period of cryopreservation. Fertilised human eggs which have been subjected to research must not be implanted into a woman's womb unless this can be done without risk of transmitting hereditary disease, defects, abnormalities or similar deformities. The purpose of this provision appears to be to permit the diagnostic biopsy of embryonic material ex utero without thereby attracting the prohibition on transfer to the uterus of embryos which have been the subject of research. The donation of fertilised eggs is prohibited by section 13(5), although by virtue of section 13(6) the Minister of Health may make further rules regarding cryopreservation and donation of human eggs, and further regulations securing donor anonymity. The legal motives specify that it is a precondition that the donation of unfertilized human eggs is only undertaken anonymously while the legislation presupposes that it will only be permissible to cryopreserve eggs for a maximum of one year. The Bill does not deal with sperm donation although administrative provisions operated through the central Danish cryopreservation facility for sperm ensure that this will only be undertaken anonymously. Civil law questions of family rights will not be effected by this legislation because those questions are deemed to lie within the domain of the Ministry of Justice. Unlike the British legislation then, the Danish Bill does not aim to be as comprehensive or wide-ranging; and in neither case does the legislation present itself as a code covering all questions of assisted conception.

Additionally, Chapter 4 section 14 prohibits cloning; the production of individuals by fusion of genetically different embryos or parts of embryos prior to implantation (nucleus substitution) and experiments whose objective is to make possible the production of living human individuals which are hybrids with a geonome containing constituent parts of other species (cross species fertilisation).

Controversial conception

There are at least three areas of particular controversy within these two pieces of legislation, which we briefly address here. A range of contested issues to which the whole programme of assisted conception gives rise lies beyond the limited scope of this present paper. The first area of difficulty is whether children born following the provision of treatment services involving donated eggs or sperm should have the right to know of the identity of the donors of those gametes. It would be possible to adopt one of at least four positions here:

a) that no identifying information be made available to such children.

b) that any information be made available provided it is with the consent of the donor.

c) that all identifying information be made available at the request of the person born following treatment services.

d) that some non-identfying information be provided.

The UK Act and its accompanying regulations provide that the fourth option is the one to be followed. On reaching the age of 18 an applicant may require HFEA to furnish information if it discloses that the applicant was or may have been born following the provision of treatment services, provided that the applicant has first been given the opportunity to receive suitable counselling.

There are interesting comparisons to be drawn with the way in which Scandinavian countries have responded to this particular problem. In Denmark donor anonymity is secured by the administrative fiat, through the way in which the public donor bank functions; the child is not entitled to be informed of the identity of the father, nor of the fact that donor insemination has taken place. The Ethical Council Report of 1990 was quite forthright on this issue. In Norway the principle of anonymity has been legally enshrined; there it was argued that the parents of the child would want anonymity and that it might be very difficult for them to accept the appearance of the biological father many years after the birth. Further, it was argued that the donor would not usually want to be associated with his child; most donors would probably refrain if the principle of anonymity was abolished. Finally it was averred that despite the difficulties for a person who did want to know of their biological origins, the possible conflicts between parents and child and the strain which such a meeting might impose on the child outweighed any benefit which could be foreseen.

However, in Sweden the position is different. There a child who is the result of donor insemination is entitled to know the identity of the donor once it has reached sufficient maturity, and the argument again has relied upon the concerns for the welfare and interests of the child. Despite initial fears and caution, the number of donations and treatment cycles with donated gametes has returned almost to the pre-1985 level, although with marked changes in the characteristics of the donors, who now tend to be older, married men rather than the younger donors of the late 1970s and early 1980s. This question of donor identity is but one manifestation of the larger concern with the status and interests of the future child, and, with the parallel development of the human geonome mapping project, the interests of future generations. How are we properly to assess the interests of the future child or the generations to which she will belong? Leave aside for the moment the difficult conceptual issues of whether future generations or the as-yet-non existant can have interests or rights, what are the ethical implications, and what role if any is law to play?

At least two contrasting approaches are possible; first, it can be argued that to assert the primacy of the benefit which assisted conception bestows on the child - life - is to approach the matter upside down. The fact that some adults wish to become parents is sometimes thought of as paramount; if they cannot have a child they may be disappointed, frustrated, grieving, angry, or any combination of these and other things. But there is no child to disappoint; as Lucretius[6] nicely put it in the related context of death, 'it is like the eternity that passed before we were born; we do not regret our non-existence, the time of not being, therefore we have nothing to fear in death' (Hanfling, 1987). In parallel, the child who is not born, or the children who were not born before the advent of modern reproductive technology, have suffered no loss. That there may be disappointed adults who are unable to have their own 'genetic' children, and that the state's interest in maintaining a stable population base and growth rate may each be harmed, are extraneous matters of little or no consequence in weighing the interests of the child.

On the other hand, it is argued that in the absence of overwhelming physical, mental and relational dysfunction,[7] it is conceptually impossible to compare non-existence with even a life lived in what has been called 'genetic bewilderment', in which the person has no knowledge of his or her parents, nor of how to discover this. This position does not deny that some people born following assisted conception, like some people who have been adopted and separated or insulated from their genetic parents, experience real suffering. This argument would hold, however, that the interest of the 'future' child should always be subordinate to the wishes of the intending or putative parents; that to extend 'welfare' considerations for future children back before their conception is to devalue the real benefit which simply flows from being alive and that nothing beyond that needs to stated. Of course, this argument is wider than that more simply contained within the parameters of the discussion of anonymity, but it provides the backdrop against which such claims need to be considered.

The approach adopted in the United Kingdom is one in which the interests of the child are regarded as particularly important but not necessarily paramount. Thus, in the Human Fertilisation and Embryology Act 1990 sec 13(5) it is provided that

> A woman shall not be provided with treatment services unless account has been taken of the welfare of any child who may be born as a result of the treatment (including the need of that child for a father) and of any other child who may be affected by the birth.

This section raises but does not address a fundamental question in respect of assisted conception. It is the second of the major issues to which the development and refinement of reproductive technologies have given rise. If all the financial and counselling hurdles are surmounted, does every one have a right to 'marry and found a family' as specified in Article 12 of the European Convention on Human Rights, or can that be circumscribed by general considerations of public policy, howsoever justified? The UK Committee of Inquiry, the Warnock Committee (1984), clearly thought that such a 'right' would be undesirable[8]

> ... many believe that the interests of the child dictate that it should be born into a home where there is a loving, stable relationship and that, therefore, the deliberate creation of a child for a woman who is not a partner in such a relationship is morally wrong ... we believe that as a general rule it is better for children to be born into a two-parent family, with both father and mother, although we recognise that it is impossible to predict with any certainty how lasting such a relationship will be.

The Danish Council of Ethics in its Second Report, *Protection of Human Gametes, Fertilised Ova, Embryos and Fetuses* reached somewhat similar conclusions. They record that artificial insemination and in vitro fertilisation should be placed on an equal footing with intercourse at least when semen and unfertilized ova from the interested couple is used and the woman herself becomes pregnant. Here, the family relationship is not changed by the use of assisted conception techniques; 'society should not impose special demands on the qualities of the expecting parents'.

A majority of the Council, however, then proceed to make two different findings. First, one majority group holds that it is desirable for a child to have parents of the opposite sex. A different majority hold, however, that it is not crucial that a child has an identifiable father from the outset of the treatment services. It ought not to be a prerequisite, they write, for artificial insemination or in vitro fertilisation that it concerns married or established cohabiting couples. There are many single women with children; this family form is becoming more recognised and accepted and, they conclude, single women ought also to have access to artificial insemination and in vitro fertilisation. Thus, for both countries the ground rules for access to treatments are comparable. A majority of the Danish Council go further, however, and comment that 'Danish society today has given lesbian couples the possibility of a marital status, from this point of view, lesbian couples ought also have the possibility of artificial fertilization. Furthermore, there ought to be no differential treatment of single women and two women who live together'.[9]

The Bill, however, does not address this point; there was no pressure for this to be included in the legislation so policy will be decided in individual hospitals. This effectively leaves this important question of medical jurisprudence solely to clinical discretion. There are those who believe that it would have been better for provision to have been made in the legislation to address this issue rather than for it to have been left to individual clinicians. In contrast, the British approach, whatever its intended effect and likely outcome has the advantage, as many see it, of subjecting clinical judgment on fundamentally ethical questions to the possibility of external review.

It is not possible within the compass of this essay to resolve this difficult question of access to treatment services. On the one side, the argument is advanced that the child has the right to a father and a mother, and that an individual's strong desire to have a child, while it may indeed help ensure a secure basis for the child's later development, is not sufficient to outweigh the interests of the child in later life. The involvement of medical science in the creation of human life means that there is the opportunity to discriminate in the interests of the child and that that opportunity should be taken. While the creation of one parent families cannot be averted, the deliberate use of assisted conception services in such circumstances offends against the rights of the individual child who will result. Here what has been called the biological determinants of family take precedence over the customary or subjective intentions of those adults involved.

In contrast, it might be urged that having children is, largely, a private area of human affairs, and that it is not for the state to decide who should and who should not be allowed to have children.[10] Parenting involves risks, both to the physical and mental health of the children and the parents. Whether a couple are married, or even whether they are of different sexes is irrelevant to their parenting abilities and the social, sexual and psychosexual development of their children.

The third 'internal' problem concerns the status of the children born following this 'reproduction revolution'; are they to be treated - even though biologically they are not - as the children of their 'social family' or should the lack of a genetic link be specifically acknowledged, and even declared on the child's birth certificate? Here, approaches have been more uniform and the prevailing consensus is against the open acknowledgement of the genetic background and status of children born following assisted conception.

Concepts, conception and regulation

These three areas together enable us to identify some of the major conceptual and ethical problems which even a tolerant acceptance of techniques of assisted conception disclose. Ruth Macklin (1991) in a recent essay has emphasised and attempted to clarify some of these concerns. She argues that artificial means of reproduction

> have rendered the term biological inadequate for making some critical conceptual distinctions, along with consequent moral decisions. The capability of separating the process of producing eggs from the act of gestation renders obsolete the use of the word biological to modify the word mother. The techniques of egg retrieval, in vitro fertilisation (IVF), and gamete intrafallopian transfer (GIFT) now make it possible for two different women to make a biological contribution to the creation of a new life.

From this she argues that a number of different determinants of what is meant by 'family' can be drawn. In addition to the 'traditional' biological vector, she suggests that law, custom and what she awkwardly calls 'subjective intentions' (more simply what people choose to do despite law or accepted custom) can all be factored to produce an understanding of what family is, or how we understand it or them to be composed. She concludes

> The effect of artificial means of reproduction on our

understanding of the family will vary, depending on which of these three determinants is chosen to have priority. There is no way to assign a priori precedence to any one of the three. ... there is no simple answer to the question of how artificial means of reproduction affect our understanding of family. We need to reflect on the variety of answers, paying special attention to what follows from answering the question one way rather than another. Since there is no single, univocal concept of the family, it is a matter for moral and social decision just which determinants of 'family' should be given priority.

Some of the broader, external questions concern the nature and status of 'infertility'; whether it is a health care issue at all, and something to which resources should be devoted; and if so whether they should be exclusively private or wholly publicly resourced. Again Montgomery has anticipated the nucleus of the challenge here

> [t]he status of infertility raises the second of the major background issues to the 1990 Act on which consensus is absent. Much rhetoric has emerged under the slogan of 'the right to reproduce' but the concept remains an obscure one. It might refer to a range of claims. It can refer to no more than the negative right not to be robbed of the capacity to procreate without just cause. At the other extreme it might be said to entail a duty on the state to provide services to help overcome infertility. Between these two versions of the right is a claim that the state should facilitate assisted reproduction by removing any rules of law which prevent individuals taking steps to overcome their inability to have children' (Montgomery, 1991).

Of course, there could be an intermediate position, which places a negative obligation on the state not to do anything which obstructs 'private ordering' attempts to overcome infertility, such as surrogacy arrangements or any aimed at circumventing infertility, such as self insemination.

The United Kingdom Royal College of Obstetricians & Gynaecologists' 1983 Report *In Vitro Fertilisation and Embryo*

Transfer argued that 'one function of medicine is to alleviate the aberrations of nature. The treatment of infertility is intended to correct such an aberration'. The assumption here is that infertility is an exclusively biological fact, an aberration of nature, without specific cultural backdrops or even established aetiology (Doyal, 1981). Yet infertility is as much a social construct as a biological fact; in Barbara Schiterman's memorable phrase 'there is no such thing as biology in the socialised world' (Schiterman, 1983).

Against this background, we may suggest that legal initiatives may be required for one or more of four reasons.[11] First, a symbolic function of law; declaring certain values and interests as worthy of protection against any infringement. In the present context, prohibitions on altering the structure of the nucleus of an embryo, cloning, cross species fertilisation, the creation of chimeras and measures to protect or safeguard the life of the unborn foetus as paradigm examples. They are part of the vocabulary of who we say we are and who we want to become. Second, a protective function; providing sanctions for abuses within the bioethical field, and for minimising risks to patients and significant others affected by the application of biotechnology - such as potential children who might be born following assisted conception (Nielsen, 1991). Third, a regulative or declarative function; there is probably no legal system with a comprehensive biomedical law. The legal status of many bioethical practices is unclear in the absence of parliamentary intervention, which is seen or appealed to as securing clarity and certainty in handling controversial areas of bioethics. Again, regulation of the permissible extent of embryo research is a paradigm example. Finally, a technical function may be required for law; to stabilise confidence between physician and patient by providing reliable rules for their relationship. One example of this might be ground rules relating to access to lawful abortion facilities, another dealing with aspects of confidentiality in respect of genetic knowledge obtained during the course of pre-natal or ante-natal screening, and a third in the (non) disclosure of the identity of gamete donors to children born as a result of assisted conception.

Introducing ethical pluralism

This essay has been in part an attempt to explore the ways in which these determinants have been manipulated in two European legal systems to produce pictures of the family. We are interested in the ways in which those legal systems have been customised to provide temporary answers and marshalling points for regulating reproduction in trying to order the response to the 'reproduction revolution'. We want to begin an investigation into what sorts of interests and values the law is being used to underscore. The use of two contrasting approaches to the regulation of reproductive technologies helps to expose not only the plurality of moral responses - which may be reflected in different legislative approaches, but also some of the ambiguities of reproductive technology and the contrasting ways in which this might impinge upon or even compromise reproductive freedoms.

This is very much an introductory and exploratory essay, in which more descriptive than analytical work has been done. It sets an agenda and, self-consciously, probes the outlines of some of the questions which we feel a European approach to the regulation, supervision and promotion of health and health care enjoins. There are, of course, serious doubts which we can express about the 'externalities' involved in different types of regulation. For example, suppose that the Danish legislation were to propose (as the German Embryo Protection Act 1990 has done) that research using human (pre-) embryos is prohibited unless for the therapeutic benefit of that individual embryo. Would that mean that citizens or inhabitants of Denmark would or should be disentitled from reaping the benefits (if any appear) of subsequent scientific work which has traded specifically on such research? This is a variant of an argument much canvassed since the Third Reich and experiments or torture performed on human beings without their consent. Is such 'knowledge' so morally tainted that to draw any benefit from it whatsoever is similarly profane and perverted? These difficult questions are ones which we want here only to identify as candidates for a much broader agenda which we intend to pursue.

Differences in legislative response and differences in the extent to which questions such as these arising from the advent and adventure of reproductive technology constitute items on public, social and legal policy agendas, will depend on permutations and nuances in tradition, religion, culture, economics and wealth. Throughout the European Community and the member states of the Council of Europe moral and legal pluralism reflecting these variations is evident. Yet, it is sometimes overlooked that that pluralism typically operates at the margins of what might be called the ethical stationery. The depth and breadth of agreement far outweighs and outpaces moral disagreement, whether the supporting reasoning is of a broadly consequentialist or of a deontological kind. However, it is at the margins of this ethical page that the lines become less clear, the text blurred and the meanings most ambiguous, oppositional and most evidently contextual. It is in these margins that legal script becomes most branded with national trademarks, and yet in the commonality of responses there are some common themes to be pursued.

In analysing this Europeanisation of ethical responses to reproductive technologies, two sorts of foundational work which have driven deep into the bedrock of ethical debate need to be surveyed, anatomised, reinforced and reconstructed. First, an attempt to declare and understand differing philosophical approaches needs to identify the background cultural theories implicated in the analysis; this is an essentially epistemological question. Second, the way in which these views have been translated into legal regulation or its functional equivalent, legislative quiescence, needs to be carefully constructed and explored. Assumptions and expectations, intentions and outcomes will need to be documented and analysed. As individual European countries increasingly debate questions arising from in vitro fertilisation and embryo research[12] it is apparent that general agreement is emerging, that common core approaches are desirable. This consensus is apparent both within the scientific community and European institutions.

But for the present there remains the difficulty of towards which position harmonisation should gravitate; it could be either towards more restrictive or more liberal or radical approaches. Which is the polar position to which plural systems should be magnetised and what are the active critical masses? Unless there is to be a 'harmonisation downwards' it is apparent that if research centres in different countries are to engage in successful, co-operative projects, then some common ethical norms, backed by harmonised sanctions, are essential. This is recognised in Articles 130F-130Q of the Single European Act, which amongst other things seeks to establish an annual European research programme with common standards for the projects involved.[13] The Commission's recent proposals for Human Genome Analysis[14] are a further example of this.

Against such diverse legal and ethical backdrops we may wonder as to the feasibility and comprehensibility of, for example, a European Bioethics Convention? Our preliminary conclusion is that this diversity makes the case for such a Convention more pressing. It would be mistaken to assume that the goal here might be accommodation by consensus; that would in effect be 'harmonisation downwards' without excuse or reason. There is, perhaps on the agenda of ethical and philosophical issues the temptation to believe that legislative attempts to secure recognition of one particular view at the expense of others is the enforcement of moral majoritarianism. Thus legislation is sometimes asked to portray or reflect a 'weakened and expansive ethics or moral conception' (Danish Council of Ethics, 1990). The relationship between ethics and law 'makes it necessary to pose two questions in connection with concrete legislation: does the legislation live up to that minimum of humanity which the society wishes to preserve and does it allow real freedom for the individual to observe stricter standards than those contained in the law? (Danish Council for Ethics). It would be impudent and impotent to believe that the continued and further use of assisted conception techniques and associated research will atrophy. This point is well made by the Haderka

> [i]t would be an illusion to think that further use of biomedical assistance to non-coital fertilisation can be stopped. Its application is so deeply rooted that it can be eradicated by no means in any of its forms, especially those connected with the use of donated gametes or embryos. No effect can be brought

by outlawing some technology in one country or in a group of countries. Artificially induced births will continue to occur because pregnancy will be available in other countries which will permit them and the world becomes more and more interconnected and travels to this aim will be quite easy (Haderka, 1991).

Of course, it would be frivolous in any comparative exercise such as that upon which we have embarked to fail to acknowledge the enormous economic, social, theological and philosophical traditions which separate Latin America, African, and Asiatic countries from those in Europe, the North Americas, and Australasia, and the different traditions within each of these federations. This means that gradual evolution of regional ethical and legal standards seems to be the most realistic way to envisage further progress in assimilation and harmonisation of legal regulation and ethical consideration of reproductive technologies. Even within Europe, where harmonisation or approximation seems more likely and perhaps desirable, the experience of the Ad Hoc Committee of Experts in Biology (CABHI) is far from reassuring; the recommendations which it proffered in its Report *Human Artificial Procreation* (1989) were not carried forward. This experience makes the comparative studies which we have here foreshadowed more important, perhaps more urgent.

As we noted in the opening quotation from St Exupery, 'our notions of separation, absence, distance, return, are reflections of a new set of realities, though the words themselves remain unchanged'. We need to be careful that the dangerous liaison between biology, technology and humanity is carefully reflected in the forms and content of legal and ethical regulation which we bring to assisted conception. This will depend in part on the view we take of technology itself; whether for example, we see it as a tool or as a system. This will affect on the one hand whether our ethical and legal evaluations are aimed not directly at the technologies themselves but at their different possible uses. Or if we believe technology to constitute a coherent system with its own incentives, gradient and vectors, then the possibility of its planned control is not a matter of course and 'technology' will appear as a

72

power which requires us to adapt to its development. This has begun to happen; external fertilisation or egg and embryo donations illustrate this. The existence of the fertilised ovum outside the woman's body has fragmented reproduction. The separation of the embryo and the woman gives rise to the belief that decisions regarding the embryo are a matter for the mother and the father or the embryologist or the recipient patient and partner if donation is contemplated. Dilemmas occasioned by disagreement between, say, intending mother and father cannot be resolved on any a priori basis. The real difficulty, we think, is that the individualisation of ethical responses, characteristic of much pluralistic westernised views of the value of life, risks 'dehumanisation' and that to grasp the meaning of the world of today we may be forced to adapt the language which we created to express the world of yesterday. This dangerous liaison will itself be an attempt to explore the possibilities behind that fear.

* Morgan, Senior Fellow in Health Care Law, Centre for Philosophy and Health Care, University College, Swansea.
** Nielsen, Associate Professor, Institute of Legal Sciences, University of Copenhagen.

1. Hansard 17.7.91 col.194.

2. Following Catherine Lalumiere (1989), 'Allocutions D'Ouverture' in Europe and Bioethics, Proceedings of the 1st Symposium of the Council of Europe on Bioethics, Strasbourg.

3. Law on the Establishment of an Ethical Council and the Regulation of Certain Forms of Bioethical Research (no 353 of 3 June 1987).

4. Council of Ethics report, p.50.

5. Kapitel 4 para. 13.

6. This is from the 1951 translation of *On the Nature of the Universe* by Latham, R. (1951), Harmondsworth, Penguin.

7. This has been addressed by the UK courts, see *Re C* [1990] 3 All ER 930 and *Re J* [1991] 2 WLR 140. There are no comparable Danish cases.

8. We reserve the whole troubling question of rights based jurisprudence, its constituents and determinants, and the question of whether appeals to such doctrines, fashionable though they have become, have any logical coherence or status.

9. For an analysis of the Registered Partnerships Act 1989 see Nielsen (1900) *Int. J. of Law and the Family* 108.

10. A strong counter-argument is presented by LaFollette (1980) and is responded to by Frisch (1982).

11. See Eser (1989), *Legal Aspects of Bioethics*, in Europe and Bioethics, Strasbourg.

12. Three straightforward examples are the UK Human Fertilisation and Embryology Act 1990 s.3 and 11, the German Embryo Protection Act 1990 cl.11.11 and 12 and the proposed Danish Bill of October 1991, (limited sanction for embryo research if the purpose is to achieve a successful IVF pregnancy).

13. See Council Decisions 87/551/EEC, OJ L334/20 (November 24, 1987) and 85/195 EEC OJ L83/1 (March 25, 1985).

14. COM (89) 532 final draft.

Regulating Sexuality: A Legislative Framework for Non-Consensual Sterilisation

The precedent set by *Re F* is that decisions of this nature will continue to be made on a case to case basis and it is *because* the details of each case differ that we would approve the process; the calls for specific legislation should, we believe, be resisted because it would, inevitably, lead to generalisation in an area where the individual is paramount' (Mason & McCall Smith, 1991, p.94 footnotes omitted).

Josephine Shaw*

Introduction

One of the most problematic interactions between law and sexuality lies at the point where a medical device for preventing conception - sterilisation - emerges as an ostensibly convenient solution to the difficulties thrown up by the exercise of sexual autonomy on the part of a group of people for whom conception is by and large seen as socially undesirable: those suffering from a mental disorder or handicap. Sterilisation challenges the law, since it represents an interference in bodily integrity and reproductive autonomy which, in the absence of the consent of the subject of the sterilistion, would be seen in liberal terms as a human rights violation, attracting the sanction of penalties under the law. Where the subject cannot consent, at least in conventional terms, the issue becomes that of balancing personal autonomy - ie not forcing upon a person something which she[1] has not agreed to - against welfare - ie not denying access to medicine to a person simply because she cannot consent.

The internal logic of a legal framework for nonconsensual

sterilisation, which will inevitably be characterised by the typically self-referential nature of legal concepts such as consent and competence, offers an incomplete response to the challenges of medical possibility and social and ethical desirability in the realm of sexuality. Statements of value about persons implicit or explicit in the legal framework (eg the ability or lack of ability to consent) are not neutral vis-à-vis wider issues such as medical power, or the construction of mental health. However, it is possible to postulate, in general terms, a certain minimum rubric within which an acceptable legal framework for nonconsensual sterilisation could be expected to operate. This rubric can be reduced to two central goals: the first is to regulate coercive sterilisations which, for ethical and historical reasons must be regarded as repugnant. The second is to provide a legal framework which strictly limits the use of involuntary but non-coercive sterilisations, providing effective substantive and procedural safeguards ensuring that mentally handicapped people - most frequently, in practice, women - are not sterilised for eugenic reasons or for the convenience of their carers.

It is perhaps inevitable that nonconsensual sterilisation will be used as a contraceptive device, but it should be available only as a mechanism of last resort, truly necessary in limited circumstances in order to avoid a greater evil; stringent restrictions must therefore be placed on its use. It must not be permitted to masquerade as a complete solution to the complex moral and practical dilemmas posed by the balance to be achieved between the right of mentally handicapped people to sexual self-expression and the need to avoid the greater physical, mental and emotional damage which they might suffer as a result of exercising that right, such as the side effects of repeated use of injected contraceptives, or the trauma of abortion and childbirth (Scroggie, 1990). In moral terms, although it can never be right to deny to mentally handicapped persons unable to give an informed consent the types of therapeutic medical interventions required to save their lives or prevent a serious deterioration of their mental or physical state, the availability of a legal mechanism which does away with consent or which substitutes a surrogate consent must not be allowed to become either a coercive measure or a substitute for alternative, less intrusive but perhaps more inconvenient and expensive measures for avoiding the undesired by-products of the exercise of sexual autonomy. Involuntary sterilisation permanently denies procreative choice, yet it can arguably be justified in certain circumstances as an acceptable means of ensuring sexual choice. In practical terms, it cannot claim to resolve all difficulties regarding sexual activity such as the risk of sexual exploitation, and exposure to sexually transmitted diseases and AIDS. There remains an unresolved conflict between paternalism, expressed through the welfare principle, and autonomy, expressed in terms of inalienable rights, since nonconsensual sterilisation promotes the former at the expense of the latter (Fennell, 1990).

A legal framework which successfully achieves these two goals will be stringent in its condemnation of forced sterilisations, modest in the claims which it makes on behalf of sterilisation as a medical device for the care of mentally handicapped persons, and clear and certain in the regulatory framework which it establishes.

This essay evaluates the legal frameworks governing the nonconsensual sterilisation of mentally handicapped persons recently elaborated in German and English law in the light of these principles. The common law position under English law is considered only briefly in the first section as a counterpoint to the statutory position under German law. The recent intervention of the legislature in Germany to ban forced sterilisations and the sterilisation of all minors, and to create a network of substantive and procedural conditions governing the legality of the giving of surrogate consent to other nonconsensual sterilisations is assessed in more detail, principally in order to throw into relief the contrasting recent developments in English law. It is argued that a legislative framework is preferable to a common law framework, and that change is all the more urgently required in English law because of the absence of a clear human rights context (for example, in the conventional form of a written constitutional guarantee) under which the interests of mentally handicapped people can be identified and given concrete form. A legislative framework remains better able to satisfy the twin demands set out above, without necessarily slipping into the generalisations feared by Mason & McCall Smith, than the judge-made law which occupies the legal terrain under English law.

77

In an earlier article, I argued that legislative intervention was desirable, not only because it provided the opportunity to put in place a defined and clear legal framework which would attempt to protect the interests of mentally handicapped persons against the abuse of their bodies and procreative capacity, but also because it gave the opportunity for a reasoned public debate about the historical and contemporary issues involved (Shaw, 1990). I contrasted the law-making by judicial fiat which has occured in England with the developments then taking place in the Federal Republic of Germany with a view to the elaboration of a statutory framework governing the non-consensual sterilisation of persons incapable of giving consent. This came within the overall context of a major overhaul of the legal provisions on guardianship for persons who are mentally handicapped, mentally ill or frail and vulnerable for some other reason, such as age. The new provisions have now been adopted and came into force in the Federal Republic on January 1 1992.[2]

This essay concludes the story of the adoption of the new legislative framework, tracing its fate in the hands of the German Parliament, and its Committee. It recapitulates the different positions put forward by those opposing and proposing the adoption of a sterilisation clause, and the nature and content of the provisions finally adopted. The general objective is, by importing a comparative perspective, to make it possible to offer a wider range of policy options in order to tempt the domestic legislature into regulating a field which, in the continuing opinion of this writer, cries out for a clear statutory framework.[3] This does not mean to say that the approach taken in the Federal Republic is necessarily one to be followed. For as Wedderburn (1991) has argued in another context, the use of the comparative dimension means

> not the foolish search for institutions to import from elsewhere but the stretching of the imagination and of the agenda by inquiry into unfamiliar legal treatments of familiar social problems and in so doing to follow the argument wherever it leads.

The point is the simple one that by following the experiences of other jurisdictions, we will strengthen our own ability to deal with parallel social developments within the domestic forum. The approach taken here represents a combination of two of the aims of comparative law recently identified, also in another context, by Collins (1991). While remaining receptive to the possibilities of legal transplants (one of the classic positivist aims of comparative law), yet sceptical of the true workability of such a project, the comparatist now focuses on increasing the level of understanding about the domestic system, as a consequence of appreciating the problems encountered and solutions devised by other systems. This form of comparative law will, however, only work successfully in circumstances where neither the specificities of legal development nor questions of underlying ideology render the domestic experience so dependent upon such highly specific national contingencies that it is in truth incomparable. In the case of nonconsensual sterilisation, although the historical background including the Nazi sterilisation laws in some respects separates the German experience from the UK experience, the basic structures of tort law premised on recognising the unlawful nature of interferences with the person which are not consented to or justified on some other ground provide a firm foundation on which to pursue a comparative project such as the present one.

A critical examination of English law

The law of consent in relation to mentally disordered persons has developed parallel streams of statute and common law in English law (Fennell, 1990). The Mental Health Act 1983, Part IV, lays down procedures for doctors to proceed without the consent or against the refusal of detained mentally disordered persons to administer treatment in relation to that mental disorder. Other medical treatment falls outside the scope of the Act, and is governed by the common law. In relation to the nonconsensual sterilisation of mentally handicapped persons for contraceptive reasons, the latter does not contain an unequivocal condemnation of coercive sterilisations. Inasmuch as certainty and clarity are afforded by the law, moreover, it is certainty and clarity in the interests of professionals and carers, whose interests are not always identical to those of those they care for. In *Re F*,[4] for instance, Lord Bridge's first concern appeared to be with the protection of the former rather than with the rights of the latter

> [i]t seems to me of first importance that the common law should be readily intelligible to and applicable by all those who undertake the care of persons lacking the capacity to consent to treatment. It would be intolerable for members of the medical, nursing and other professions devoted to the care of the sick that, in caring for those lacking the capacity to consent to treatment they should be put in the dilemma that, if they administer the treatment which they believe to be in the patient's best interests, they run the risk of being held guilty of trespass to the person, but if they withhold that treatment, they may be in breach of a duty of care owed to the patient.[5]

In *Re F* the House of Lords held that the English courts have no jurisdiction to give surrogate consent to the sterilisation of a mentally handicapped adult, which would be the equivalent to the statutory wardship jurisdiction for minors, or the common law *parens patriae* jurisdiction for incompetent adults which continues to exist, for example, in Canada.[6] However, the sterilisation of a mentally handicapped adult without her consent will not be unlawful provided it is in the best interests of the patient. The operation would be in her best interests if it is carried out in order to save her life or to ensure improvement or prevent deterioration in her physical and mental health.[7] A doctor will be held to have acted in the best interests of the patient if he or she has acted in accordance with a responsible body of medical opinion - the so-called *Bolam*[8] test used to determine the standard of care in medical negligence cases.[9] Although it is not obligatory, it is certainly highly desirable as a matter of good practice for the proposed sterilisation of a mentally handicapped adult to be brought before a court, and for the court to issue a declaration if it believes the sterilisation to be lawful.[10]

The decision in *Re F*, like the earlier House of Lords decision in *Re B*[11] sanctioning the sterilisation of a minor under the statutory wardship jurisdiction, and subsequent first instance decisions sanctioning the sterilisation of mentally handicapped girls,[12] has been subjected to a good deal of adverse academic criticism (On *Re B*: Freeman, 1988; Lee & Morgan, 1988; Montgomery, 1989b; Bainham, 1987; De Cruz, 1988; On *Re P*: Brazier, 1990; on *Re F*: Scroggie, 1990; Ogbourne & Ward, 1989; Carson, 1989; Morgan, 1990). Much of the comment has focused on the apparent inadequacy of the common law, in the hands of the judges, to the task of creating a mandatory protective jurisdiction to ensure that the interests of the mentally handicapped person are fully taken into account in the decision-making process and of elaborating acceptable standards of human rights protection. The apparent ease with which the courts have reached their decisions, dealing, seemingly in passing, with some of the most intractable moral issues of our time, such as the conflict between sexual and procreative freedom, the conflict between paternalism and autonomy and the continuing influence of eugenicist and discriminatory thinking, allowing simple assertion to become the substitute for argument, (eg the curt dismissal of the influence of eugenics by Lord Hailsham in *Re B*[13]) and the generalised acceptance of sterilisation as an appropriate solution to the 'problems' thrown up by the sexuality of mentally handicapped persons have all been a cause for concern.

Particularly vehement criticism has been directed at the decision in *Re F* to use the *Bolam* test of clinical judgment as the standard by which to judge the doctor's evaluation of the 'best interests' of the patient (Morgan, 1990; Jones, 1989). While on the one hand the judges have declared that it is good clinical practice to have the decision to sterilise judicially evaluated by means of the procedure for a declaration, with the other hand they have handed the entire decision-making process back to the doctors by making the test governing the legality of the clinical <u>assessment</u> of the best interests of the patient a test of medical <u>competence</u>. The *Bolam* 'responsible body of medical opinion' test is concerned less with the process of seeking the reconciliation of possibly competing individual rights to proceative and sexual freedom in the light of the perceived best interests of the patient, and more with the operation of interprofessional solidarity between the medical and legal professions and the willingness of the English judiciary to accept, largely at face-value, assertions of professional competence by the doctors. Carson's comment in this regard is perhaps most damning

> [i]s it imaginable that any other group of people (other than those with learning difficulties) could have their *best* interests restated as merely the right not to have others make negligent decisions in relation to them? (1990, p.372).

Surprisingly, little criticism has been directed at the absence of any outright prohibition of coercive sterilisations in cases such as *Re F*. Yet no attempt was made in that case to define the limits of 'best interests' in circumstances where the patient is actively resisting a medical intervention, for example, because of a generalised fear of 'white coats'. Gardner (1991) asserts that the paternalism of the House of Lords' decision in *Re F* is a weak form of paternalism, concerned with the (inevitably fictional) discovery of what the 'victim' would have wanted had she been able to consent, rather than the stronger version of paternalism which simply disregards the self-determination of the victim in pursuit of what are deemed to be their best interests. However, he acknowledges that misgivings must surround the determination of 'best interests' in the approach of the House of Lords since the invocation of the *Bolam* standard seems to indicate that it is more a case of what (some) doctors want rather than what the patient herself would have wanted.

In reality, however, the patient deemed incapable of consenting may have little opportunity to express opposition - thereby clarifying what she does not want, for the purposes of the best interests test - because there is no requirement that her carers attempt to explain what is to happen. Of course, where the patient has not been informed in any way of what is to happen to her, she has little opportunity to make objections. It is implicit in the English case law that the evaluation of competence to give consent may be judged without an attempt necessarily being made to see if she can in fact understand. Yet under the common law of consent, the nonconsensual sterilisation of a person competent to give consent constitutes an unlawful battery and will be regarded as coercive in that sense regardless of whether or not consent was first sought. Should mentally handicapped people not have the same right to say 'no' in similar circumstances, irrespective of their capacity to consent? It is submitted that the best interests model used in *Re F* veers towards a stronger and morally unacceptable form of paternalism than that postulated by Gardner.

Since the decision in *Re F*, sterilisation may have disappeared from the front pages of the newspapers,[14] but disturbing legal developments have still been occurring. In two decisions in early 1991, it was held that therapeutic hysterectomies required on pure 'medical' grounds by both mentally handicapped minors and adults, which have the incidental result of rendering the patient sterile, do not require the consent of the court.[15] They fall outside the ambit of both the declaration procedure for adults and the wardship jurisdiction for minors. Contraceptive sterilisation had itself in 1989 already been the subject of a Practice Direction issued by the Official Solicitor.[16] This set out detailed guidelines on the procedure to be followed for obtaining the declaration of the court on the legality of the proposed course of conduct. The Practice Direction states that

> [t]he sterilisation of a minor or a mentally incompetent adult ('the patient') will in virtually all cases require the prior sanction of a High Court judge.

The proceedings must commence by a summons for directions heard by a High Court judge. This would be followed by a full adversarial hearing, at which the evidence would be considered. The purpose of the procedure is defined as establishing 'whether or not the proposed sterilisation is in the best interests of the patient' and ensuring that 'those proposing sterilisation are seeking it in good faith and that their paramount concern is for the best interests of the patient rather than their own or the public's convenience'. The role of the Official Solicitor is to act 'as an independent and disinterested guardian representing the interests of the patient'. Finally, a non-exhaustive list is given of the types of matters about which the Official Solicitor would anticipate that the judge would need to be satisfied before making the declaration. These fall under four heads - the assessment of the competence of the patient, the likelihood of conception, the risk of damage to the patient and the necessity of sterilisation rather than a less intrusive alternative.

The Practice Direction was considered by Thorpe J in *J* v *C*.[17] He cast serious doubts upon whether there would in fact be two hearings in all cases of sterilisation. He stated that if, after the initial summons for directions

> the case appears straightforward and without contention, (the judge) may dispose of it there and then without further adjournment. For although the gravity of the issues and consequences in sterilisation cases call for appropriate safeguards against hasty or ill-considered conclusions, many such cases involve a real degree of urgency. The longer the litigation, the longer the period in which the patient may be exposed to risk. Furthermore, in cases of emergency the originating summons can always be preceded by an initial application ex parte when the court, on an undertaking to issue the originating summons forthwith, may consider abridging time limits or dispensing with procedures generally appropriate.

This decision has rightly been criticised as considerably diminishing the legal protection provided by the sanction procedure and of creating a situation in which mentally handicapped children and adults may be deprived of minimum standards of dignity and respect (De Cruz, 1990). It amply illustrates the fluidity of the guidelines laid down by the appellate courts in *Re F* and the inadequacy of the Practice Direction, as a source of legal rights. The Practice Direction itself has been amended following *J* v *C*.[18] It now states

> The proceedings will normally involve a thorough adversarial investigation of all possible viewpoints and any possible alternatives to sterilisation. Nevertheless, straightforward cases proceeding without dissent may be disposed of at the hearing for directions without oral evidence.

There are, therefore, two categories of case exempted from the requirement of an adversarial hearing - the 'urgent' case and the 'straightforward' case. Few of the sterilisation cases reveal any great inclination on the part of the judiciary to undertake the type of critical analysis required to dissect the apparently innocuous but in truth highly ambiguous labels of the 'urgent' and 'straightforward' cases. Thorpe J assumes that both types of case are conceptually and practically unproblematic and that judges will be able to identify such cases, without difficulty and on the basis of the facts as presented to them. He does not assume a need to question the facts and assumptions on the basis of which the urgency or lack of controversy are asserted. One of the primary aims of the Practice Direction and the appellate court judgments on which it is based is to prevent the sterilisation of mentally handicapped persons for the convenience of their carers; yet they are the very people who most probably will be arguing that the case is urgent or straightforward, or both. Thorpe J has in fact opened the door to sterilisations on convenience grounds, for unless the judges are prepared to look more closely at the events leading up to the 'emergency' - who or what caused the emergency? was it brought about by some person's earlier dilatory behaviour? - and to challenge the construction of a situation as an emergency, even a good faith failure to bring the case to court until there is a real danger of pregnancy can easily lead to a slide down the slippery slopes of convenience.

The regulation of sterilisation in the Federal Republic of Germany

Legal developments in the Federal Republic of Germany present a contrasting picture. There, the argument in favour of statutory intervention needs to be seen in the context of the earlier legal and factual uncertainties besetting nonconsensual sterilisation.

A situation of legal and factual uncertainty

Whereas the figure placed upon the number of sterilisations of mentally handicapped women carried out annually in the Federal Republic by the Federal Ministry of Justice (1987), just over 1,000, compares somewhat unfavourably with the position in the United Kingdom where figures are available only in respect of mentally handicapped minors - 'some dozens' (Dyer, 1987) - the impression of the extent of the 'problem' of sterilisation as it emerges from submissions made to the Legal Committee of the Federal Parliament (*'Bundestag'*) when it considered the draft guardianship law is rather mixed (Protocol, 1990). One prominent opponent of the sterilisation clause, Prof. Dörner, argued that in his practical experience there was no widespread practice of sterilising adults incapable of giving consent to such a procedure. His argument against the introduction of a sterilisation clause was that it would operate as a Trojan Horse, encouraging the use of sterilisation procedures for competent mentally handicapped persons above and beyond the level currently thought appropriate (Protocol, 1990, p.215). In contrast, a number of respected organisations concerned with the interests of mentally handicapped persons, such as the *Vormundschaftsgerichtstag*, a body formed in 1988 in view of the reform of the guardianship laws to facilitate debate amongst guardianship judges, did claim that there was widespread and uncontrolled sterilisation of mentally handicapped women (Protocol, 1990, p.310).

The difficulty of determining the number of sterilisations undertaken should now diminish, since it will be possible to discover, via questions in the *Bundestag*, the number of sterilisations authorised through the new statutory procedures. The Federal Government is also required to report every four years to the *Bundestag* on the operation of the new law.[19] However, the full picture regarding the use of sterilisation will not emerge since the new law does not cover consensual sterilisations, and will not reveal how many are carried out with the 'consent' of a mentally handicapped person which may have been obtained as a result of the influence and pressure of family and carers.

The legal position regarding nonconsensual sterilisations has long been the subject of even greater uncertainty than the factual position, and a topic of considerable controversy and diversity of opinion in the Federal Republic under both criminal law and constitutional law (Shaw, 1990, p.94). The position with regard to forced sterilisations is, at least, clear. Forced sterilisations can be defined as those undertaken without the consent of a person capable of giving consent, or undertaken against the will of a person not capable of giving consent and without the surrogate consent of his or her legal representative (Pieroth, 1990). Since the time of the repeal of the eugenicist Nazi sterilisation law of 1933[20] by the occupying powers in 1946,[21] and the adoption of a comprehensive catalogue of fundamental rights in the 1948 Constitution, the unconstitutionality of forced sterilisations has not seriously been called into question. The rights to human dignity (Article 1), to self determination (Article 2(1)) and to the integrity of the person (Article 2(2)) unconditionally prohibit the forced removal of procreative capacity.

For nonconsensual sterilisations undertaken with the surrogate consent of a parent or guardian and where there is no expressed opposition on the part of the patient, positions put forward by academic commentators have varied from an almost total prohibition allowing only a limited exception for life-threatening danger (Reis, 1988; Mahnkopf & Spengler-Sadowski, 1984; Horn, 1983; Finger, 1988) via a wider exception in the broader interests of the physical and mental health of the patient (Pieroth, 1990), to a general acceptance of surrogate consent as adequate provided it is exercised in the best interests of the patient (Hirsch & Hiersche, 1987; Laufs, 1984). The position has been exacerbated since for the most part courts have refused to pass judgment on the matter, arguing that there is no statutory jurisdiction to authorise sterilisations.[22] The absence of both statutory and case law rules created unacceptable levels of uncertainty under which different interpretations of the legal position seemed equally plausible. Statements by legal commentators and interest groupings of what the law was easily shaded into what the law ought to be, a question which is bound to be coloured by personal moral and social precepts. That this was the case is supported by the fact that in the submissions made to the Legal Committee of the *Bundestag* each of the positions set out above formed the basis of at least one submission as to what the new law ought to be.

The linkage between the reality of nonconsensual sterilisation as practiced by the medical profession and the plasticity of the law prior to the introduction of the new statutory regime is perhaps most starkly illustrated by the two sets of Guidelines issued by medical interest groupings - the *Deutsche Arztekammer*[23] and the *Deutsche Gesellschaft für Medizinrecht*[24] - on carrying out sterilisations without the consent of the patient. Both sets of Guidelines were the subject of vigorous criticism, *inter alia* on the grounds that they embodied unacceptably eugenicist premises and paid insufficient attention to the autonomy of mentally handicapped persons (Köttgen, 1988; Finger, 1988; Reis, 1988).

Taking, for example, the Guidelines of the *Deutsche Arztekammer*, these are not only of historical interest as representative of the most 'permissive' position taken on nonconsensual sterilisation prior to the new law, but they also raise the question of how doctors might act in practice when faced with the much more restrictive statutory regime. The suspicion cannot easily be suppressed that the reality of the application of the new regime may have at its core the presuppositions of the old Guidelines.

Under the *Deutsche Arztekammer* Guidelines, two substantive conditions must be satisfied:

> the operation must be necessary in order to prevent reproduction by the patient (ie only sterilisation of women is envisaged) and must be in the best interests of the patient;

> the conditions under which abortion is decriminalised (para. 218a II of the Criminal Code) must be applied by analogy in order to determine whether or not the sterilisation is justified.

Abortion is decriminalised under German criminal law if one of the following 'indications' is satisfied: danger to the life or health of the woman; substantial risk of the foetus being severely handicapped; rape; and 'general emergency'. In the latter case, the pregnancy provokes a situation of emergency for the pregnant woman if it renders the carrying of the foetus to term an intolerable burden for her (Eser, 1986).

In addition, a number of formal or procedural conditions had to be satisfied, such as the obtaining of the surrogate consent of the patient or guardian and an up-to-date expert psychiatric/neurological report on the patient's condition and capacity to consent. Perhaps more revealing, however, were the requirements that the sterilisation should not be undertaken against the expressed will of the mentally handicapped person - but only if she was capable of insight into the proposed operation - and that the procedure must be fully documented in writing, to protect the doctor in any future legal action. The latter conditions exhibited a preoccupation with upholding the professional interests of the doctor, potentially at the expense of the rights of the patient, and finds a regrettable parallel in English law in the adoption of the *Bolam* test in *Re F*.

The new Guardianship Law of September 1990 and the sterilisation clause

The climate of uncertainty with regard to the legality of nonconsensual sterilisation sketched out in this section forms the background to the initiative of the Federal Ministry of Justice to include the statutory regulation of nonconsensual sterilisations within the new Guardianship Law. According to the Ministry's working party, a failure to use that opportunity to clarify the legal position of nonconsensual sterilisations would have amounted to dereliction of duty on the part of the legislature.

The new Guardianship Law itself constituted the culmination of a long-term project to reorganise and reconceptualise the socially and politically troublesome legal provisions which regulate the lives of those lacking full social, mental and physical capacity. The earlier provisions (Coester, 1991) dating from the time of the adoption of the Civil Code at the beginning of this century, focused on the removal of legal capacity and the running of the affairs of incompetents, in the interests of the protection of property and of the public. They used what the Ministry working party saw as outdated and, in some cases, socially discriminatory conceptions such as 'mental weakness', 'spendthrift', 'alcoholism' and 'infirmity'. Neither *Vormundschaft*, the most drastic form of guardianship, based on a classical conception of patriarchal power giving the right to one person to act for another on the basis of an authoritarian but protective relationship and closely linked to loss of legal capacity under the general provisions of the Civil Code,[25] nor *Pflegschaft*, which required the prior consent of the ward and existed separately to the loss of legal capacity, gave the courts the appropriate legal instruments with which to deal flexibly and sensitively with issues of mental and physical disability.

Since 1975, reform had been on the political agenda, and in 1986 the Federal Ministry of Justice set up an interdisciplinary working party which in 1987 and 1988 produced a series of preliminary drafts. Under the new law, *Vormundschaft* has been removed, and *Pflegschaft* superceded by the new concept of *'Betreuung'*. Although in terms of personal scope, the new law covers many of the same categories of persons, it subjects them to a very different legal regime, one which is now separated from the concept of legal capacity. The need for *'Betreuung'*[26] is defined by reference to the inability of the ward (*'Betreute'*), on the grounds of psychiatric illness or physical, mental or psychological disability fully to manage his or her own affairs (para. 1896 *et seq* BGB). This leads to the appointment of a guardian (*'Betreuer'*) by the Guardianship Court who will act on behalf of the *Betreute* within those limited fields determined by the Court, where surrogate action is <u>necessary</u>, necessity being one of the underlying principles of the reform (Lachwitz, 1990). *Betreuung* is, therefore, in all cases subject to the basic constitutional principle of proportionality, whereby a measure should always be appropriate to the end it pursues, and no more restrictive than absolutely necessary. This applies equally to the sterilisation issue.

The welfare of the *Betreute* is always paramount. Para. 1901 BGB requires the *Betreuer* to manage the affairs of the *Betreute* in accordance his or her best interests, giving the latter the opportunity, wherever possible, of exercising a maximum of choice and autonomy, within the limits of his or her capacities. From this general principle it must follow that whenever the *Betreute* is, in a particular instance, capable of autonomous action - eg of consenting or not consenting to medical treatment or sterilisation - he or she must be allowed to do so.[27] The inspiration of the reform is, therefore, while inevitably paternalist, nonetheless liberal in its approach to autonomy: the German Constitution or Basic Law (*Grundgesetz*) draws no distinction between those with and without disabilities - whatever their cause - as regards the possession and exercise of the core human rights, such as human dignity and self-determination. The new law aims to create a satisfactory legal framework within which those rights can be exercised as fully as possible by those unable to act at all times autonomously within the social sphere, and in which the emphasis is not on the passive administration of the effects and interests of the incompetent person, but on an active interrelationship between *Betreuer* and *Betreute*.

In that sense the guardianship law undoubtedly represents a historic modernisation of the law and the context of the debates was one of the awareness that the new statutory framework would remain in place for some considerable time. This awareness also coloured some contributions to the sterilisation debate, where it was argued that within the foreseeable future, advances in medical technology may render the need for measures involving a permanent removal of procreative capacity a thing of the past.[28] This is one of a number of arguments advanced by those who opposed the inclusion of a clause specifically legalising nonconsensual sterilisations undertaken under certain conditions, they regretted that the creation of an emancipatory legal framework should be accompanied by the restrictive regulation of the sexuality of mentally handicapped persons.[29]

The new regulatory framework for sterilisation in fact inserts a number of provisions into the BGB prohibiting all sterilisations of minors (para. 1631c BGB), legalising the nonconsensual sterilisation of adults subject to *Betreuung* under certain conditions (para. 1905 BGB) and introducing a range of procedural guarantees which govern the giving of surrogate consent by the *Betreuer* and the approval of that consent by the Guardianship Court. Para. 1905 BGB now provides

(1) If the medical intervention consists of the sterilisation of the *Betreute* to which the latter cannot consent, then the *Betreuer* may only give consent where:

1. the sterilisation is not being performed against the will of the *Betreute*;
2. the *Betreute* will remain permanently incapable of consenting;
3. it can be assumed that pregnancy will occur if the sterilisation is not carried out;
4. in consequence of such pregnancy, there is a risk of danger to the life, or of a serious damage to the physical or mental

health of the pregnant woman, which cannot reasonably be averted in any other way;
5. the pregnancy cannot be avoided through other acceptable means.

A serious risk to the mental health of the pregnant woman also includes the serious and continuing distress with which she would be threatened, because guardianship court proceedings relating to a separation from her child would have to be taken against her (paras. 1666, 1666a).

(2) The consent requires the authorisation of the Guardianship Court. The sterilisation may only be undertaken two weeks after the authorisation has become effective. In the case of sterilisation, the method which allows the greatest chance of refertilisation must always be used.

Para. 1905 needs to be situated amidst the other amendments to the BGB which provide for restrictions of the rights and liberties of mentally handicapped persons. In particular, the new para. 1904 BGB requires the authorisation of the Guardianship Court in addition to the surrogate consent of the *Betreuer* for all medical treatment and diagnostical measures involving a recognised danger of death or serious and lasting injury to the health of the *Betreute*. This would not appear to cover all medical interventions involving general anaesthetic, notwithstanding the inherent risks of anaesthesia (Schwab, 1990, p.686; Zimmermann & Damrau, 1991, p.541). It is unclear whether only the surrogate consent of the *Betreuer* is needed for nonconsensual abortions, despite the intensely personal nature of the intervention (Kern, 1991, p.70). It is interesting to note that Lord Donaldson in *Re F*[30] explicitly bracketed together sterilisation and abortion. Coester (1991, p.8) has argued that the *Betreuer* is entirely unrestricted in relation to the giving of consent to abortion, and that in the absence of a provision parallel to para. 1905(1) No. 1 above in para. 1904, an abortion can be undertaken even against the expressed opposition of a patient deemed unable to give consent. Treatment and diagnostical measures involving danger to life and health can be undertaken without court authorisation if danger will result from postponement.[31] Para. 1905 operates as a *lex specialis vis-à-vis* para. 1904. It is not clear whether this will mean that hysterectomies undertaken on medical grounds will need to surmount the hurdles in para. 1905 as well as para. 1904, purely because sterilisation will be an incidental result of the operation. This cannot have been the result intended by the legislature, since para. 1905 is by its very terms aimed at <u>contraceptive</u> sterilisations.

In addition, the new para. 1906 BGB allows for the restriction or removal of the liberty of the *Betreute* where this is in his or her best interests to prevent the self-infliction of physical injury or suicide, and to allow for the medical procedures to be undertaken which otherwise would not be possible. Measures taken under para. 1906 are subject to the authorisation of the Guardianship Court. Again there is uncertainty in the relationship between the two provisions, since it is not clear whether measures could be taken under para. 1906 to carry out a sterilisation under para. 1905, given the express prohibition on forced sterilisations in para. 1905(1) No. 1.

Complementary to the substantive conditions, are the procedural guarantees which have also been introduced by the new law. These include amendments to the law on matters relating to non-contentious jurisdiction[32] requiring the appointment of a special *Betreuer* to deal with the proposed sterilisation, a personal hearing for the *Betreute*, compulsory legal representation, and the provision of expert witness reports regarding the medical, psychological and social prognosis for the *Betreute* by experts, who themselves have interviewed the *Betreute*. The doctor who undertakes the sterilisation may not be one of the expert witnesses.

The legislative history of para. 1905

The first draft of the new law which was issued in November 1987[33] contained an almost identical prohibition on the sterilisation of all minors and a clause regulating the sterilisation of mentally handicapped adults which, with the exception of one amendment and one addition,[34] was the same as that ultimately adopted in late 1990, notwithstanding a lengthy consultation process.

The original draft of para. 1905 referred, like the *Deutsche*

Arztekammer Guidelines, to the criminal law provisions on abortion, stating that surrogate consent to sterilisation would be sufficient if the pregnancy which risked occurring if there were no sterilisation could lawfully be terminated. Only rape - ie the possibility or probability that the mentally handicapped woman would become pregnant as a result of physical abuse - was excluded from consideration as a ground for justifying prophylactic sterilisation.[35] The controversial 'general emergency' and eugenics grounds for abortion were thus filtered into the law on sterilisation, in addition to the more generally accepted ground for sterilisation of risk of harm to the physical or mental health of the mother. The link with abortion as representing a satisfactory analogy for determining the legality of nonconsensual sterilisations was broken only when the argument put forward by the Federal Ministry of Justice in its Explanatory Memorandum (Federal Ministry of Justice, 1987: 537-538) namely that it was widely accepted that the statutory representative of a person suffering from permanent incapacity was entitled to give surrogate consent to an abortion, was successfully challenged by opponents of the sterilisation law. They were able to show a considerable element of doubt in the law (Reis, 1988, p.321; *Deustcher Caritasverband*, 1990). By the time the second draft was issued in February 1989 for consideration by the *Bundesrat*,[36] that part of the new clause had reached its final form. As we have seen, it refers only to a danger to the life or physical or mental health of a woman whose pregnancy could be anticipated if sterilisation was not undertaken (usually but not necessarily the *Betreute* whose sterilisation is proposed). As an example, it gives the distress which she would risk suffering if measures were taken after the birth to separate her from her child.

In November 1989, the draft law entered the final stage of the consultation process before the Legal Committee of the *Bundestag* prior to consideration and adoption in plenary session. This stage was crucial, since before the Committee started work it remained highly uncertain whether the sterilisation clause would be adopted (Shaw, 1990:105). No clear parliamentary majority in favour of nonconsensual sterilisations existed, for both the Greens and the Social Democratic Party ('SPD') appeared to be opposed to the adoption of a law in the form proposed by the Federal Government.

The Greens demonstrated their unconditional opposition to almost all nonconsensual sterilisations by signing a petition organised against the draft sterilisation clause,[37] and by sponsoring a conference of interested parties where a wide range of alternative means of addressing the issues raised by the sexuality and procreative capacities of mentally handicapped persons were canvassed (Greens, 1988). The SPD had also consistently opposed legalising sterilisation except under a strict medical indication - ie serious risk to the life of the mother.[38] In letters to the organisers of the petition dated as late as October 17 1989, SPD officials were stating that they could not countenance the prospect, against the background of historical experience, of nonconsensual sterilisation being permitted in the Federal Republic of Germany (Wunder, 1990).

Yet para. 1905 emerged from the Committee not only in almost identical form to that in which it went in, but also with a bipartisan commitment to its adoption encompassing the governing coalition partners (the Christian Democrats and the Free Democrats) and the SPD. The single addition to the draft was one motivated by a suggestion of the *Bundesrat* which was accepted by the Federal Government[39] to the effect that the method of sterilisation offering the best chances of refertilisation should always be chosen. Prompted by the Federal Government, the Legal Committee also considered a proposal of the *Bundesrat* to define the expression of 'natural will' by the patient in opposition to sterilisation in para. 1905 (1) No. 1 as the natural will 'expressed through gestures, expressions of feeling, opposition and similar conduct'. It was felt that the concept of 'natural will' was sufficiently precise as not to require further definition or explanation; the provision was left unchanged (Protocol, 1990).

In switching its position, SPD concluded that the approach in the Government-sponsored draft was the 'least bad' solution to an undoubted problem (*Bundestag*, 1990, p.75). It saw two advantages in the draft: it avoided the danger that a complete prohibition on nonconsensual sterilisations would lead to the fictitious 'invention' of legal capacity to consent where none existed, and it removed an existing area of legal uncertainty. It drew support for its position from the treatment given in the Legal Committee to evidence brought before the Committee by opponents of the sterilisation clause regarding the legal position in Switzerland. Guidelines drawn up by the Swiss Academy of Medical Sciences on the medical ethics of sterilisation[40] appeared to outlaw nonconsensual sterilisations altogether on the grounds that consent is a right which can only be exercised personally under Swiss Constitutional law. However, on further investigation of the situation, the majority of the Legal Committee concluded that although a prohibition existed in theory in Switzerland, in practice it was not observed as sterilisations were in fact undertaken and regarded as inevitable (*Bundestag*, 1990, p.67-68). The Legal Committee wished to avoid the repetition of this situation in the Federal Republic.

With bipartisan agreement in the Legal Committee, the main hurdles to the enactment of the sterilisation clause were overcome, and it was adopted by the *Bundestag* with just one member of the SPD voting with the Greens, who continued their opposition to the end (Wunder, 1990; Schwab, 1990, p.686). The loss of the support of the SPD is symptomatic of the generally unsuccessful campaign to mobilise opposition to the sterilisation clause. Wunder (1990) attributes the failure of the campaign against the sterilisation law to the failure to convince public opinion of the parallels in eugenicist and human rights terms between the new law and the Nazi law, which itself provided for a range of procedural safeguards - although these meant little in practice. On the other hand, opponents of the draft were certainly well represented amongst those intervening through official consultation procedures in the legislative process. These included prominent representatives of the Catholic Church including the *Deutscher Caritasverband*, the *Sozialdienst katholischer Frauen* and the *Komissariat der Deutschen Bischöfen* (Protocol, 1990, p.162 *et seq* and 352 *et seq*; Reis, 1988), representatives of the Protestant Church -*Diakonisches Werk der Evangelischen Kirche in Deutschland* - (Protocol, 1990, p.207), groups campaigning for alternative social support mechanisms for mentally handicapped persons wishing to have children - *Aktion Autonom Leben* - (Protocol, 1990: 1 *et seq*; Wunder, 1988; Schumacher & Jürgens, 1988), individual oppositionists such as Prof. Dörner, and, most significantly, the *Vormundschaftsgerichtstag* presenting the views of Guardianship

Court judges. All these groups put forward arguments either entirely opposed to the legalisation of non-consenual sterilisations or in favour of only a very limited exception for life-threatening physical danger. It cannot be said, therefore, that lack of input into the legislative process was responsible for the failure to prevent the adoption of the sterilisation clause.

The arguments for and against the sterilisation clause

Arguments raised against the draft ranged from the conservative, the religious and the moral to the emancipatory. The first group of arguments stressed the ideal of non-interference with procreative capacity and opposition to the destruction of unborn life, drawing support from the parallel issue of nonconsensual abortion. Since the rights to self-determination in the Basic Law is universally applicable, and it incorporates, arguably, the right to reproduce, it is important to avoid the slippery slopes leading to abuse of legalised nonconsensual sterilisations and, potentially, to even more serious infringements of the right of self-determination such as euthanasia and the coercive use of genetic engineering. In the second group of arguments, the need to maintain an open debate on the sexuality of mentally handicapped people was considered paramount. If sterilisations were permitted, the sexuality of mentally handicapped people would continue to be a taboo subject. Discussion would be solely behind the closed doors of hospitals, courts, homes and care institutions and would be conducted principally in terms of preventing pregnancy, rather than of facilitating full enjoyment of life. Implicitly, allowing sterilisation gives one 'easy' solution to a difficult problem which will discourage the promotion of other, less invasive solutions which would require a greater input of time and resources, such as the careful supervision of the administering of oral contraceptives, the supply of condoms to the sexual partners of the mentally handicapped woman, a generally enhanced level of sex education and an increase in support for projects which assist mentally handicapped people to become parents. Moreover, in historical terms, it was regretted that barely has the subject of forced sterilisation begun to be publicly debated in the context of the classification of victims of Nazi eugenics as victims of Nazi 'Unrecht' (Wunder, 1988, 1990) than it is abruptly closed off again. The allegedly overhasty adoption of the sterilisation clause was not thought likely to be conducive to increasing the confidence of mentally handicapped persons in either the law or the medical profession.

Arguments in favour of allowing sterilisations were, in contrast, largely of a pragmatic nature. In the absence of a legislative framework, it was argued, sterilisations would continue in the shadow of the law and perhaps in greater numbers than under the new regulatory framework. If, on the contrary, nonconsensual sterilisations were forbidden, sterilisations would probably be undertaken abroad, or in secrecy. Regulating sterilisation under strict legal conditions, as has arguably occurred through the adoption of para. 1905, makes it clear that it is an instrument of last resort which may not lightly be used. Ultimately, it was argued, nonconsensual sterilisation is a useful option without which the difficulties thrown up by the sexuality of mentally handicapped people will be much greater (Bundesvereinigung Lebenshilfe, 1988; Protocol, 1990, p.128 *et seq*).

In the event, of course, it was the pragmatists who prevailed. Prominent in this group was the *Bundesvereinigung Lebenshilfe*, an organisation concerned with problems of mentally handicapped people, which *inter alia* represents the interests of parents on whom the greatest burden of caring for the mentally handicapped continues to fall. It is the latter who were, for precisely that reason, amongst the most vehement proponents of sterilisation. Support came also from by a majority of bodies representing professional interests, especially doctors and lawyers. Their arguments were buttressed by an interpretation of the Constitution which regards forced sterilisations as prohibited but permits 'best interests' sterilisations based on surrogate consent subject to clear limitations and procedural safeguards (Pieroth, 1989, 1990). Crucial to the success of that argument is the assertion that the right to self-determination under Article 2(1) of the Basic Law can validly be exercised by one person on behalf of another. In contrast, the argument canvassed in *Re B* regarding the valid exercise of the 'right to reproduce', namely that a right is meaningless without the capacity properly to exercise it,[41] has, thankfully, not prevailed. Nor has the contention that consent is a right which can only be exercised personally found support great support amongst mainstream constitutional lawyers in the Federal Republic notwithstanding its role in Swiss constitutional law. This contention makes a nonsense of the right to physical well-being since it cannot be maintained consistently with the need to provide emergency treatment in appropriate circumstances to all patients regardless of capacity to consent.

However, even amongst the pragmatic proponents of a sterilisation law, unanimity has not prevailed as to the precise terms and scope of the provisions which it was desirable to enact. Some feel that the conditions to be satisfied under para. 1905 are so strict that recourse to the Guardianship Court will be rare and sterilisations in future will frequently be undertaken with the (fictitious) 'consent' of the patient. This argument has some justification. Para. 1905 only regulates nonconsensual sterilisations. It does not regulate whether and how it is permissible to obtain consent from those whose capacity to consent is limited and who require a very specific type of explanation before they are able to understand the nature of what it is they are consenting to. Such situations fall under the general rules on informed consent, or the doctor's duty to disclose - but those principles were not developed with a view to the special problems posed by limited capacity to consent (Shaw, 1986).

In contrast others argue - and in this they are joined by opponents of sterilisation in so far as they have critiqued the actual terms of the clause - that the terms of para. 1905 are too loose, in particular in so far as they contain ill-defined concepts such as 'capacity to consent' and 'natural will'. As a consequence, legal capacity is now defined at three levels - legal capacity (in relation to the formation of contracts etc., which may be full or partial legal capacity), capacity to consent (which is normally defined in accordance with the criminal law case law on capacity to consent (Schönke/Schröder, 1985, para. 223), and the 'natural will' - each with its attendent uncertainties. For example, it is very difficult to determine when the actions of a person are driven by their 'will' as opposed to being instinctual, or motivated by fear.

The particular opposition of the *Vormundschaftsgerichtstag* has also focused on the difficulties inherent in determining in advance that the risk of pregnancy in general would lead to a specific pregnancy resulting in separation proceedings following birth or that the putatively pregnant woman would suffer distress as a result of the separation. These are decisions, it is argued, that can only ever be taken in a concrete and individual case. Nor is it clear from the terms of the law whether financial factors may be taken into account either for the purposes of determining the probability of the removal of the child from the mentally handicapped parents, because of the insufficiency of outside assistance, or for the purposes of determining the feasibility of less drastic alternatives to sterilisation such as extensive counselling and support systems in relation to sex education and sexual practices for mentally handicapped people and their carers, in particular, parents. Finally, no guidance is given as to whether measures taken under the two provisions flanking para. 1905 BGB, namely an abortion under para. 1904 and or measure of deprivation of liberty under para. 1906, can ever be regarded as acceptable and more 'proportionate' alternatives to sterilisation.

The conclusions to be drawn from this review of the terms of the new sterilisation clause and of the arguments of proponents and opponents are mixed. Returning to the principles set out in the introduction to this essay, one requirement appears clearly to be met. The new provisions do contain a blanket prohibition on forced sterilisations, although it might have been preferable for the legislature to have given further thought to what it considered represented the 'natural will' of the patient. As regards the third condition, namely the clarity and certainty of the legal framework, although the substantive conditions set out in para. 1905 itself may not be models of clarity, the arrangements for *Betreuung*, the giving of surrogate consent, and the granting of the authorisation of the Guardianship Court are each accompanied by procedural requirements which tend towards the cumbersome and bureaucratic and are incapable of easy circumvention, and do provide for considerable input from a variety of sources, including the patient herself. These points, along with the second condition - the limited role of sterilisation in the care of the mentally handicapped - are reviewed in the final section, which reassesses the efficacy of the procedures governing nonconsensual sterilisation in German and English law.

A reassessment of sterilisation procedures

It will be recalled that the starting point for this exposition of the German law on nonconsensual sterilisations was the unsatisfactory legal position in the United Kingdom of mentally handicapped minors and adults whom it is proposed to sterilise without their consent. I argued not only that the outline framework of the law based on substituting 'best interests' for consent as set out in the House of Lords cases of *Re B* and *Re F* itself was barely sufficient to ensure that justice can be done in the consideration of the various competing interests, but also that the watering down of the Practice Direction issued by the Official Solicitor by the decision of Thorpe J in *J* v *C*[42] and the subsequent amendments to that document made it even less likely that justice was <u>seen</u> to be done. The decision-making process appears to be almost entirely in the hands of the medical profession - who are protected against legal sanction by the doctrines of necessity, best interests and an internally defined notion of professional competence. A look at the legislative processes and consultative discussions which have occurred during the last four years in the Federal Republic of Germany has, it is hoped, thrown the experience in English law into sharper relief and added weight to the call for legislative intervention.

Yet on the face of it, there remains a striking similarity between the position in the Federal Republic and the position under English law, at least in so far as it is set out in the Practice Direction.[43] For each of the four general heads which the judge should take into account before issuing the declaration, clear parallels can be found in para. 1905 BGB: first, there is the assessment of competence, in which, according to the Practice Direction 'it should be borne in mind that the fact that a person is legally incompetent for some purposes does not mean that he or she necessarily lacks the capacity to make a decision about sterilisation'.[44] Compare with this the partial nature of *Betreuung* as a method of guardianship which does not necessarily lead to removal of the right to decide. Second, in both systems there needs to be a concrete risk of pregnancy, a risk which arises only where sexual intercourse is occurring or is very likely to occur and where there is procreative capacity in both partners. Third, in both cases there must be a probability of substantial damage to the patient as a result of the pregnancy. Finally, in neither case may sterilisation be undertaken if a less intrusive alternative is available. Thus the principle of proportionality plays a role in both systems. Looked at from the perspective of the Practice Direction, therefore, the situation under English law does not compare so unfavourably with that now reached by German law. This superficial similarity, however, conceals a number of crucial points of difference. More detailed comparison between the approach taken in German and English law can assist those uneasy about the developments in the English courts to focus their objections.

First, there is the general inadequacy of the procedures provided for under English law, which is exacerbated by the non-binding nature of the Practice Direction. The Practice Direction merely elucidates in a more discursive form the operation of the best interests standard articulated by the judiciary, from the House of Lords downwards. Yet even with the Practice Direction but without a clear catalogue of rights by reference to which the interests of the subjects of nonconsensual sterilisations can be measured, the welfare standard remains an indeterminate and ineffective means of ensuring proper human rights protection. Thorpe J had little difficulty in introducing the notion of an emergency in order to sidestep the requirement for two hearings, and in order, where appropriate, to sanction the abrogation of procedures. Yet there must be a fine line indeed between a situation where there is a concrete risk of pregnancy, required to justify sterilisation in the first place, and a concrete risk of pregnancy which has turned into an emergency. Judicial non-intervention in such circumstances could lead to the declaration procedures set up by the House of Lords falling entirely into disuse.

Even the non-binding guidelines in the Practice Direction are not themselves always observed by the judiciary. *J* v *C* illustrates this point, and the indeterminacies of judicial discretion in factual evaluation are emphasised by two cases decided before the Practice Direction was issued. In *Re F* there was no concrete of proof of risk of pregnancy, since there was no evidence that F had in fact had sexual intercourse or that she was fertile. *Re P*,[45] a case where sterilisation could not have been sanctioned under the German system (P was a minor), the decision to sterilise was approved even though the judge accepted that she might one day achieve the requisite capacity to marry. Yet the Practice Direction states that the judge should take into account 'that in the case of a minor his or her youth and potential for development may make it difficult or impossible to make the relevant finding of incapacity.' P, however, was not given the chance to develop and to decide for herself.

Para. 1905 BGB, in contrast, is binding law, and when the two sets of provisions are carefully compared, it becomes clear that the procedures set up by the German legislation are a good deal more complex than those required by English law, and that no provision has been made for sidestepping these requirements in either urgent or straightforward cases. The procedure involves two separate visits to court. First, the Guardianship Court must establish the need for *Betreuung* in general, and appoint a special *Betreuer* competent solely in relation to the decision to sterilise. The *Betreuer* must then assess the capacity of the *Betreute* to consent, and ensure that the other conditions in para. 1905 are met before he or she actually takes a decision to give surrogate consent. Implicit in the evaluation of the capacity to consent, and the recognition that the sterilisation must not take place against the natural will of the *Betreute*, is the assumption that the *Betreute* will have been told what it is proposed to do. The matter then returns to the Guardianship Court which calls for independent expert witness reports, appoints a legal representative for the *Betreute*, if she does not already have one, and hears the patient in person. The Court must then approve the consent of the *Betreuer*, looking again at all the conditions in para. 1905. Finally, two weeks must elapse before the sterilisation can be carried out by a doctor who has not previously provided an expert witness report, and whose impartiality cannot thereby be impugned. It can be concluded, therefore, that para. 1905 does render the sterilisation process more visible by giving it a particular locus within the legal system.

Second, medical knowledge and medical power - in particular in the form of clinical judgment which is raised in *Re F* to a standard for evaluating the conduct of the medical profession in relation to the human rights of the mentally handicapped patient - has achieved a primacy in the English cases which the explicitly interdisciplinary nature of the expert witness reports and the greater weight placed on the critical evaluation by the Guardianship Court of the mandatory conditions under para. 1905 would appear to preclude, at least in principle, in the Federal Republic.

Third, English law offers no guarantee against the performance of forced sterilisations since there is no provision for giving those deemed unable to consent the opportunity to express opposition. There is no guarantee at all that the patient will have been told what is to happen to her. Scroggie (1990) asserts that that English courts have attended to the practical need to find a solution to the problem of the sexuality of mentally handicapped persons without paying sufficient attention to the moral difficulties underlying that problem. While the concern of the German legislature to provide an explicit guarantee against forced sterilisations may be explicable in the light of historical experience, that does not absolve the English law-maker from responsibility for considering the possibility that forced sterilisations may occur under the guise of the operation of the best interests standard. By departing from the classic formulation of consent as the primary justification for interferences with the person, and developing instead a wider field for the doctrine of necessity, the courts have left less space for the assertion of the counterpart of consent - refusal.

Finally, the best interests standard is a seriously flawed instrument for evaluating the lawfulness of sterilisation, as it concentrates merely on the paternalistic elements of welfare. The definition of best interests used in para. 1901 BGB to define the basic principle of *Betreuung* is an explicitly emancipatory one - the best interests of the patient include the exercise of choice wherever possible. This principle binds also the interpretation of the sterilisation provisions. The difference in conception of the welfare principle is almost certainly attributable to the influence of constitutional principles embodied in enforceable human rights guaranteed by the Constitution under German law. The result is that greater weight is placed on autonomy as opposed to paternalism. Thus in comparison to the legal framework constructed under German law, the operation of the best interests standard in English law, in conjunction with the more detailed elaboration in the Practice Direction, provides a seriously inadequate mechanism for protecting the human rights of mentally handicapped persons whose procreative capacity it is proposed to remove.

English law thus falls down most seriously when compared to German law in relation to the first and third conditions used in this essay to assess sterilisation provisions. It is hoped that the comparative analysis in this paper has demonstrated the urgent need for a legislative framework in the United Kingdom which is explicitly based on human rights rather than professional interests.

The evaluation of the second condition, however, calls in both systems for a more critical assessment of the impact of legislative regulation of nonconsensual sterilisations. The normative impact of law extends not just to determining what is legally permissible, but influences also what is seen as socially desirable. The effect of legalising such sterilisations, whether through case law or legislation, is to offer an apparently complete solution to the problems and conflicts associated with the sexuality of mentally handicapped people. Critics in both the United Kingdom (Scroggie, 1990) and the Federal Republic of Germany (Protocol, 1990, p.1) have stressed the foreclosure effect of legalising nonconsensual sterilisation. As a purportedly 'complete solution' to the problem, the law thereby absolves itself of responsibility for both the practical issues which it does not solve and the so-called 'moral remainder' - the issues which remain unresolved wherever a moral dilemma throws into conflict two or more competing sets of rights and interests (Scroggie, 1990). Sterilisation, most obviously, does not prevent sexual exploitation, rape, the passage of sexually transmitted diseases, infection with HIV and AIDS or the possibility of explicitly sexual behaviour in inappropriate circumstances which those whose own sexual conduct and expectations of the sexual conduct of others have been normalised through socialisation might find embarassing. In addition, it tends to give primacy to contraception in preference always to conception. There is a spillover from that policy choice into policy-making as regards, for example, the resources and support made available to those mentally handicapped persons who are capable of making choices about sterilisation and reproduction and who may choose to have children. The effect of a legislative framework such as that adopted in the Federal Republic is, therefore, to create as many unhappy dilemmas as the case law solution operating under English law. The conclusion of this analysis must therefore be although the case must continue to be made for a greater human rights input into the legal regulation of nonconsensual sterilisation in English law, with this instrumentalised in the form of legislative guarantees of the interests of mentally handicapped persons, as much if not more emphasis needs to be placed upon the strictly limited role of law in resolving issues of sexuality.

* Lecturer in Law, Keele University. I would like to thank the *Bundesvereinigung Lebenshilfe für geistig Behinderte* and the Institute of Medical and Pharmaceutical Law, University of Göttingen, for supplying me with materials.

1. Throughout this paper, the female pronoun is used to describe the mentally handicapped person whom it is proposed to sterilise, in explicit recognition of the gendered nature of the legal rules under discussion.

2. *Gesetz zur Reform des Rechts der Vormundschaft und Pflegschaft für Volljährige (Betreuungsgesetz - BtG)* of September 12 1990, *Bundesgesetzblatt* I, p.2002.

3. See also proposals for legislative intervention mooted in the Canadian province of Alberta: Rivet, 1990:1156 *et seq*. Even prior to *Re F*, Fortin, 1988:642 was arguing in favour of legislative clarification of the consent issue.

4. [1990] 2 A.C. 1; [1989] 2 All ER 545. All references with page numbers alone are to the Appeal Cases Report of *Re F*.

5. At p.52.

6. *Re Eve* (1987) 31 D.L.R. (4d) 1.

7. Per Lord Brandon, at p.55. See also Lord Bridge: 'It seems to me to be axiomatic that treatment which is necessary to preserve the life, health or well-being of the patient may lawfully be given without consent', at p.52.

8. *Bolam* v *Friern HMC* [1957] 2 All ER 118.

9. Per Lord Bridge, at p.52; per Lord Brandon, at p68; per Lord Goff, at p.78; per Lord Jauncey, at p.83.

10. Cf Lord Griffiths, at p.70 who argued that 'the time has now come for a further development to forbid, again in the public interest, the sterilisation of a woman with healthy reproductive organs who, either through mental incompetence or youth, is incapable of giving her fully informed consent unless such an operation has been inquired into and sanctioned by the High Court.'

11. [1988] A.C. 199; [1987] 2 All ER 211.

12. E.g. *Re M (A Minor) (Wardship: Sterilisation)* [1988] 2 F.L.R. 997; *Re P (A Minor) (Wardship: Sterilisation)* [1989] 1 F.L.R. 182.

13. [1988] 1 A.C. 203.

14. A recent study of the difficulty of 'letting go' for the parents of a young woman with Down's Syndrome in the *Independent on Sunday* (August 18 1991) referred to the emergence of her sexual feelings but without saying what contraceptive precautions had been taken.

15. *Re E (A minor)* The Times, February 22 1991; *F* v *F* The Times, April 29 1991 (adult).

16. [1989] 2 F.L.R. 447.

17. [1990] 3 All ER 735.

18. [1990] N.L.J.R. 1273.

19. Resolution of the *Bundestag* of May 11 1990, on *Bundesrat Drucksache* 316/90.

20. *Gesetz zur Verhütung des erbkranken Nachwuchses* of July 14 1933, Reichsgesetzblatt I p.529.

21. *Gesetz No. 11*, Kontrollrat (January 30 1946).

22. E.g. OLG Hamm NJW 1983, 295; LG Düsseldorf FamRZ 1981, 95; AG Alzey FamRZ 1984, 208.

23. *Bundesärztekammer* (German Chamber of Doctors), 'Zulässigkeit einer Sterilisation geistig Behinderter aus eugenischer oder sozialer Indikation', Deutsches Arzteblatt 84 (1987) B1979.

24. Einbecker Expertengespräch der Deutschen Gesellschaft für Medizinrecht: 'Empfehlungen zur Sterilisation geistig Behinderter', Der Frauenarzt 1988, p.139.

25. *Bürgerliches Gesetzbuch* ("BGB"), paras. 104 and 105.

26. As this and related expressions refer to very specific legal arrangements, and cannot easily be translated into English, the terms will be used in this paper in the original language.

27. Para. 1904 BGB which provides for surrogate consent to medical treatment specifically referred in its earliest draft to the right of the *Betreute* to consent if he or she was capable of doing so. This phrase was subsequently removed on the grounds that it was self-evident.

28. Cf *Re P* [1989] 1 F.L.R. 182 where Eastham J used the alleged reversibility of certain forms of sterilisation operation as one ground for giving consent to the sterilisation of a minor.

29. Although the sterilisation provisions do not refer specifically to mentally handicapped persons they will in practice be limited to this category of *Betreute*.

30. At p.19.

31. This provision parallels para. 1903 BGB which subjects similarly serious decisions regarding the property of the *Betreute* to court authorisation.

32. *Gesetz über die Angelegenheiten der freiwilligen Gerichtsbarkeit*, para. 65 *et seq*; hereinafter 'FGG'. These provisions apply also to other measures for which consent of the Guardianship Court is required.

33. Reprinted in *Der Frauenrat* 1988, p.533.

34. There were also a number of minor amendments to the procedural provisions which are not considered here.

35. Para. 218a(2) No. 2 of the Criminal Code.

36. Upper House of the Federal Parliament, containing the representatives of the *Länder*.

37. Appell des Arbeitskreises zur Aufarbeitung der Geschichte der Euthanasie, *Kein neues Sterilisationsgesetz in der Bundesrepublik*, March 12 1988.

38. See for example the call for the creation of better guardianship arrangements and improved rights for mentally handicapped persons by the SPD of August 6 1987, *Bundestag Drucksache* 11/669.

39. *Bundestag Drucksache* 11/4528, May 11 1989, Opinion of the *Bundesrat*, p.209, No. 23; counterstatement by the Federal Government, p.228.

40. *Schweizerische Artzezeitung/Bulletin des médecins suisses* 1982, p.624.

41. See, most vehemently, Lord Hailsham in *Re B* at [1988] 1 A.C. 204.

Law, Health and Medical Regulation

42. [1990] 3 All ER 735.

43. [1989] 2 F.L.R 447, [1990] N.L.J.R. 1273, para. 8.

44. 8(1)(i).

45. [1989] 1 F.L.R. 182.

Policy, Rights and the HIV Positive Prisoner

Thus, too, they came to know the incorrigible sorrow of all prisoners and exiles, which is to live in the company of a memory that serves no purpose. Even the past, of which they thought incessantly, had a savour only of regret. For they would have wished to add to it all that they regretted having left undone ... And thus there was always something missing in their lives. Hostile to the past, impatient of the present, and cheated of the future, we were much like those whom men's justice, or hatred, forces to live behind prison bars (Camus, 1962).

AIDS victims should be locked up (Independent Newspaper, 1987).

Jean McHale and Alison Young.

Introduction

There is a vast literature on the subject of HIV infection and AIDS, ranging through personal accounts of living with seropositivity (Mordaunt, 1989, Grimshaw, 1989), analyses of the lack of political intervention to find a cause, vaccine or cure (Shilts, 1988, Watney, 1989), moral and philosophical debates (Almond, 1990, Jonson, 1988, Guttmacher, 1990, Illingworth, 1990), and accounts specifically of its predicted effect on the heterosexual population (Masters et al 1988). However, there exists a lacuna within this literature: very little attention has been directed toward the situation of individuals who are or who may be seropositive within institutions such as prisons. In this essay, we propose to examine a number of issues arising from the fact that there are individuals in prison who have HIV infection or HIV disease (Redfield et al 1989). These issues are: first, whether antibody testing should be mandatory or voluntary; second, the question of confidentiality arising out of testing; and third, the participation of prisoners in drug trials and research; finally, the extent to which prisoners are able to obtain the medical treatment of their choice within prison. We have called these issues 'the dilemmas of the HIV positive prisoner' to connote both the management concerns confronting prison authorities and the Home Office, and also the intense physical and psychological burdens upon such a prisoner. To provide a degree of context to the four areas under examination, we will also consider differences in general, national, penal policy, comparing in particular England, Scotland and the United States.

HIV infection is still often portrayed as if it were a direct result of being gay, black, poor or an intravenous drug-user. Many still fail to distinguish between 'high-risk activities' (unprotected anal or vaginal intercourse and the sharing of unsterilised needles in particular) and 'high-risk groups' (the inaccurate and unwarranted label applied to groups who currently appear to show a high incidence of HIV infection). This deeply entrenched attitude produces discriminatory and oppressive policies. A corpus of material is developing which is dedicated to criticising this perspective and advocating other ways of responding to HIV infection (Dalton et al 1990, Montgomery, 1990, Moran, 1988). However, the need to follow this critical lead is even greater when we look at the dilemmas of the HIV positive prisoner. The marginal and disadvantaged of society meet in concentrated numbers in overcrowded prisons, where 'risk behaviours' are the norm (Carvel et al 1990), and categories such as 'homosexuality' and 'heterosexuality' are not fixed but amorphous and shifting (Vaid, 1987).

In the process of considering the dilemmas of the HIV positive prisoner, we shall also raise the question of the appropriateness and efficacy of rights-based arguments in this context. The term 'prisoners' rights' has passed into the discursive commonplace; it is accepted and recognised in many different institutions. Debates within the field which has developed around the notion of prisoners' rights tend to be 'issue-specific'; that is, discrete demands are raised, argued for, and, sometimes, met. For example, there have been long and contentious struggles over legal representation, disciplinary hearings, and medical care (Maguire et al 1985). Commentators have written extensively on these demands and struggles (Richardson, 1984, Jacobs, 1980). Rights debates are also becoming familiar in the context of HIV infection: texts cover the rights of the healthy, of HIV positive individuals, of medical personnel and of 'society in general'.

Within the issue-specific realm of debates on prisoners' rights, HIV infection is not just another problem. HIV infection yells to us of our mortality, our fragile categories of sexuality, and our class-oriented social structures. Within the prison system, HIV infection makes visible and explicit the hidden and implicit links between conceptions of disease and criminality. Both are seen as (symbolically or literally) life-threatening. The HIV positive prisoner is a deadly icon of a psycho-social malaise. Such an ideological agenda, inflected with homophobia, racism, censures based on gender and class, produces particular kinds of prison policy. Prisoners represent (and are sometimes called) 'undeserving' of society (Conrad, 1982). Attempts to produce guidelines for standards of care in prison regimes, to reform the parole system in order to alleviate overcrowding (Casale, 1984), are often met with outrage from the penologically repressive, who confuse sending an individual to prison as punishment with sending an individual to prison for further punishment once there. HIV positive prisoners therefore constitute a specific pariah class within the general pariah class of prisoners.

Many of the responses to HIV infection from prison authorities are the product of the widespread image of the HIV positive prisoner; he is the least worthwhile of the undeserving. In England and Wales, HIV positive prisoners have been segregated in solitary confinement with denial of exercise and work (Advisory Council Report on AIDS, 1989). In the state of New Jersey, prisoners with AIDS were shackled to their beds for six months and denied visits from their families. In Texas, four prisoners with AIDS were hospitalised with prisoners who had infectious diseases; this could kill a person with AIDS, whose immune system can easily succumb to opportunistic infections. The existence of such brutal regimes should be understood and criticised as part of an ideological nexus which conjoins a fear of fatal disease, a widespread homophobia, a horror of drug-users and their supposed lack of self-control, and a disdain for the lived experiences of prisoners.

HIV infection at the moment links disparate marginal groups: homosexuals, drug-users, babies and women. Some have written with sympathy and insight on the bizarre and cruel situation which makes allies of such dissimilar groups. Others, however, have responded more viciously: a right-wing politician, Sir Alfred Sherman, asserted in a letter published in The Times, that HIV positive individuals are merely 'sodomites and drug-abusers, together with numbers of women who voluntarily associate with this sexual underworld'.[1] Such attitudes should be challenged both in their general manifestations and also in application to discrete situations. It is our aim here both to challenge such attitudes and also examine certain questions relating to medical provision for HIV positive prisoners in the light of arguments about prisoners' rights. We shall now consider these in turn.

Medical provision within the penal system

Testing for HIV infection

> Yet it is seldom remarked that, for anyone in a vulnerable group, taking the test is an act of enormous courage (Goldstein, 1989).

Decisions about whom to test for HIV infection and about what to do with the test results, raise as yet unresolved problems. Reflex responses about the benefit to the patient need careful re-examination in relation to HIV. Benefit may be much more likely to accrue to the tester rather than the individual tested. The consequences of a test result which reveals the presence of HIV antibodies, signifying infection by the virus, are far-reaching and life-altering. The individual's health prognosis will appear extremely poor and both physical and emotional problems can arise. Employment prospects may suffer. Social and economic stigmatisation, such as loss of insurance or ostracism by family and acquaintances, are also possible. The reasons for testing are crucial here. In the prison system, antibody testing may take place for three reasons: to enable a diagnosis of HIV infection to be made, to collect epidemiological information on HIV infection, or to identify and isolate HIV positive individuals.

Testing in order to diagnose is the most straightforward. If the test is requested by the prisoner or recommended by a medical officer and then consented to, if it is preceded by careful counselling and followed up (if possible) with support and help (both clinical and emotional), few problems should arise (Nooney, 1990). To this extent, we support the resolution of the British Medical Association, made at its 1988 conference, which stated

> HIV testing should be performed only on clinical grounds and with the specific consent of the patient ... As a positive HIV test has serious implications, counselling of patients prior to carrying out the test is essential, and further counselling must be offered if the test proves positive.

If this is the recommended standard to be maintained in the community, there is no reason why the same standard should not be relevant to prisoners considering taking the test. Failure to meet this standard would, strictly, be a breach of a duty of care and actionable in negligence. The difficulty for any plaintiff would be to prove damage and to quantify any loss.

Testing in order to establish the epidemiological prevalence of HIV infection in prisons and testing in order to identify and isolate HIV positive prisoners raise more difficult questions. With regard to the generation of epidemiological information, Vaid has written that this is

> ... justifiable if such testing is anonymous and voluntary. Proponents of such screening argue correctly that prison administrators can more accurately anticipate their needs for staffing, budgeting, AIDS education and health care, if they know how many seropositive inmates live in their prisons (Vaid, 1987).

British prison authorities seem close to approval of mass

epidemiological screening. In 1989, the then Director of the Prison Medical Services stated

> ... the number of HIV antibody positives reported to me is, in my honest belief, and with skills of an experienced epidemiologist, probably one third to one tenth of the real numbers. I cannot be more precise at present because the law of the land does not permit compulsory blood testing of prison inmates.

Dr. Kilgour went on to state that prison communities would be included in the mass anonymous screening of the population

> We shall have for the first time a solid indication of how many HIV antibody positives there really are, as opposed to those that are reported to me ... I look forward to having better information on which to base management decisions (Kilgour, 1989).

This seems to be only a partial account of the situation. While this data would certainly be of use to prison administrations in order to plan the running of their institutions, the practical operation of health care facilities, drugs for treatment and hospital wings for HIV patients, it cannot be properly used where it is generated as a result of anonymous and voluntary screening. Anonymous screening, such as the type that is now in operation in Britain with regard to the random testing of blood samples, can only provide statistical data which is of no benefit whatsoever, except in providing abstract numbers of HIV positive individuals. It completely ignores the question of which inmates will receive the benefit of health care facilities or bear the brunt of segregational strategies. This form of antibody testing has dangerous implications: either benign and beneficial practices will only be extended to the symptomatic HIV patient who has been voluntarily tested; or already tested prisoners together with those presumed to be HIV positive (drug users and homosexuals) will be subjected to degrading and stigmatising forms of treatment (such as segregation). The British authorities thus participate in the erroneous assumption that mass anonymous testing can be of use in the making and implementing of management decisions.

Those who support mass epidemiological screening may also come to support the third form of testing which may occur in prison. This position holds that governments should screen prisoners to identify HIV positive prisoners, in order to segregate and isolate them, in the belief that this will prevent the transmission of the virus within prison. From the very beginning of the official labelling of HIV infection as an 'epidemic',[2] there has been continual pressure to force HIV testing on some groups and to require the identification of those who test positive, at least to health care personnel and sometimes also to families, employers, insurance companies and the state. This argument has not had any generalised success to date, since most people recognise that this would drive many 'underground'. However, the captive population that lives in prison is still in danger of being subjected to compulsory screening.

There are many reasons why this form of testing is indefensible. A seropositive individual is often in good health and may feel well for years, indeed, emphasising this should be an important part of individual and institutional responses to HIV infection. If segregation for seropositives is the only outcome of mass testing, as opposed to support, counselling or health care options such as advice on medication, stress or diet, then no effort is being made to improve the emotional and physical situation of the HIV positive prisoner. Isolation may increase the likelihood of illness due to the stress and depression that it may engender. Casual contact does not spread infection; indeed there are few day-to-day situations which could constitute a health risk for prison officers or for other prisoners (Curran, 1990). Arguments that screening followed by segregation would halt transmission are also unfounded. Individuals do not produce antibodies immediately after infection and screening would therefore need to be continually repeated on all who test negative. Those who propose segregation would also need to justify the isolation of individuals who falsely test positive. It is recommended by the medical profession that follow-up tests be done on all initial positive results and, even then, there still exists the statistical risk of a false positive. Mass mandatory screening of the prison population, as with any social group, cannot be justified and we strongly oppose any argument in favour of it.

Unfortunately, the British prison authorities seem to support mass testing more than many other jurisdictions. The United States National Institute of Justice (NIJ) has identified a shift from seeing mass screening as a tool in infection control to an integral part of medical treatment, designed to allow earlier medical intervention. Many correctional systems also now offer voluntary or on-request testing. In the Netherlands and France for example mass testing is considered of little worth; both operate a policy of testing on request. However, the British attitude seems very different. Dr. John Kilgour expressed the opinion of British prison authorities thus: 'We have a duty to care for [HIV positive prisoners] and that's sometimes going to drive us into situations which look like segregation but they are not - they are care and support ... for their own safety' (Kilgour, 1989).

It seems to us that the only way in which antibody testing can be supported in the prison system is when it occurs as a result of the individual's voluntary consent to and understanding of the process. Counselling should be provided before and after testing. One prisoner has told how his test result was communicated to him in the most blunt fashion possible: 'you're positive', to be followed with no immediate counselling or support whatsoever (Bennett, 1990). Confidentiality also needs to be considered. The systemic existence of disincentives identified at a general social level by Moran (1990), can be discovered in a highly specific form within prisons. Segregation policies can lead to HIV positive prisoners being forced to live in appalling conditions, on occasions locked up for twenty four hours. Denial of work and sport also occurs. The prisoner is also permanently identified and therefore stigmatised as an HIV positive individual: a generalised lack of compassion and understanding among both officers and prisoners can mean that prison life becomes intolerable. In addition to the burden of the knowledge of seropositivity, a prisoner may be subjected to physical and verbal abuse (for example, at one time in Saughton Prison in Edinburgh, HIV positive prisoners were known as 'riddlers', because they were said to be 'riddled' with disease, Bennett, 1990).

It is essential that prison administrations remove these systemic disincentives to voluntary testing, by instituting facilities for counselling, education, support and training (for all, not just those taking the test). If this does not occur, it will be impossible to deny that the situation in prison exemplifies an intolerance which will have devastating effects. Firstly, individuals will be deterred from voluntary testing and HIV positive prisoners will be unable to obtain medical help. Second, any figures as to the extent of HIV infection in prison will be dangerously inaccurate. Finally, such a failure to institute positive support for HIV positive prisoners seems tacitly to align the prison authorities with the represssive regimes of segregation, abuse and vilification.

Confidentiality and the HIV positive prisoner

The obligation to preserve patient confidentiality has long formed part of the medical profession's ethical code. This obligation is owed by practitioners to all patients (GMC, 1988), and extends to the prisoner-patient. But, to talk in such a generalised way as this ignores the reality of the complex situation which exists within the prison.

The prisoner-patient is subject to the care, not of an ordinary general practitioner, but of a Prison Medical Officer. While the Prison Medical Officer is a registered medical practitioner and is thus subject to the ethical code of the General Medical Council, as an employee of the Home Office, he is subject to other constraints (Bowden, 1976). The first part comprises those activities which he undertakes which form part of the conventional doctor-patient relationship; the care of sick persons. The second part is activities he performs which support the prison institution. These include advice as to what type of institution the prisoner is physically and mentally suited and whether the prisoner is fit for work, education or for confinement as part of a disciplinary measure. The third and final part is those activities which support the state, such as informing the governor of information revealed by a medical examination which will assist in the identification of a prisoner. Thus, while the Prison Medical Officer has the same basic ethical obligations as any other medical practitioner, institutional considerations may lead him to a different conclusion as to the precise obligation of confidentiality which he owes his patients.

At present, Home Office policy is that information regarding HIV and patients should only be disclosed on a 'need to know' basis (Advisory Council Report, 1989). In practice, however, it appears that the confidentiality of such information is rarely preserved. The Home Office operates what are known as Viral Infectivity Restrictions (VIR). Those patients who test HIV positive have VIR written on their file. The Prison Medical Officer takes decisions as to what steps should be taken regarding such prisoners, for example, exclusion from work, recreational activities and segregation. A majority of these prisoners have been made the subject of segregation provisions, thus losing the chance of retaining the confidentiality of their HIV positive status.

The right of the prisoner-patient to confidentiality in English law is unclear. An action for the equitable remedy of breach of confidence will arise when one individual has given information to another individual in a situation imposing a duty of confidence and the person to whom the information has been given discloses it, without the consent of the person who has imparted the information. However, while the remedy has been used to restrain the unauthorised disclosure of information relating to AIDs patients, it does not provide blanket protection for all confidential information (*X v Y*).[3] The Court of Appeal in *W v Egdell*[4] affirmed that a medical practitioner may break confidence where it is in the public interest to do so. As a result of this decision the position of a prisoner-patient with HIV is unclear, although such a prisoner has been granted legal aid to bring a breach of confidence action.

Should then the notion of doctor-patient confidentiality within the prison system be abandoned? Is it simply illusory? While there are those who still hold to the traditional view of it as some absolute intransigent obligation (Kottow, 1986), in recent years such a view has come increasingly to be seen as unrealistic. The general requirement to keep patients' confidences has been held to be subject to so many exceptions that the suggestion has even been made that the concept be abandoned (Swanick, 1989). Others have argued that, while medical confidentiality is justifiable on the utilitarian grounds of ensuring that patients are willing to go to their medical practitioners for treatment; at the same time, exceptions, such as the need to prevent likely or serious harm to another person, are justifiable, similarly on utilitarian grounds (Lesser et al 1990). Arguments advanced, justifying confidentiality on the grounds of the patient's innate human right to privacy can be subjected to criticism - not least because such rights may be over-borne by other 'rights' and interests.

Is there then any future for such an uncertain concept in the prison system? There are two arguments which can be advanced in its favour. Firstly, the promise of confidentiality may be essential for a prisoner-patient to come forward for care if he fears that he may have contracted HIV. Without it, the prisoner may be deterred from seeking care frightened of the personal repercussions he may face once publicly 'stigmatised' (Grimshaw, 1990). It can be argued that to remove this stigma from HIV we need to accept persons who have contracted the virus. Acceptance will eradicate the need for secrecy. Such acceptance, though a desirable measure, will not take place instantly. Is it not better to provide the individual in the meantime with the choice of whether to reveal his HIV positive status. This step would maximise patient autonomy. It is encouraging that the need for confidentiality for prisoner-patients with HIV or Aids was emphasised in the Woolf Report (1990). While not making any detailed recommendations relating to the treatment of such prisoners, the report criticised the use of Viral Infectivity Restrictions.

Second, confidentiality is a notion which has been seen as worthy of protection in law. This has led to the development of the equitable remedy of breach of confidence. The efficacy of that remedy in the situation of the prisoner-patient has been questioned above. But we have also arguably an obligation to recognise confidentiality as part of the right to privacy through our international obligations under the European Convention of Human Rights. Article 8 of the Convention has been interpreted as affording a right to privacy. Neither Article 8, nor the equitable remedy of breach of confidence are panaceas for the problems of confidentiality and the HIV positive prisoner. Both are limited by public policy considerations. But, at the same time, the increase in use of these legal remedies are indicative of a trend towards safeguarding personal autonomy. Such raised consciousness is important in highlighting the dilemma of the HIV positive prisoner.

Experimental Drug Trials

> Drugs are now being tested in the hope that one can be found to safely arrest the progress of HIV infection. Whether that search will be totally successful is highly uncertain. Thus neither potential vaccines nor drug therapies offer much hope in the near future for altering the course of the epidemic (Advisory Council, 1989).

The considerations and procedures that should govern trials of new drugs have been widely argued. It was not until well into the twentieth century that controlled clinical trials began to be accepted as a method of evaluation of new drugs and procedures. After the Second World War, the principle of randomisation was introduced into clinical research. Randomised controlled trials' (RCTs) are widely used. Very often, the participants are not even aware that they are taking part in a trial. This means that the principle of informed consent has been dispensed with (Faulder, 1985).

An attempt to justify this would assert that when a drug is being tested which will eliminate a life-threatening disease from a patient's system or control its advance, such a drug could be immeasurably important to those who suffer from such an illness. Even if a doctor explains that no-one knows whether the drug works or whether it produces unacceptable side-effects, there are many patients who would still want to seize any opportunity of treatment, however uncertain its outcome. On one hand, they might accept the principle of randomisation; on the other their understandable desire to live might make them unable to accept it for themselves. Patients who feel like this cannot be entered into a trial, according to the medical profession. Informing patients of all the procedures and protocols within RCTs therefore risks the study finding insufficient participants to go ahead. Thus are RCTs conventionally justified.

Placebos are frequently used in drug trials as an alternative to the experimental drug, and, almost without exception, it is a condition of the trial that patients should not be informed that they are receiving a placebo instead of a specific form of treatment. This is justified on the grounds that researchers cannot get a fair comparison between the two 'treatments' if patients suspect that one is a placebo. Further, to provide this information might destroy the trial, since many patients would refuse their consent. In a 'double blind' trial, doctors know that a placebo is one of the options, but they do not know which patients receive it.

There are many ethical objections to this form of trial. Firstly, the patient is being denied the opportunity to act as an autonomous individual. Second, doctors are abusing patients' trust by entering them in trials without telling them about the risk of receiving a placebo. Finally, in the context of HIV infection, the actual 'cost' can be very great. In a trial for the drug azdothymidine (brand name Zidovudine, also known as Retrovir and AZT), one thousand patients received AZT while one thousand others received placebos. While some psychosomatic benefit from appearing to receive treatment may accrue to the individual receiving the placebo, it still cannot be denied that nothing is being done to prevent the onset of AIDS for these participants. This is the 'Concorde 1' AZT trial, an AngloFrench initiative which aimed to discover whether AZT does retard the development of AIDS in people with HIV infection. The 'blind' nature of the trial (whereby neither doctor nor participant knew if the drug or a placebo was being dispensed) was claimed to be necessary in order to test the drug's efficacy. It is sometimes said to be unethical to give everyone AZT since the drug has a high risk of toxicity. Researchers rarely question the ethical nature of giving one thousand people a placebo. Although alternatives have been suggested - such as recruiting a group of people who were sure that they did not want to take AZT to act as a control - no such trial has been developed. At the moment, a large number of people continue to take a placebo instead of AZT - in the belief that they are being given access to a possible cure.

In the United States, the Federal Department of Health and Human Services incorporates a number of agencies which promote the development of new drugs and treatments. The most important are the Food and Drug Administration (FDA) and the National Institutes of Health (NIH). Federal approval for the sale of a new drug takes on average eight years and until that point, a drug is unavailable for public use, even for a terminally ill person. In 1986, media pressure about the rumoured efficacy of AZT moved the FDA and the NIH to accelerate the licensing procedure: as a result, AZT was licensed for sale in the spring of 1987. Its extremely high cost makes it unavailable to some HIV positive individuals (and to many institutions such as prisons). Dissatisfaction with federal procedure over the search for a cure has led some organisations, such as Project Inform in San Francisco, to advise HIV positive people on substances not approved by the FDA. Other organisations help individuals to obtain drugs from abroad or from illicit domestic sources (Stoddard, 1989). Frustration has also led to the creation of private organisations that assist in the testing of treatments; for example, the Community Research Initiative in New York. For the HIV positive prisoner, access to such alternative sources of treatment is, of course, impossible.

Within almost all prisons in the United States, AZT is available to some inmates. The Philadelphia system has developed a plan to offer AZT to all asymptomatic HIV positive inmates. However, only twenty-five per cent of Canadian systems offer AZT. In both Canada and the United States, it is not clear whether all those who meet the eliqibility criterion (a T-cell blood count of below 500) are receiving AZT. Figures from the National Institute of Justice (NIJ) suggest that 'there may be many inmates eligible to receive AZT who are not receiving it'. A number of experimental drugs are in various stages of clinical trials in the United States. However, NIJ survey results show that very few systems give prisoners access to experimental therapeutic drugs. Federal regulations were developed which strictly limited the use of prisoners in any kind of medical research. These were designed to protect inmates from abuse, but in the light of the often gloomy prognoses faced by HIV positive prisoners, many now wish to see the regulations liberalised to allow inmates access to these experimental drugs. There is support for this from the medical profession, if protections as to confidentiality and consent are maintained (although, as we argued above, it is unclear whether these can exist at all within prisons).

In Britain, AZT is becoming available for HIV positive prisoners along with the T-cell test used to monitor when treatment should begin (Jolliffe, 1990). Dr. Kilgour, former director of the Prison Medical Service, expressed hopes that the availability of AZT would encourage prisoners to reveal their seropositivity, claiming that 'it would be to their advantage' (Kilgour, 1988). However, we will question later the straightforwardness of this assertion, by means of a comparison between English and Scottish prison policy.

The Council of Europe has noted that 'prisoners may not be submitted to medical or scientific experiments which may result in physical or moral injury to their persons' (Council of Europe, 1988). Such a provision would presumably rule out the participation of prisoners in drug trials such as the Concord 1. In the absence to date of a cure for HIV infection, and as numbers of HIV infected prisoners rise, it seems likely that cases will be brought to challenge such protective rules, since prisoners may well feel that their interests have changed due to HIV infection. Even if prisoners are allowed to take part of their own volition, in experimental trials, the conflict between care and treatment, and research interests remains unresolved. While drug trials continue to be organised in the form of RCTs or double blind trials with placebos, it is apparent that the researcher is more interested in a putative scientific objectivity than in the provision of care for the individual. Those who continue to organise trials around the use of placebos and randomisation are privileging a notion of 'science' over a regard for the physical symptoms of the HIV positive individual. Drug trials are essential in order to find a cure for HIV infection, but it is equally essential to pay critical attention to the ways in which trials are organised. HIV positive individuals, whether prisoners or not, are not simply statistics, and the offering of a placebo or the prevention from participation in a drug trial will reduce that individual's chance to resist their illness.

A choice of care

Curran (1990) has said 'it is the aim of the Prison service that prisoners with HIV should receive as good care as is available outside. The notion that prisoners should receive the same standard of medical care as those patients outside prison is a concept the English Courts have not yet been prepared to accept. This was clearly illustrated by the case of *Knight v Home Office*.[5] This case concerned an unsuccessful action brought by the relatives of Paul Worrall, an inmate, held on remand in Brixton Prison who committed suicide - for negligence against the Prison authorities. In giving judgment Pill J. held

> I am unable to accept the submission that the law requires the standard of care in a prison hospital to be as high as the standard of care for all purposes in a psychiatric hospital outside prison.

But should the standard of care in a prison hospital be as high as that in a hospital outside the prison regime? Should the choice of care be as good? If the view is taken that, once sentenced, a prisoner is detained as punishment, not for punishment, then surely there should be no difference? The importance of ensuring that there was no such difference was emphasised by the Chief Inspector of Prisons in his annual report and was confirmed by the Woolf Report. However, in practice, a considerable difference does exist in both choice of care and standard of care in relation to prisoners with HIV.

There is a far wider choice of care for a patient with HIV outside prison than inside. Such a patient while still unable to obtain a 'cure' for the virus may seek treatment to delay its progression, or seek a cure for any of the illnesses which he may contract if he developed AIDS. He may attend his general practitioner or a hospital consultant. Should he fall seriously ill, he may be taken into hospital. He may have the opportunity to spend his last days in a hospice. In addition he may seek psychotherapeutic care and counselling to bring him to terms with the fact that he has HIV. If he has the means, he may also obtain care from 'alternative' medical practitioners and other 'private' practitioners.

In contrast, the prisoner has, as his only option, care from the Prison Medical Service. The service has however constraints upon its therapeutic role. It has the task of operating the Viral Infectivity Restrictions, which inhibit patient care by the denial of medical confidentiality. There is less opportunity for a doctor-patient relationship to be built up since a prisoner may be moved to a different prison, a step which may have the effect of inhibiting treatment. For a prisoner who goes on to develop AIDS, a healthy environment and a balanced diet are both necessary. These are difficult to obtain in prison. The squalor of many of Britain's overcrowded prisons is well documented - the potential for transfer of infection is great. An education programme is now underway which should ensure that all prison medical staff are fully capable of assisting prisoners who develop HIV (Wool, 1990). But, the very fact of increased expertise will have to be assessed in relation to the constraints which existing conditions place on care.

The English approach can be compared with that in the United States. There, the standard of medical care of prisoners may be subject to challenge under the US Constitution. In the leading case of Estelle v Gamble,[6] the court held that there existed a constitutional right to adequate medical care

> [t]he principles [related to the Constitutional guarantee against cruel and unusual punishment] establish the government's obligation to provide medical care to those whom it is punishing by incarceration. An inmate must rely on prison authorities to treat his medical needs; if the authorities fail to do so, those needs will not be met.

The constitution has been invoked by prisoners with HIV, claiming that they have not received an adequate standard of care. In November 1989 the release on bond of a prisoner with AIDS, from a Federal prison in Miami was ordered on the grounds that he could not receive adequate medical treatment in the institution. An action by the inmate, alleging inadequate medical care is now in progress. A class action is being brought by prisoners in New York State who are HIV infected. They claim that State policy and

> ....its disregard of the right of privacy have caused and continue to cause an accumulation of class members' death, an inexcusable increase in their suffering and a loss of their very humanity.[7]

Pressure from the courts have led to alterations in prison regimes.

As will be seen later, segregation has been reduced. The United States' position is epitomised by the statement of the US Department of Justice that

> ....legally correctional medical care must meet community standards. That is, it must be equivalent to generally acceptable medical practice in the outside community. Prisoners may not be entitled to state of the art treatment, but they should have access to all approved therapeutic drugs and generally employed treatment strategies.

While the exact stance taken varies across the United States, as the discussion below in relation to prevention policy will illustrate, many advances have been made. AZT is available to some inmates in 90 per cent of prison systems and 77 per cent of jail systems. In addition there are a range of counselling and supportive systems in operation.

Given that any lack of choice of medical care for prisoners with HIV is unlikely to spawn successful litigation in this country in the absence of a constitutional list of rights against which isolations can be measured, it is even more vital that the policies of treatment and care adopted by the Prison Medical Service are satisfactory. Choice, in the sense of a free full choice of all types of medical treatment is an unrealistic aspiration. Few patients outside prison possess sufficient financial resources to command such medical attention. An adequate standard of care is a more realistic aim. What then are the component parts of such a standard of care? First, there is a need for adequate psychotherapeutic care and counselling, bringing the patients to terms with his diagnosis. To discover HIV positive status may cause a patient a high degree of stress and anxiety. Second, there is a need for confidential access to care - otherwise the doctor-patient relationship within the prison system will have been devalued, and finally there is a need for access to drugs and treatments, as these become available to combat the virus.

Care for those who have HIV or have gone on to develop AIDS will become an increasingly important part of the role of the Prison Medical Service. It is, however, only part of the general strategy adopted in relation to the problem of HIV and AIDS both in prison and outside. The need to combat HIV through education, prevention and other policy measures has come to have a high profile in the debate.

Home Office policy and the prisoner with aids

Are we neglecting prevention?

The perception of an AIDS epidemic has led to introduction of measures designed to curb the spread of the virus. These have taken two forms: first, the encouragement of the use of 'safer sex' practices, and second, the introduction of needle exchange schemes. Safer sex practices advocated have included statements concerning alleged promiscuity and the importance of using proper methods of protection against infection. Health Authorities were provided by the government with £1 million to establish needle exchange agencies. As their name suggests they are places where drug users may exchange used needles and hypodermic syringes in exchange for sterile equipment. They also have a health education role, and are involved in other activities such as HIV testing.

Despite these measures taken with the aim of curbing the spread of the virus, the Home Office response to the need for preventive measures to be introduced within the prison system today has been frosty. Home Office reticence in this area may be attributed to problems which full recognition of the need for prevention might bring. The first of these is related to the extent to which homosexual activities taking place in prison are legal. The decriminalisation of homosexual behaviour in 1967 only applies where that homosexual behaviour takes place in private. It is debatable as to whether homosexual activity in prison amounts to a private or a public place; if the latter it is an illegal activity. The Home Office may be placed in a difficult position in that supplying condoms could amount to aiding and abetting criminal activity. Also, if the prison authorities were to provide sterile equipment for the proposed injections they may be regarded as condoning the illegal activity of drug abuse. Moreover, supply of equipment other than clean needles and hypodermic syringes may fall foul of the provisions of the Misuse of Drugs Act 1971, sec 9A. Thomas has suggested that this reticence concerning prevention is not motivated by totally legal considerations (Thomas, 1990). He notes a concern with issues of morality, quoting from individuals such as the governor of Winson Green prison, whose view on giving condoms to prisoners was that it would be 'reprehensible and terribly immoral'.

The problem of how to prevent the spread of AIDS in prison was addressed by the Advisory Council on the Misuse of Drugs in their report on AIDS and Drug Misuse. As far as the provision of condoms was concerned, the report asked for a realisation that homosexual activity did take place in prison and that although the safest course of action was for inmates to avoid anal intercourse, even with good health eduction, it would still occur. They recommended that the prison department give urgent consideration to means of providing confidential but easy access to condoms. As far as the provision of equipment for injections was concerned, the Report said that they could not recommend this as a realistic option. However they commented that 'the Government's forward-looking approach in setting up the pilot syringe exchange scheme provides a constrast to the approach of the prison department'. Since then, however, there has been no alteration in the present position.

It is interesting to contrast the English position with that elsewhere. The United States jurisdiction has not followed a uniform approach. Considerable controversy was generated in Philadelphia before the present policy was adopted of making condoms available to inmates, on admission through prison medical officers and through the AIDS education programme (Hornblum, 1990). Four others Mississippi, Vermont, New York City and San Francisco County, provide condoms to inmates. As far as needle-exchanges are concerned, no correctional systems provide these. A few prison systems do however acknowledge that needle-sharing takes place and address needle-cleaning methods in their AIDS programmes. Europe has moved further in the direction of prevention than the United States and in 17 European countries it has been found that just over half distribute condoms to inmates (Harding, 1987). Again no country made syringes or clean needles available. However, in Switzerland a needle-cleaning kit was being designed which would be distributed to inmates in the same way as condoms.

Given that drug abuse does occur in prison as does homosexual activity, perhaps thought should be given to the adoption of measures aimed at weaning drug users off their activity. In addition perhaps it is time for Home Office policy concerning conjugal visits to be reviewed. In the short-term however given the urgency of the situation, perhaps the Home Office should reassess its position concerning the provision of condoms, at the very least in the light of the Advisory Committee's report.

Segregation or inclusion

If a prisoner in an English jail tests HIV positive, then he will become subject to Home Office Viral Infectivity Restrictions. The exact nature of these restrictions, undertaken on the recommendations of the prison medical officer may vary. Prisoners can be segregated by being placed in a single cell or by being placed with other segregated prisoners on a separate landing, or in the prison hospital. The restrictions were originally devised for Hepatitis B sufferers (a disease more infectious than HIV). The restrictions represent a fear of the spread of the virus, and of the risk the virus presents, but the value of such restrictions is questionable. It also has the effect of reinforcing the negative attitude taken towards those with HIV - to have developed HIV is to be stigmatised. In addition, any enforced restriction creates a further divide between the approach to HIV taken within and without the prison walls. How far this division will continue is dependent upon the interpretations given to the Public Health (Control of Infectious Diseases) Act 1988. The implementation of Viral Infectivity Restrictions has had a considerable impact. In September 1989, only 27 per cent of the 63 prisoners who were known to have HIV in the prisons of England and Wales were at normal locations.

Elsewhere, there have been conflicting approaches as to whether the segregation of HIV infected persons should take place. In the United States there is at present a trend away from segregation.

Just over one-third (39 per cent) of prison systems segregate all prisoners with AIDS. There are only four prison systems (those of Alabama, Colorado, Connecticut and Nevada) which segregate all categories of HIV infected individuals. In 1985 only two state/federal systems did not segregate prisoners with HIV - by 1989, the figure was 18. Several law suits have been fought over segregation with diverse results. In New York State a claim that segregation was unconstitutional was rejected (*Cordera v Coughlin*).[8] In contrast in Connecticut, California and Colorado class action law suits have led to changes in segregation policy. A settlement of an action brought over segregation of a prisoner with AIDS and the requirement that prisoners with AIDS wear red wrist bands to identify the need for blood and body fluid precautions took place in Oregon. Other actions concerning claims over segregation are pending.

One prison system which has sought to challenge the notion that segregation is an automatic requirement in cases of HIV is Scotland.[9] In Edinburgh Prison one of the HIV/AIDs management groups policy objectives was that of the full integration of all prisoners unless it was considered medically inappropriate to do so. Where prisoners are found to be HIV positive they are kept in the general prison system, until such time as hospitalisation is necessary. Confidentiality is treated as of paramount importance, although some HIV positive prisoners have been willing to come out into the open concerning their illness. In order to ensure that other inmates may become aware of their HIV positive status by prisoners travelling to a local hospital, a fortnightly clinic is held in the hospital for HIV inmates by a senior specialist consultant from the Edinburgh City Hospital.

In view of the medical evidence which suggests that many of the fears regarding the transmission of HIV have been greatly exaggerated, widespread segregation of those prisoners with HIV is, perhaps, unjustified. While segregation may be needed, should a HIV positive prisoner pose a real threat to prisoners and staff within the prison, blanket segregation perpetuates the stigma which surrounds HIV positive individuals. Integration of the prisoner with HIV into the prison system will require several steps. First, a radical change in the policy of confidentiality which operates in prison will be needed. It is arguable as to whether such a policy will require alteration in the structure of the prison medical service. One solution advanced by commentators such as Dr. Paul Bowden is that of care of prisoner-patients being undertaken by medical practitioners who are full members of the NHS and employees of the Home Office (Bowden, 1976). Total independence may help to reinforce the doctor-patient obligations. An alternative approach may arise from the revitalisation of the prison medical service in the manner suggested by the Royal College of Physicians (Bluglass, 1990). They have advocated the development of prison medicine as a full medical speciality and that along with this a competent career structure could be established. Such a development may lead to a redefinition of the doctor-patient role. However, such a radical change may not be needed if prison authorities are willing to recognise the inviolate nature of confidentiality as has happened in Edinburgh Prison.

Second, any reassessment will need to take into account the fact that a point may be reached where some special care is needed for the prisoner with HIV separate from that of the rest of the prison population. Some steps down this road have already been taken. A unit which will accommodate nine patients in an interim period before they are moved to hospital is almost completed at Brixton Prison. But this is obviously at present a very small scale development. This step should only be taken where, on medical grounds, it is necessary to do so and such a decision should be made taking into consideration that subsequent re-inclusion of the prisoner within the rest of the prison population would be difficult. Perhaps there are lessons to be learnt from the approach taken in the United States. In late 1985 an 18-bed hospice ward was established at the Oregon Correctional Unit. It included a lounge furnished with rocking chairs, plants, a small patio and yard. In New York the prisoner with AIDS is first put into a prison hospital. Then, if he becomes sick, he is transferred to the nearest AIDS Centre located in hospitals in the area. Prisoners transferred to such a centre are rarely transferred back. In Edinburgh a care and support unit is to be established with 22 beds to deal with illnesses developed as a result of AIDS and to look after those who are in remission. Such a development would obviously require considerable capital expenditure. But it is necessary if the Prison Medical service is to adequately perform its role of caring for the prisoner.

A policy of education?

It is now widely recognised that efforts to educate individuals about HIV infection is of major importance within prisons. The need for such education is urgent. For example, despite some efforts at education in the past few years, confusion still exists, particularly as to the methods of transmission of HIV infection. A survey by the NIJ in 1989 showed that in Virginia, 20 per cent of inmates did not know that HIV is transmitted through semen and 25-50 per cent thought that HIV could be transmitted by the sharing of eating and drinking utensils, by insect bites and through contact with sweat, tears or urine. In Britain, although leaflets such as the government-produced 'AIDS -Don't Die Of Ignorance' were made available to prisons, it is alleged that their distribution did not always occur. It is therefore to be predicted that the types of uncertainty and confusion found by the NIJ survey will also be present in British prisons.

However, the need to counteract such confusion is not the only reason for educative efforts. Studies show a high incidence of 'risk behaviours' in the prison community. For example, in a 1990 study of intravenous drug users which aimed to establish the degree of illicit drug use in prison and the prevalence of risk behaviour, it was found that a significant proportion of the respondents appeared to have taken part in activities which are highly efficient means of HIV transmission. Out of 50 respondents (42 men and 8 women), 33 had injected drugs while in prison and 26 of these had shared equipment. Within this group, 1 woman and 4 men had augmented the risk of engaging in unprotected anal, vaginal and oral intercourse with more than one partner. The researchers in this study expressed the view that the presently limited access to treatment, counselling, methadone programmes and health education, compounded the situation. The Parole Release Scheme estimates that 10,000 prisoners in Britain each year take prohibited drugs in prison. Of this figure, a considerable proportion inject by means of shared equipment. The NIJ survey found that over 40 per cent of South Carolina inmates reported personal knowledge of needlesharing in prison and over 60 per cent had personal knowledge of sexual activity among inmates.

It seems clear that education is necessary to reduce or, ideally, prevent the occurrence of these activities. Indeed, most authorities will concur that education is worthwhile and necessary. However, what is not agreed upon is, firstly, the content of such education and, secondly, its status and position within an overall institutional response to HIV infection. As far as the first of these questions is concerned, it is clear that educative efforts should attempt to reduce stereotyping, break down prejudices and defuse myths about HIV. For example, it is important to emphasise that HIV cannot be transmitted through casual contact, but is passed through unprotected sexual activity and through exposure to infected blood, usually through needle-sharing. In women's prisons, information should be given on mother-foetus transmission and on the greater risk for women than men in heterosexual intercourse. It is relatively straightforward to recommend techniques for avoiding infection upon return to the outside community; however, many authorities have felt legally constrained from outlining such techniques for avoiding HIV infection in prison. As we have noted above, under criminal law, homosexual acts in prison could be construed as illegal.

The Home Office have made a video for inmates on HIV infection. Entitled 'AIDS Inside and Out', it attempts to dispel myths about HIV, and is successful to the extent that it emphasises the lack of danger from casual or social contact. With regard to proposing strategies for avoiding infection through more risky activities, the video becomes coy and confusing. It opens with the warning that prisoners who commit homosexual acts 'may be breaking the criminal law', without informing the audience that from April 1989, homosexual behaviour at least ceased to be a disciplinary offence in prisons. General guidance on safer sex and safer injecting practice is given, although the stress is on the relevance of this information after leaving the institution. For example, the video advertises the availability of clean syringes and needles from chemists, but no corresponding advice is given on how to clean needles in prison.

This video should be contrasted with the educational material prepared for prisoners in Saughton Prison in Edinburgh. Information is conveyed in a frank tone, using an argot more recognisable to prisoners than that of medical officers. Fears about encouraging prohibited activities and the need to educate about risk behaviour also seem to have been juggled more successfully in American educational programmes. For example, in Cook County, Illinois, AIDS educators tell prisoners that during their imprisonment they should clean needles with soap and water as a (less efficient) substitute for bleach. San Francisco County's AIDS educators advise inmates that condoms are available, while emphasising that sexual activity in prison is a felony.

Such a recognition and acceptance of the inevitability of these practices, together with an attempt to encourage their safer practising seems much more useful than the Home Office strategy, which has been to claim the minimal extent of these activities and to be elliptical as to risk-reducing techniques. The general attitude displayed by the Home Office towards the content of their educative endeavour is reflected in its status within the overall English response to HIV infection in prisons. The key strategy in English prison policy continues to be segregation: more than half of all known HIV positive prisoners in England and Wales are in segregation, whether formally under VIR or informally under Rule 43. Although official enthusiasm has been expressed for the role education should take in a generalised response to HIV infection, in practice it is still subordinated to the perceived need to segregate and isolate.

American authorities emphasise that 'because there is no vaccine or cure for the disease, education and training programs are the cornerstone of efforts to curb the spread of AIDS in prisons and jails'. Saughton Prison in Edinburgh practises a regime in which education does constitute the cornerstone of the official response. This may be due in part to Edinburgh's extremely high rate of HIV infection in general; it may also be due to the non-segregative policy operated by the prison authorities, which undoubtedly encourages prisoners to be either voluntarily tested or to declare their HIV status to the medical officer. In 1988, prison officers were in favour of segregation; however, the governor, John Pearce, recognised that this was, at the least, bad management and opted instead to provide education and training for prisoners and officers. This involves the distribution of leaflets to all inmates upon reception, the regular showing of videos, staff training and the establishment of a support group for HIV positive inmates. A hospital ward is planned: this will provide beds not only for prisoners with AIDS but also for relatives who need to stay overnight.

The Saughton regime has been criticised for having a humane HIV policy without a concomitantly effective AIDS policy (Shaw, 1990); that is, for being inadequately prepared for the numbers that could begin to die in prison in the next few years. However, its response to HIV and AIDS is to date the most admirable attempt to develop a policy that will retain respect for the situation of the HIV positive prisoner, hopefully reduce the numbers who become HIV positive in prison and defuse fears that could otherwise create tensions within prison.

Implications for the prisoners' rights debate

As a result of the above discussion of specific questions arising out of the dilemmas of the HIV positive prisoner, there are clear ramifications for the prisoners' rights debate. First, the framing of political struggles within a discourse of rights can produce unwanted effects. For example, as we showed above, in an effort to protect prisoners from abusive medical research, regulations were created which enshrine the rights of prisoners not to be subjected to medical treatment which risks their physical or mental health. This now leads to the difficult situation in which prisoners still wish to be protected from abuse, yet may also wish to enter into research trials in order to have a chance of controlling their HIV infection. A protection framed as a right, has become a prohibition.

We therefore disagree with the optimism shown by commentators such as Richardson

... the argument here will proceed on the assumption that basic

137

> rights exist ... that they provide necessary protection for the individual against any state irrespective of ideological hue ... and that they should be recognised at law. This positive attitude is encouraged by the present subject matter: the case for prisoners' rights is particularly strong (Richardson, 1985).

It is inadvisable to proceed with any argument on the assumption that a crucial aspect of it exists; too many questions are begged. And while the case for substantive changes in the lived experiences of prisoners is indeed strong, we are unconvinced that a rights-based argument is the only or even appropriate basis on which to proceed.

Richardson is correct to note 'the powerful political impact of the assertion of a right', but the examples above of the slipperiness of rights arguments lead us to conclude that great care must be taken when arguing for change based on a claim to a right. Successful interventions have been made by and on behalf of prisoners through a discourse of rights; however, it must also be acknowledged that rights are 'all things to all people' (Carlen, 1983). This inherent volatility of rights arguments produces our second concluding point: that the employment of such arguments should be limited to very specific and clearly defined demands.

Rights arguments can backfire on their proponents, with unexpected and deleterious consequences. Further, seeking the recognition of prisoners' rights legitimates the legal system which places people in prison: the rights of prisoners depend inexorably upon the right of society to imprison. We require an analysis which proceeds in terms of 'oppression' as heuristic trope rather than rights. Prisoners should be able to specify which behaviours are overly oppressive; underlying this should be the acceptance that imprisonment is not a societal right and cannot be justified in most cases. Its institutional operation should be criticised in every case. The debate would therefore be shifted from the emotive subject of prisoners (which usually inspires reactionary responses) to the question of what is collectively acceptable behaviour towards prisoners (a more self-reflexive position). This should be defined by prisoners themselves wherever possible.

Arguments about prisoners' rights can be emotive, powerful and occasionally effective. Organisations such as PROP (Preservation of the Rights of Prisoners) depend upon and exploit the notion of prisoners' rights. However, this same notion is equally capable of producing statements such as that made by Lord Wilberforce in *Raymond v. Honey*;[10] 'a prisoner retains all civil rights which are not taken away expressly or by necessary implication'. As Moran says of rights, 'we should see them primarily as a mere act of faith, a devotion to a dangerous orthodoxy ... A rights based engagement in the politics of HIV/AIDS will necessarily need to understand the struggle over meaning that is being waged in the production of knowledge of HIV/AIDS' (Moran, 1988). The struggles that can be won by a rights argument are limited. To move beyond the sphere of piecemeal interventions, we must look to an analysis that attempts to understand the operation of moralism, homophobia, metaphors of dirt and disease and their subtle links with criminality, both in framing arguments to improve the situation of the HIV positive prisoner and in criticising the discursive responses of official agencies within the criminal justice system.

Rights arguments will retain an importance; however, their framing should be carefully theorised. For the HIV positive prisoner, as for all prisoners, there should exist a right to health. This right is identical to that enjoyed by any individual. 'Prisoner' should not be the defining term from which all practices are allowed to flow. Instead, our emphasis is on 'health'. A prisoner has a right to health, which should be fulfilled in every situation to the limits of the authorities' capabilities. It may be that litigation will be unavoidable to determine the exact details of this in practice; however, the benefit of such a framing is that, for once, the onus will be on the authorities to prove that they have acted to the best of their available resources. The prisoner will no longer be required to establish degrees of harm and amounts of suffering. It is our contention that the future utility of prisoners' rights arguments lies in this direction.

*Mchale, Lecturer in law, Nottingham University.
** Young, Lecturer in law, Lancaster University.

1. Letter to The Times, 14 December.

2. The term epidemic is used ironically: the describing of HIV infection as an epidemic enabled government, agencies, the media and the individual to deploy particular mechanisms of control and quarantine, embellished with a hompohobic and racist ideology. For a discussion of the term epidemic see Foucault (1976).

3. [1983] 3 All ER 545.

4. [1990] 2 WLR 472.

5. (1990) NLJ Feb 16.

6. (1976) 97 Si Ct 285.

7. NLJ (1989) p. 68.

8. (1984) 607 F.Supp 9 (SDNY).

9. This is well documented in the Prison Service Journal of Spring 1990.

10. [1982] 1 All ER 756.

Doctors' Handmaidens:

The Legal Contribution

Jonathan Montgomery*

Introduction

The relationship between nurses and doctors has long been a controversial matter. From one perspective, hospitals are places in which doctors compete with nurses and midwives to maximise their influence over the way in which health care is delivered. By and large the medical profession has come out best, at least at the formal level. Nurses and midwives may successfully play the 'doctor-nurse' game so as to exercise power informally and unobtrusively (Porter, 1991), but this does little to challenge the assumptions on which medical supremacy is based. It is itself a form of 'hierarchy maintenance' (Kitzinger et al 1990, p.156). The National Health Service (NHS) has remained dominated by doctors (Klein, 1989, Stacey, 1988b, p.116-132, 176-193), and this has generally been at the expense of the other professions. This essay has arisen out of the convergence of an interest in this aspect of the politics of health care with the study of the doctrines that lawyers use to analyse the work of the professions in question. It seeks to consider how far and in what ways the law supports the dominance of medicine over nursing and midwifery.

This essay is therefore concerned with the way in which the power of the health care professions is structured by the law. Its subject matter is narrow. It examines only one aspect of legal regulation, the relative positions of medicine and of nursing and midwifery, and the law itself is only a small piece of a complex jigsaw puzzle displaying the nature of professional power. Nevertheless, the relationship between medicine and nursing is a autonomy. Consideration of the contribution of the law can provide a stimulating addition to the now considerable body of literature examining the sociological aspects of the matter.

Sociologists have identified the concepts of autonomy and dominance as central to understanding the place of professions in modern society (Turner, 1987, p.131-156, Elston, 1991). The traditional image of medicine is based on nineteenth century practice where the individual patient consulted an independent doctor on his professional opinion. Even in 1985, Lord Templeman asserted that the root of the doctor-patient relationship was contractual despite the absence of a contract between them under the NHS (*Sidaway v Bethlem RHG*).[1] This image portrays doctors as unconstrained by administrative regulation; early state intervention, in the form of a professional register, served to protect the medical profession against encroachment by other occupational groups rather than to scrutinise the quality of its practice. In such a context medicine can be seen as a paradigm of professional power: possessing an occupational monopoly in which doctors defined both the needs of their clients and also the manner in which those needs were to be met (Johnson, 1972).

The advent of bureaucratic systems for the delivery of health care, particularly in Britain the NHS, has produced a number of threats to this autonomy. One is presented by the possibility of administrative oversight, whereby doctors might become more like employees than independent practitioners. At least until recently, British doctors have successfully resisted managerial control over their work. The official position under the structure introduced in 1974 was that the nature of the clinical responsibility held by doctors was such that they could not be held accountable to managers (DHSS 1972: para. 1.18). It remains to be seen whether the reorganisation of 1991 will bring significant alterations to this approach. However, while the explicit recognition of medical autonomy has been reduced, the real power of doctors in the hospital hierarchy may be little diminished (Elston, 1991). This aspect of the debate over the nature of medical hegemony in contemporary British health care cannot be fully addressed through the materials discussed here, but the second main threat to the power of doctors can.

In addition to increasing the scope for bureaucratic control of the health professions, the NHS provided an opportunity for non-medical professions to seek to establish their own autonomous status. Freidson's early work suggested a model of professional dominance whereby, in order to maintain the clinical freedom that they coveted, doctors had to ensure that they continued to dominate the other occupational groups working in health care (Freidson, 1970a, p.127-164, 1970b, p.47-70). From this perspective, autonomy on the part of other health professions undermines the power of the medical profession. Thus some commentators have suggested that medical autonomy has been compromised by the interdisciplinary nature of modern health care. Armstrong (1976) has argued that increasing official concern with the position of other health professions indicated a loosening of medical influence over the NHS. Others have pointed out that a more sophisticated framework is required and that an increase in the autonomy of non-medical health professionals does not necessarily entail a reduction in medical power. Ovretveite (1985) has observed that there is little evidence that increased involvement of physiotherapists in decision making processes has led to them having a significant influence on the outcome. In addition, other professions may have considerable autonomy in their spheres of practice without undermining medical dominance if those spheres are defined by the medical profession and if their ability to practise their skills depends on medical referral or supervision. Thus Freidson (1977) has described a pattern of medical domination in which doctors are the key profession from whom the legitimacy of other professions flows, and who provide the authoritative interpretation and evaluation of their contribution. Closer analysis of the development of the paramedical professions shows that it would be wrong to conclude from the dominance of medicine that subordinate professions are powerless, but the limited control wrestled by such groups from medicine does not necessarily destroy the power of doctors (Larkin, 1983).

An analysis of the way in which the relationship between professions is mediated in the law can contribute to the debate over the nature of professional power. There is no doubt that the legal system acknowledges the practice of nurses and midwives, but this does not necessarily dilute the dominance of medicine. A detailed examination of the mechanisms by which medical power is replicated is called for to see how far the models of dominance fit.

Turner (1987, p.141) has identified three modes of medical domination: subordination, by which doctors treat the other professions as their servants whose authority arises through medical delegation; limitation, by which the practice of the dominated profession is contained within limits established and maintained by doctors; and exclusion, whereby the medical profession prevents others from practising at all within its domain. At one level these strategies can be traced through the schemes of professional regulation. First in the way in which occupational monopolies are guaranteed by law, but shared with medicine. Thus, for example, midwifery may be practised only by registered midwives and medical practitioners (Nurses, Midwives and Health Visitors Act 1979, s. 17). Further, the involvement of doctors in the governing bodies of other professions also guarantees continuing medical influence (although not complete control) over their work.[2] The materials discussed here are concerned with the less elevated legal rules that govern everyday practice. They relate primarily to the strategy of subordination and illustrate the extent to which the relationship between doctors, nurses and midwives remains characterised as one of medical dominance.

A case study

The relative position of nurses and doctors came explicitly before the courts in *RCN v DHSS*[3] The case concerned the termination of pregnancy by prostaglandin. In essence this drug induces labour and causes the foetus to be expelled. It is prescribed by a doctor and administered over a period of time during which the woman's condition will usually be monitored by a nurse. In cases of 'maximum nurse participation' the doctor will be responsible only for prescribing the prostaglandin and inserting the catheter through which it is to be administered. The actual administration, which leads to the ending of the pregnancy, will be done by a nurse. The doctor's contribution would have no effect on the pregnancy without the subsequent nursing intervention.

The Royal College of Nursing was concerned that in this situation nurses might not be protected against prosecutions for illegal abortion. The College therefore challenged a DHSS circular which advised that nurses were covered by the defences under the Abortion Act 1967. These are available when 'a pregnancy is terminated by a registered medical practitioner'. In order to justify the Department's position it was necessary to construe the actions of the nurses as being those of the doctors in the eyes of the law. This was precisely what the House of Lords did. They held that, providing the procedure was initiated by a doctor and a doctor was on call should the nurses desire their assistance, for the purposes of the Abortion Act 1967 the termination was being carried out by a registered medical practitioner. In doing so their Lordships characterised the relationship between the two professionals as one in which the nurse is little more than the doctor's handmaiden.

It might be argued that it would be wrc ¬ ₃ to place too great a weight on this decision. It is perhaps best seen as based on expediency rather than as a considered view of the status of nursing. However, this sanguine view sits uneasily with the recent Parliamentary reform of the Abortion Act. With effect from April 1991 the law has been reshaped and a new defence to allegations of child destruction under the Infant Life (Preservation) Act 1929 has been created. The operative words are 'no offence under the Infant Life (Preservation) Act 1929 shall be committed by a registered medical practitioner who terminates a pregnancy in accordance with the provisions of this Act' (Abortion Act 1967 s. 5(1) as substituted by the Human Fertilisation and Embryology Act 1990 s. 37(4)). This defence extends only to doctors. Unlike the phrase interpreted in *RCN v DHSS* it is not who terminates the pregnancy that is in issue, but who may claim the defence. Parliament has once more ignored the position of nurses. It is difficult to see how the courts will be able to stretch the meaning of the new provision in the way they did in the *RCN* case. This will have significant practical effects. It means that nurses would be ill-advised to assist in terminations after about twenty-two weeks of pregnancy. If the foetus is capable of being born alive, which requires only the capacity to survive for a few hours (*Rance v Mid-*

Downs H.A.,[4] then doctors may terminate pregnancies under the Abortion Act 1967 without risk of prosecution for child destruction but nurses may not. For present purposes, however, it is the symbolic significance of continuing the implicit characterisation of nurses as the largely invisible handmaidens of the medical profession that is important. Parliament's continuing failure to recognise the involvement of nurses suggests that the RCN case may represent a more general legal devaluing of nursing skills.

The purpose of this essay is to examine whether this view of nurses as subordinated to doctors is one that the law adopts generally and to consider the legal doctrines that reinforce it. The abortion case highlights a number of themes that call for scrutiny. The judicial discussion illustrates two important assumptions about the relationship between the professions that underpin the dominance of medicine over nursing. Lord Diplock justified the decision through the concept of <u>responsibility</u>, arguing that even though the actions were those of the nurse, responsibility lay with the doctor. On this view, the independence of nursing is constrained because it is the doctor, not the nurse who is legally accountable for mishaps. If this is so, then it is said to be unjust to the medical profession to deny them the power to determine how care is offered, for that is the only way they can protect themselves against liability. The issue of responsibility is perhaps best considered through the law governing malpractice. The extent to which doctors can be made responsible for the actions of nurses is crucial.

The second assumption made by their lordships is almost the converse of the first, it emphasises the degree of <u>control</u> that doctors have over nurses. Lord Roskill argued that it was in law the doctor who performed the termination because the nurse's 'participation in it is at all times under the control of the doctor even though the doctor is not present throughout the entirety of the treatment'. Lord Keith articulated a similar view, describing the nurses' actions as 'done in a ministerial capacity and on the doctor's orders'. This issue of control can be examined by considering the extent of the duty of a nurse to obey instructions given by doctors. The stronger this duty, the more the law supports the dominance of medicine. The wider the exceptions to the duty of obedience, the more the law recognises the independent professional skills of nurses.

A third issue concerns the degree to which nurses are treated by the legal system as professionals with independent clinical expertise rather than ordinary employees. Jacob's (1988, p.152-153) analysis of the decision in *RCN* suggests that it illustrates a failure of the courts to recognise nursing as a profession with its own normative values. Instead of allowing nurses to work in accordance with their professional ethics, fixed and maintained by the profession itself, he presents the case as indicating a utilitarian method of control under which nurses are expected to pursue the values that their employing organisation imposes on them. The crucial factor is the extent to which nurses are free to exercise their own <u>clinical judgment</u>. This matter can be pursued through the consideration of nurses' rights to opt out of courses of treatment favoured by the medical staff.

These three themes of responsibility, control and clinical judgment provide a structure for the examination of the division of health labour between nurses and doctors. Pursuing them requires analysis of a range of legal sources, judicial decisions, statutory provisions passed by Parliament and ministerial regulations. It is also necessary to consider the implications of administrative arrangements within the health service in order to understand the practical implications of the legal principles. When these disparate materials are collected together, the extent to which English law is riddled with assumptions about the dominant status of medicine and the weaker position of nurses can become clear.

Responsibility

The respective responsibilities of members of the health care team is an important issue in medical accident litigation. Most mishaps occur in situations where a number of professionals have been involved in the patient's care. If the patient wishes to sue, [s]he needs to decide against whom to bring the action. In practice this is usually the health authority or the doctor rather than the nurse or midwife. This is probably because there is a greater risk that nurses may not be insured. In theory, the doctor or health authority may claim indemnity for any damages that they are required to pay as a result of nurses' negligence, and this issue raises the allocation of responsibility within the team. As will be seen the law has not been given the chance to take this matter very far.

The second area of interest is the application of the 'captain of the ship' doctrine. In its fullest sense this makes one member of the health care team responsible for all mishaps irrespective of personal fault. If this was applied so as to make doctors responsible for nurses' mistakes, it would clearly indicate a hierarchy of professionals with doctors at its head. Finally comes the question of whether the doctrine that allows junior practitioners to escape liability by calling in their seniors works in a way that implies the subordination of nurses to doctors. If nurses can rely on calling in doctors to cover their inexperience as nurses (as opposed to recognising that the issue requires medical not nursing expertise), then there is an implicit assumption of medical supremacy in that it implies that doctors possess superior nursing skills.

Apportionment of liability

Untangling the way in which liability for paying damages in cases of accident is distributed is complex. Both legal doctrine and the administration of malpractice litigation by those representing the medical profession need to be examined. The general principles governing the apportionment of liability are first that a successful plaintiff may obtain the whole of the damages from any one of the defendants to the case and second that the defendant may sue the others for their share of the money paid. The amount of the share depends on the degree of responsibility each party holds for the accident (Civil Liability (Contribution) Act 1978). Cases brought to determine the apportionment of liability between health professionals would therefore provide an important indicator of their respective responsibilities. The more that nurses are seen by the courts as independent practitioners, the more cases would identify them as primarily responsible for the payment of damages.

The operation of these principles in the health care context can be seen in two cases concerning pharmacists and doctors. In *Dwyer v Roderick*,[5] the doctor had made a gross mistake in making out the prescription. The pharmacist dispensed the drugs as instructed. The patient took them and suffered a fatal overdose. Negligence was admitted and the litigation concerned the apportionment of responsibility between the professionals. The doctor was held to be liable for 45 per cent of the damages and the chemist for the rest. In a second case the pharmacist misread the doctor's handwriting and dispensed a drug that caused irreversible brain damage (*Prendergast v Sam & Dee Ltd*).[6] The doctor was found to be negligent for writing illegibly, but the court found that this amounted to only one quarter of the responsibility. The chemist was primarily responsible as the dosage prescribed should have alerted him to the fact that there was a misunderstanding and he should have queried the instructions.

After the former decision, Finch (1982) advised pharmacists that they had 'no choice but to query a prescription... if there is any cause for doubt whatever. They must be instructed to ignore any adverse response if the doctor finds it unpleasant to have his word put into question'. He argues that the effect of such decisions is to allow doctors to pass the blame for their own errors on to other professionals. In addition, however, the law is encouraging and legitimating professional independence on the part of chemists. Doctors can no longer dismiss challenges to their decisions, as anecdotal evidence suggests they do in relation to nurses, by arguing that it is they who will be held legally responsible and therefore what they say must go. In the context of nursing, the implications of being found partly liable for accidents might be both positive and negative. Being sued is never pleasant, but at least their professional responsibility would be recognised.

In fact, however, the courts have never been given the chance to consider the extent to which nurses are independently responsible for actions taken as part of a health care team. Most cases concerning allegations of nursing negligence are brought against health authorities, who are vicariously liable for their errors. A deal struck between the medical defence societies and the health authorities has kept the apportionment of liability away from the courts and confined them to secret negotiations in which nurses' advisers have no part (Ministry of Health, 1954). The parties agreed not to sue each other for contributions but to determine the proportions each would pay privately, splitting the amount equally if no agreement could be reached. With effect from January 1990 this deal has been superseded by a system of NHS indemnity for hospital doctors, so that the health authority pays all of any damages awarded, irrespective of the exact apportionment of liability between staff (Department of Health, 1989c). Both professions are now effectively in the same position and their respective contributions are irrelevant as the health authority pays either way. Nevertheless, the old approach has prevented the matter of the relative position of nurses, midwives and doctors being considered by the courts and has removed the most obvious mechanism by which the independent legal responsibility of nurses could be established.

The 'captain of the ship' doctrine

The 'captain of the ship' doctrine raises the relationship between doctors and nurses in a particularly acute form. This principle is a means of making one person (the 'captain') responsible for all mishaps occurring under her or his jurisdiction. Personal fault is not in issue, superiors are liable even if they did nothing wrong. If the health care team can be conceived as a ship and the doctor is properly said to be its captain, then nurses are defined as subordinates for whose actions the doctor is responsible. A distinction should be made between a weak and a strong sense of this doctrine. The weak sense describes the duty of 'captains' to oversee the procedure in question and be alert to the possibility of errors being made. In addition to carrying out their work properly they must monitor the work of other members of the team. However, they will only be liable for an accident if they have exercised this oversight negligently. Under the strong version, the doctrine fixes liability for mistakes on those with overall responsibility irrespective of their personal role in causing them. It is enough to show that the defendant in a malpractice action was in charge of the team, it does not matter whether it was they or another member who was negligent. In a sense, this treats those other members as analogous to employees of the 'captain', who is vicariously liable for their mistakes. Although this doctrine has been used in some US jurisdictions to make physicians responsible for the actions of nurses, its application in England is uncertain.

Tucker J has held, in a pre-NHS case concerning a Harley Street consultant hired by the patient to operate on him in a local hospital, that 'it is well established as a matter of law that the resident medical officers... and the nursing staff, are not the agents of a specialist surgeon ... at any rate in so far as they are performing the ordinary duties which have to be carried out at a hospital of this kind' (*Morris v Winsbury-White*).[7] As the mishap in question might have occurred in the course of these routine duties he held that the plaintiff had failed to show that the surgeon was liable. This case denies the application of either the weak or the strong version of the 'captain of the ship' doctrine to the routine support and after-care that a hospital provides.

In relation to the operating theatre the courts have been less reluctant to accept the doctor's overall responsibility. *Mahon v Osborne*[8] concerned a swab that had been left inside the patient causing his death. The court was required to consider whether the surgeon could escape liability by arguing that the fault lay with the nurse. Standard procedures existed to protect against the possibility of a swab being missed. Each swab was attached to a clip and was counted in and out, the count being recorded by a nurse on a blackboard. Scott LJ accepted there was a risk of the clip becoming detached from the swab and that this risk was 'wholly external... to the surgeon... [who] can neither control it nor know it' Nonetheless, the surgeon could not excuse himself from bearing this risk by relying on the nurse; he had a personal responsibility to check that no swabs remained before sewing up the incision (see also *Urry v Biere*[9] and *James v Dunlop*[10]). In a sense, the surgeon is responsible for nursing errors. This responsibility is limited, however. It requires doctors to search personally to check that no foreign body is left before closing the wound. But this does not make them liable for the nurse's mistake it makes them responsible for their own. If there was an urgent need to complete the operation quickly because the patient's condition was deteriorating this might absolve the surgeon from the duty to search

(*Mahon v Osborne*). The doctor's defence is not, however, that he was relying on the nurse but that he did everything that a responsible practitioner would have done in the circumstances. This case gives some support to the contention that the 'captain of the ship' doctrine applies. It does extend the doctor's responsibility to all aspects of the operation. But it could be contended that it is only an application of the ordinary standard of care. If it is an example of the doctrine it must be stressed that it is a weak version.

A number of cases suggest that the captain of ship doctrine does not exist in the strong sense. It has been held that an anaesthetist was not responsible for a nurse's error in drawing up a dose of anaesthetic despite the fact that he was responsible for anaesthesia (*Fussell v Beddard*).[11] In an older case, surgeons were held not to be liable for the negligence of nurses who were bathing a patient on their instructions (*Perionowsky v Freeman*).[12] It was accepted practice to leave the supervision of baths to nurses and the surgeons were not responsible for the fact that the water had been too hot. The best view of the cases is that both doctors and nurses have personal responsibility. Neither can rely entirely on the other to carry out their duties competently, both have a duty to look out for potential problems. However, this is not responsibility for another's mistake. Liability exists only where professionals fail to carry out their own duties satisfactorily.

If there is a captain of the ship doctrine in the strong sense, it applies not to doctors but to hospitals and health authorities. A developing area of law, to this effect, is that of the direct liability of hospitals for the care they offer (Bettle, 1987, Montgomery 1987). The decisions in *Roe v Ministry of Health*[13] and *Cassidy v Ministry of Health*[14] set out the principles on which liability is based. Under this doctrine, where a hospital holds itself out as offering services of a particular type it is bound to offer treatment with reasonable care and it is liable for breaches of that duty regardless of who was responsible. The Court of Appeal has indicated support for this approach in *Wilsher v Essex AHA*,[15] but the matter has not yet come up for formal decision in this country. It is a strong version of the 'captain of the ship' in that it makes the hospital responsible for the actions of others. It can perhaps been seen as an example of the law recognising the increasingly bureaucratic context of health care in which professionals are employees rather than independent contractors. This matter will be raised again in the discussion of the impact of hospital policies on clinical freedom. At this point it should merely be noted that there is little evidence for the existence in English law of a 'captain of the ship' doctrine that makes doctors responsible for the errors of nurses.

Passing the buck

A further aspect of the issue of responsibility concerns the extent to which nurses can pass the buck to doctors, and in the process absolve themselves of responsibility. To the extent that this is a recognition of the different spheres of professional expertise such a doctrine would not suggest subordination, but partnership. Where it is used in relation to areas within the competence of nurses the implications would be rather different. This can be illustrated by reference to the case of *Wilsher v Essex AHA*, which concerned allegations of negligence on the part of doctors in a neonatal care unit. Martin Wilsher was born nearly three months prematurely and at the time of the hearing was nearly blind. It was alleged that the blindness had been caused by his being given an excess of oxygen in the course of his care. The reason for this excess was that the instrument monitoring his oxygen levels had been inserted into a vein instead of an artery, so that it registered oxygen levels lower than were in fact present. The doctors had increased the oxygen supplied until the readings were at the intended level without appreciating that the real levels were much higher.

The House of Lords held that no causal link between the negligence and the blindness had been proved and Martin Wilsher therefore lost his case. No criticism was made, however, of the finding of negligence. It is the approach taken to this issue that is significant for present purposes. Negligence might have occurred at a number of points, but two were the most significant. The court held that the senior house officer who inserted the catheter was not negligent in doing so wrongly, because the error was one that competent doctors might make. It could not therefore be said that he had fallen below the standard expected of a responsible medical practitioner (*Bolam v Friern HMC*).[16] In order to confirm the position of the catheter, an X-ray was taken. The senior house officer examined the X-ray and, being uncertain, called in the registrar to check it. Both doctors failed to see that the catheter was incorrectly placed. It was found that this was not a mistake that a responsible doctor, working in a neonatal unit would have made. However, the Court of Appeal found that while the house officer had made mistakes, these mistakes did not amount to negligence as 'the inexperienced doctor, called on to exercise a specialist skill will, as part of that skill, seek the advice and help of his superiors when he does or may need it. If he does seek such help, he will often have satisfied the test, even though he may himself have made a mistake'. By calling in the registrar he showed that he had exercised his judgment carefully (ibid p. 818). The registrar had no such excuse and was found to be negligent.

This is a method of passing responsibility which assumes a hierarchy. The subordinate professional may escape liability either by meeting the required standard of care or by recognising their incompetence and calling for assistance. If nurses invoke this principle by seeking the assistance of doctors, they are acknowledging the legitimacy of medical dominance. This was the crux of the decision of the United Kingdom Central Council for Nursing, Midwifery and Health Visiting (UKCC) to strike off a nurse for reporting an error to a doctor rather than to the nurse to whom she was responsible (*Hefferon v UKCC*).[17] The nurse had wrongly administered an additional immunisation to a baby. When she realised her error, she sought advice from a doctor and passed on to the mother his reassurance that there would be no lasting adverse effects, although the child's temperature might be raised briefly. The professional conduct committee of the UKCC decided that this constituted misconduct and struck the nurse off the register. She appealed to the High Court, which found that there was no evidence on which this conclusion could be properly based. The court held that no system had been established that required the nurse to report to her nursing superior. In its absence, it was quite proper for a nurse to conduct herself by seeking advice from a doctor rather than a nurse. The nurse's actions could be interpreted in two ways. It might be a recognition of the separate clinical expertise of the doctor, indicating a demarcation of responsibility between the professions rather than a hierarchy. It could also be seen as a deference to the superiority of medicine even in relation to nursing expertise. The UKCC seems to have concluded that it was the latter, and that her actions as such undermined the nursing establishment's campaign for greater professional autonomy. The court thought differently.

Control

There is a direct connection between medical liability under the captain of the ship doctrine and the legitimacy of doctors expecting nurses to carry out their orders. Two rather different claims can be made. The first is made by the nurse, that she is not responsible because she is only doing what she was told. At first glance, the suggestion that nurses can escape liability by pleading doctor's orders is beneficial to them. Like the protection from having to defend actions for contributions to payment of damages, it reduces their exposure to litigation. However, also like that protection, it implicitly bolsters the subordinate position of nursing. The second is that she is obliged to carry out the instructions of a doctor, even if she believes them to be imprudent. If this is the true legal position, then the position of nurses as the handmaidens of doctors is clear.

The most common context in which this issue arises is the administration of medicines. The Code of Professional Conduct for the Nurse, Midwife and Health Visitor obliges nurses to safeguard the well being of patients and to ensure that nothing within their influence harms patients (UKCC 1984: clauses 1 & 2). Where a nurse believes that a doctor's prescription puts the patient's welfare at risk these duties seem to require them to withdraw their co-operation. Their professional body advises them to request the doctor to administer the drug herself in such circumstances (UKCC,1989, Clause G.4; the earlier document UKCC:1986 does not deal with this point). The views of the judiciary are less clear. Nurses have a duty to check, and if necessary, challenge instructions that they believe to be wrong (*Strangeways-Lesmere v Clayton*).[18] What is less certain is what a nurse should do when the doctor confirms the instructions that the nurse believes threaten the patient's interests. A number of cases have indicated that nurses would not be liable for what might otherwise be negligence if they had not been following the instructions of a doctor. In *Pickering v Governors of United Leeds Hospital*[19] it was found that nurses who had allowed the patient to get bedsores were not negligent because they had refrained from turning her on the express instructions of the surgeon who had operated on her. In another case, nurses who incorrectly believed they were carrying out the instructions of a doctor were not liable for administering an overdose of the drug (*Smith v Brighton and Lewes HMC*).[20] This does not oblige nurses to do what doctors instruct them to do, but it gives them a major incentive. An alternative approach, which would conceptualise the issue as a matter of independent professional judgment, would be to ask whether a reasonably competent nurse would have carried out the doctor's instructions. The nurse's defence would then be that she was acting in accordance with acceptable professional practice, and therefore not negligent, not that she was doing what she was told.

This approach might in fact be a better interpretation of the law. In *Gold v Essex*[21] Goddard LJ examined the nature of the nurse's duty. He argued that 'if the surgeon gives a direction to the nurse, which she carries out, she is not guilty of negligence, even if the direction is improper'. However, Goddard LJ did not accept an earlier proposition that it did not matter how negligent the instructions were, the nurse would always be protected (*Hillyer v Governors of St. Bartholomew's Hospital*).[22] He suggested that 'if a doctor in a moment of carelessness... ordered a dose which to an experienced ward sister was obviously incorrect and dangerous, I think it might well be negligence if she administered it without obtaining confirmation from the doctor or higher authority'. Clearly, blind obedience is not enough, the nurse retains personal responsibility for her actions, but the implication is still that if confirmation were forthcoming then the nurse would be absolved from negligence.

In some cases, the nurse's duty might extend further. In *Junor* v *McNicol*,[23] the House of Lords suggested that where instructions were 'manifestly wrong' then it might be negligent to carry them out. The case concerned a junior doctor who had been instructed to treat a fracture, but had not been told to administer penicillin. In fact she gave the patient the drug, evidence that she was aware that there was a problem, but in insufficient quantities to prevent gangrene setting in. She was sued for negligence, but was absolved by the court because she was following the instructions of a superior. Suspicion that a senior colleague's instructions were 'unsuitable and improper' was not enough to outweigh the duty to follow their orders. This would seem to suggest that unless the error was obviously gross it would not be negligent to follow the instructions of a doctor once confirmed. It is also probable that if they were 'manifestly wrong' then a nurse could argue that they were no longer 'lawful instructions' because they required an act of negligence and therefore she was not obliged to carry them out.

The main constraint that the law imposes on nurses in relation to the use of medicines lies in the way in which it allocates responsibility for the different parts of the process. Decisions about which drugs to use and the dose that should be given are secured to the medical profession through their monopoly on prescribing. The Medicines Act 1968 defines a category of prescription-only drugs and section 58 of that Act makes it an offence to administer a prescription-only drug save under the direction of a doctor or dentist. There are strictly limited exceptions to this monopoly for midwives and occupational health nurses (Medicines Act 1986 s.58(4), Misuse of Drugs Regulations 1985, SI 1985 No. 2066, r. 11, and Medicines (Products Other Than Veterinary Drugs) (Prescription Only) Order 1983, SI 1983 No. 1212, art. 9 & Sch. 3), but even these carry the shadow of medical control. Thus the midwives' exemption only permits them to have prescription-only drugs in their possession on the basis of a 'midwife's supply order' that has been signed by a doctor or their supervisor of midwives (Misuse of Drugs Regulations 1985, SI 1985 No. 2066, r. 11(2),(3)).[24] Occupational health nurses may use prescription-only drugs without immediate direction, but only in circumstances specified in writing by a medical practitioner (Medicines (Products Other Than Veterinary Drugs) (Prescription Only) Order 1983, SI

1983 No. 1212, art 9 & Sch. 3, Part III para. 5). In practice, medicines will usually be administered by nurses, not because they are nurses but because a doctor has directed them to do so. No legal restrictions exist on administration other than the need for medical direction (Misuse of Drugs Regulations 1985 r. 7). The aspect of the medication process that is normally left to nurses is not recognised by the law as requiring special skill at all. As a consequence of this, the law on prescribed drugs can be said to recognise the professional expertise of doctors but not that of nurses, who may only practise their art under medical control.

This restrictive approach to the nursing role in the use of medicines sits uneasily with both the practical reality and the expertise in drug use that experienced nurses build up. The crux of the matter lies in the power to prescribe rather than the provisions dealing with administration, for it is at the former stage that clinical judgment is exercised. There have been a number of calls for the recognition of nursing skills through giving them powers to prescribe (DHSS, 1986, DoH, 1990b). A private member's bill to set up a limited formulary of drugs that nurses could prescribe was introduced to Parliament in 1991. Although it is not giving its support to the bill itself, the Government is committed in principle to setting up a nursing formulary during the 1990s. Enquiries have been instigated into the cost effectiveness of nurse prescribing, the training requirements of introducing such a scheme, the drugs which might be included in the formulary and the administrative details (debate on the Nurse Prescribing Bill, Hansard HC Vol. 190 Col. 593-97, 3 May 1991). Nurse prescribing would be a recognition of the independent clinical freedom of nurses without denying that of doctors. It would, however, alter the mode of legal entrenchment of medical authority over nursing practice from a combination of exclusion and subordination to one of limitation. The extent to which it remained a mode of domination would depend on the limits placed on nursing powers and who had the main influence on their definition.

Clinical judgment

The clinical freedom of health professionals is mediated by the law in a number of different ways. I have sought elsewhere to trace its ambit in relation to malpractice, consent, and in licensing schemes set up to regulate technological advances but which maintain clinical dominance (Montgomery, 1988, 1989, and 1991). Here the concern is with clinical freedom and the employment status of health professionals. In the first half of the twentieth century a considerable amount of litigation against hospitals raised the issue of the extent of their liability for the negligence of their staff (O. Kahn-Freund, 1951; C. Grunfeld, 1954; Goodhart, 1938). Prevailing doctrine used, inter alia, a test based on the degree of control that was exercised by the hospital to determine whether vicarious liability could be established. Thus for a period it was the case that hospitals were liable for (and therefore seen by the law as in control of) the actions of nurses, but not of consultants. Nurses were thus subordinate to the hospital hierarchy, but doctors were not; the professional independence of medicine was recognised, but not that of nursing. These issues are now only of historical interest. In the modern context two issues can be singled out as indicative of the nature of clinical autonomy in the workplace; the ability of professionals to opt out of treatment to which they object and the extent to which the exercise of their judgment is constrained by policies established by their employers. In both cases the main issue concerns the freedom of doctors, nurses and midwives in relation to their employers, but it also has practical implications for inter-professional relationships.

Conscientious objection

All employees have a contractual obligation to obey lawful and reasonable instructions from their employers. In the case of professionals this obligation is problematic in that they are employed precisely for skills of judgment, which the employer will not have. The extent to which their contracts require them to act in accordance with detailed instructions is therefore an indication of the degree of clinical freedom that they possess. Professionals who are entitled to opt out of treatment of which they disapprove are given greater freedom than those who are not. Statutory rights of conscientious objection exist in relation to abortion, embryo research and some types of infertility treatment (Abortion Act 1967 s. 4, Human Fertilisation and Embryology Act 1990 s. 38). These extend to professionals asked to participate in treatment, although not to administrative support staff (*Janaway v Salford H.A.*).[25] In general, however, professionals are not entitled to opt out of treatment they dislike and may be dismissed if they seek to do so.

This principle can be seen in operation in the well known *Owen* case.[26] Owen, a registered mental nurse, objected to the use of electro-convulsive therapy (ECT). After formal warnings he persisted in refusing to participate in its administration and was dismissed. He brought proceedings for unfair dismissal. The Court of Appeal upheld his dismissal. They found that he was in breach of his implied contractual obligation to obey lawful and reasonable instructions. It is important to note that decisions to use ECT would be made by doctors and the case deems the instructions of doctors to be those of the nurse's employers for the purposes of the duty of obedience. While the Court of Appeal suggested that the decision turned on its particular facts, they offer no argument for this contention. It might be possible to point to the provisions of Part IV of the Mental Health Act 1983 that establish the respective responsibilities of doctors and nurses in relation to the administration of ECT and to suggest that this is the basis for the case being exceptional. However, the Court made no reference to them and in any event they apply only to detained patients and Owen's objection was not restricted to that context. It would therefore seem that the case is of general importance. Owen's own view was that it 'demolished all the claims of nurses right across the country to have any clinical judgment whatever'.[27]

Owen also made a slightly different form of claim. He argued that his dismissal had resulted from a refusal to administer ECT to a particular patient whom he believed to be dying and whose interests would be compromised. The Court of Appeal recognised that this was a stronger type of claim because it was based on the conflict between the duty to safeguard the interests of clients and the duty to obey lawful and reasonable instructions. The Court of Appeal refused to accept this was the proper interpretation of the facts. They found that he had been dismissed for opposition to the policy of using ECT, not for his views on the particular patient. They did, however, give brief consideration to the question of whether it would be proper for a nurse to challenge the decision of the doctor when it would appear to be inappropriate. Bingham LJ examined the codes of professional conduct that govern nursing and found

> nothing... which suggested that nurses are entitled to override or contradict the professional judgment of those with the clinical responsibility for the care of the patient. It is of course their duty to give the doctors the benefit of their professional judgment, experience and observation, but the final decision is that of the doctors. Only in the most extraordinary circumstances could a nurse be justified in intervening, and this was not such a case.

He then cited with approval the statement made in evidence by the nursing officer in charge of the psychiatric department that 'at the end of the day it is the responsibility of the medical staff to decide whether such treatment should be applied to a particular patient....' This suggests that nurses are obliged to defer to medical decisions if they are unable to persuade the doctors that they are jeopardising the patient's welfare. Clinical freedom is thus preserved for doctors but not nurses.

An interesting comparison with the position in which Owen was placed is provided by the provisions of the Mental Health Act 1983 that deal with consent to specified types of treatment, including ECT (Mental Health Act 1983, ss. 57, 58; Code of Practice: Mental Health Act 1983 section 16). The legalistic approach that characterises the 1983 Act is largely the product of public suspicion of medical power (Unsworth, 1987, p.315-351). Nevertheless, the constraints that the Act placed on medical autonomy do nothing to secure an equal status for nursing. A doctor may not proceed with treatment when the special provisions of sections 57 and 58 apply unless he has a second medical opinion. The second doctor must consult two people, one of whom has to be a nurse. But the obligation is only to consult, and the doctor is free to ignore the nurse's opinion without stating a reason. It would have been a simple matter to require the agreement of all consultees, giving each a veto. This would be similar to the second opinion necessary before pregnancies can be terminated under the Abortion Act 1967 or to the need for confirmation from a medical colleague that the 1983 Act imposes. Such a veto would provide for equal status for both professions, and would restrict but not deny the clinical freedom of both. The provisions, as they stand, restrict that freedom for doctors, and deny it for nurses.

Policies

The development of hospital policies also has a significant effect on the autonomy of the professions. When work is governed by such guidelines, rather than the judgment of the practitioner concerned, clinical freedom is restricted. Policies are given legal force in a number of ways. The obligation to obey reasonable instructions, discussed above, would be one. In addition, it has been held that a nurse who failed to follow the prescribed procedure for referring a patient complaining of a lump in her breast was for that reason negligent (*Sutton v Population Family Planning Programme Ltd*).[28] It is unclear that it would be right to assert that departure from a hospital policy automatically constituted negligence. The proper approach is probably to say that it raises a prima facie case of negligence and unless the circumstances indicate that there were good reasons for departing from the usual practice the professional would be found liable (*Clark v Maclennan*[29] as interpreted in *Wilsher v Essex AHA*). Finally, it should be noted that failure to abide by the policy for drug administration set down by the hospital might provide the basis for disciplinary proceedings before the relevant professional body. Such an allegation, together with other charges, has resulted in a nurse being struck off the professional register (*Singh v UKCC*),[30] although it must be doubtful whether the General Medical Council would proceed in the same way.

The doctrinal basis for the law's reinforcement of the constraints imposed by health authority policies is largely neutral between the professions. It is likely that in practice it operates more restrictively on nurses and midwives than it does on doctors. There is evidence to suggest that it is more likely that policies exist in relation to the former. One study found that while all the consultant maternity units surveyed had policy documents, in one third of them they did not apply to medical staff (Garcia et al, 1991, p.28). These policies themselves are likely to be perceived by midwives as impairing their ability to exercise their skills (Robinson, 1989). Although policies vary in nature and it is usual for midwives to have a significant input into their drafting, in places where doctors were responsible for them (even though they govern midwifery practice) they tended to be rigid and restrictive (Garcia et al 1991). In these latter circumstances, policies can be seen as an instrument of medical dominance and so far as their impact is strengthened by legal sanctions, the law is contributing to the subordination of nursing. Even without medical control of the drawing up of guidelines, policies contribute to the limitation of professional clinical autonomy.

Conclusion

This essay has traversed a wide range of ground in the course of mapping out the rules of law that give an indication of way in which the law reinforces the division of health labour. The search has required an examination of a range of applicable law, the decisions of the courts, the terms of statutes and the details of secondary legislation made under them. In the course of the study the pervasive traces of favourable views on the clinical autonomy of doctors and distrust of the same latitude being given to nurses has become clear. The picture is not unequivocal, but taken as a whole can be said to assume a hierarchy of the professions.

When these legal rules are related to the sociological concepts of autonomy and dominance it can be seen that there is some evidence that medical power has been diluted by legal recognition of the work of nurses and midwives, but that in general domination remains despite the multi-disciplinary context of modern health care. Some rules even go so far as to deny the professional status of nursing and midwifery. Thus the abortion case and the laws governing the administration of medicines simply ignore the expertise of nurses, treating them as lay persons.

Other areas make the subordination of nurses more explicit, although it has been argued that one of the starkest examples of medical dominance, the 'captain of the ship doctrine', has not been adopted by the English courts. The *Owen* case shows that the practical effect of the employee's obligation to obey instructions does directly enshrine the subordination of nurses. The working out of the standard of care in negligence also implicitly reinforces this position. While doctors are not responsible for nursing negligence, it has been shown that a nurse may be protected from liability by relying on medical instructions, but that the converse is not true. This implies that nursing expertise is a subset of medical expertise, emphasising Freidson's point that the legitimacy of nursing autonomy conceived as derived from the supervision of the medical profession.

Legislative interventions have also tended to preserve the privileged status of medicine. In the case of the abortion reforms introduced in 1991 this is perhaps an oversight rather than a conscious differentiation. The medical monopoly over the use of drugs enshrines the existing division of labour and ignores rather than defines the skills of nurses. The results of the inquiry into nurse prescribing should give a clearer indication of Government and Parliamentary views. At present it is absence of provisions as much as their presence that contributes to maintaining the subordination of nurses. A number of other silences have contributed to the process. The most important is the absence of case law on the apportionment of liability. This has occurred as a result of administrative arrangements, negotiated by the representatives of the medical profession, not because of the legal rules themselves.

The application of the rules on apportionment to pharmacists demonstrate how important this is. The effect of *Dwyer v Roderick* was to establish that the responsibility of the pharmacist was independent of that of the doctor, not derived from it. Thus while the position of chemists is limited to the lesser role of dispensing drugs as prescribed by doctors, it is recognisably a separate, autonomous, field of professional work. The nursing role in the process is not recognised as a professional one. The law has recognised that pharmacy has legitimate control over its sphere of practice, although it remains under a degree of medical dominance because of the need for a prescription. Nursing lacks even this control. In Turner's terminology, dominance over pharmacy takes the form of limitation, but nursing is subordinated to medical supervision.

Finally, consideration of the scope of clinical judgment for the different professions demonstrates that working within a bureaucratic framework has placed significant restrictions on the professional autonomy of nurses, and has served to reinforce the dominance of doctors. Health authority policies operate to restrict nursing autonomy, but their content is often determined by medical staff. The *Owen* case demonstrates that control of clinical decisions ultimately lies with the doctor and that the right of nurses to exercise independent clinical judgment is minimal. Thus working within the managerial structure has had a real impact on the professional autonomy of nurses, but not doctors and the suggestion that medical hegemony has been undermined by the managers is not made out in relation to the legal framework of clinical freedom.

The focus of this essay has been on the details of specific legal provisions. It has sought to show that, while the picture is complex, the law reinforces an implicit division of health labour in which the professions of nursing and midwifery are subordinated to that of medicine. The origins of this situation are of course complex. It reflects the actual division of health labour, which has been shaped by the history of health care in this country. It is also a feature of a general refusal to recognise the value of the work of women, the product of the supremacy of 'scientific' biomedicine over other approaches to healing (Stacey, 1988b), and a reflection of the way in which those who are ill are constructed as 'patients' not people, carriers of their conditions with a new 'more onerous citizenship' (Foucault, 1976, Sontag, 1978, Sontag, 1989). The suggestion here is that the law has been shaped by the politics of health care. Although it would be overstating the case to say that the areas considered here demonstrate that law has been the tool by which medical dominance has been created, it is certainly fair to argue that the potential of using these areas of law to challenge that position has been neutralised.

The essay has concentrated on aspects of normal health care.

The power of medicine over other health professions is so strong precisely because of the degree of control that doctors have over the everyday operation of NHS. The abortion context provided a useful starting point because it raised the problem so clearly, but the argument has been designed to show that the special circumstances, which could be argued to lie behind the decision in *RCN v DHSS*, are not in fact extraordinary. The assumptions made by the court in that case are also to be found in many areas of the law. So long as they continue, the law provides a buttress for the occupational dominance of medicine and should be counted among the obstructions to the recognition of the skills of nurses and midwives.

* Lecturer in Law, Southampton University. I am grateful to Elsa Montgomery for her comments on this paper in her capacities as spouse, nurse and midwife.

1. [1985] 1 All ER 643, 665.

2. See Encyclopedia of Health Services and Medical Law, Sweet and Maxwell, 1978-1991, para. 1-031 - 1-043 for a summary of the provisions and for discussion: G.Larkin (1983) and Stacey (1988a).

3. [1981] 1 All ER 545.

4. [1991] 1 All ER 801.

5. (1983) 127 SJ 806, (1983) 80 LSG 3003 (CA).

6. [1989] 1 Med LR 36.

7. [1937] 4 All ER 494, 497-98.

8. [1939] 1 All ER 535.

9. (1955) The Times, 15 July

10. [1931] 1 B.M.J. 730.

11. [1942] 2 B.M.J. 411.

12. (1866) 4 F & F 977, 176 ER 873.

13. [1954] 2 QB 66.

14. [1951] 2 KB 343.

15. [1986] 3 All ER 801 (CA), [1988] 1 All ER 871 (HL).

16. [1957] 2 All ER 118.

17. (1988) The Times, 11 March, The Independent, 21 March.

18. [1936] 2 KB 11.

19. [1954] 1 Lancet 1075.

20. (1958) The Times, 2 May.

21. [1942] 2 All ER 237.

22. [1909] 2 KB 820.

23. (1959) The Times, 26 March.

24. The supervisor of midwives is an experienced midwife appointed under Nurses, Midwives and Health Visitors Act 1979, s.16; see Nurses, Midwives and health Visitors Rules Approval Order 1983, SI 1983 No. 873, r.44 for the qualifications required of a supervisor.

25. [1988] 3 All ER 1079).

26. Owen v Coventry HA, 19 December 1986, unreported.

27. 'Nurse loses appeal over refusing to give ECT' Nursing Standard, 31 December 1986.

28. 30 October 1981, unreported.

29. [1983] 1 All ER 416.

30. 26 June 1985, unreported.

Doctors as Allocators - The Bald Facts

Robert Lee*

Introduction

A National Health Service, which, recent reforms notwithstanding, Britain still claims as its primary mode of health care delivery, is a simple concept. State ownership and control of medical resources allows their allocation at zero price, at the point of consumption. Thus, we can say that health care is available 'freely', although we shall see that there may be certain costs involved in the take-up of health care. The notion of freely available health care is linked closely with the desire to improve the state of the nation's health. Thus, the National Health Service Act 1946 promoted a comprehensive health service which, it claimed, would improve both the physical and mental health of the population by, diagnosing and treating illness through the provision of these freely available services. This involves the assumption - which does not always appear to be correct - that where services are available at zero price, there will be no barrier to the take-up of available provision, with consequent improvement in the standards of health. This belief is important, since it helps explain the ambitious nature of the 1946 reform. In part, the then Labour Government felt that health care resources could be made freely available, precisely because, as its impact was felt, the population would benefit from health improvements (Foot, 1973, vol. 11). These improvements in health would prevent large scale expenditure of recurrent costs, perhaps to the point of reducing the health care budget (Doyal, 1979; Wilcocks, 1967).

It is clear that this has not proved to be case; this can be seen from the unsuccessful attempts to reduce waiting lists for treatment year after year, notwithstanding increasing expenditure on health care. Yet various indicators seem to verify improvements in our

169

general health and welfare. Having said that, patterns of disease clearly change over time, and there is no shortage of modern killers including coronary heart disease, cancers and other environmentally-related disorders, degenerative and stress-related diseases - even to the point of suicide (Stewart, 1971). Yet, in 1946 at the time of the development of the National Health Service, the major killers were infectious diseases and bacterial infection. In modern times, with some clear exceptions, pharmaceuticals and vaccines make it relatively easy to cope with such problems. By 1946, there must have been some hope that this could be so, but the growth of new and novel epidemics, of which aids provides the most stark example, was less predictable. Moreover, the fact that medical progress allows essentially lethal disorders to be treated does not lessen the demand of many such treatments (Illich, 1981, Ch. 1). Advance seems often to imply expenditure.

Demand

Thus there are continuing, and increasing, if evolving, patterns of demand in spite of a technical capacity to treat a wider range of disorders. To this, must be added a review of the economic underpinning of the NHS which is fundamental to understanding its functioning. This relates to the notion that costs might be curtailed as the population grows healthier, whereas, in economic theory, zero prices, as opposed to prices set by marginal costs, suggest significant increases in demand (Pigou, 1928). For certain items, price elasticity approaches zero since demand is finite. The demand for health care is not finite but potentially infinite. However healthy we are, we may desire to be healthier. In the author's own case, much of the writing of this essay has been undertaken whilst suffering from premature (in his view) hair-loss. It is true that occasionally the author's pre-occupation with the onset of this disorder is deflected by more serious worries about a 'flu bug or food poisoning. However, once cured of these ailments, it does not take long for the concerns regarding baldness to return.

But I should deny strongly that my concern with baldness is in any way odd or quirky. Since other baldies are not so open about their feelings it is difficult to produce survey evidence, but my suspicion is that, like me, they would mainly prefer to have more hair. What is unusual about my position is that I demand regularly that resources be expended to research and eventually treat my ailment - others are not so vociferous. Thus there is a distinction to be made between the demand for health and the demand for health care. The latter may be derived from the former and the former itself may be derived from other demands, the take-up of which may require adequate health. This itself tells us something of health as an investment good (in that it can bring consequential benefits - for instance in the form of earnings in the wider market place) (McGuire, Fenn and Mayhew, 1991a). Yet no-one suggests that my investment opportunities as a writer, or even as a lecturer, will be improved by more hair. To that extent health is a consumption good from which I derive some direct utility. Of course if I had realised my true potential and become a television celebrity or film star then I might worry about my hair loss -as do certain wig-wearing TV presenters who, for legal reasons, I shall not name. In such a case, it might have been prudent of me, at a stage of more luxuriant hair growth, to have taken precautions against its loss, or, in the event of this not being possible, insured myself against the loss of earnings consequent upon the handicap of a head that shines under the studio lights.

Thus within the health sector, it becomes necessary to differentiate between demand for: (i) health; (ii) health care; and (iii) health insurance. These demands may be interlinked in complex patterns depending upon available health care systems. Thus in private health care systems demand for health insurance and health care may be met, at least in part, by the same purchase. Equally state systems may fail to cope with the demand for health insurance (Besley, 1991), however well they meet demands for health or health care. And even where health care is freely available, the opportunity cost of take-up may prove a disincentive to treatment, notwithstanding the potential to meet a health demand (Lee, 1986). An understanding of the complexity of patterns of demand is of assistance any debate concerning allocations - but in the case of market allocations the concepts become vital since expressions of consumer preference are taken as the mechanism for improvement of allocative efficiency. The marginal cost of the commodity should reflect its marginal valuation.

The question is whether this typical market analysis rests on assumptions which are less likely to apply in the health sector. One objection which may be raised is that if the commodity is health, we are unlikely to wish to trade. In practice, however, this does not seem to be true. If pushed, I have to admit to a preference for being a balding film star than a hairy lawyer. Moreover, in spite of my desire for more hair, I damage my precious remaining stock constantly by over-frequent washing of it, which results from regular sporting activity - which incidentally is now beginning to cause quite severe pains in my right knee. The truth is that, valuable though health is, we trade it quite regularly for other pleasures, opportunities and activities. Indeed this tradability of health is as significant in understanding state systems as market systems of health allocation. Certainly the fact that patient value choices differ, and that the doctor's perception of the 'best' result does not necessarily reflect the most important inputs into the patient's decision is vital to an understanding of the tension between medical paternalism and patient autonomy within the NHS system of provision.

If, as was stated earlier, health is an investment good, then demand for health (or health care or health insurance) may depend upon available investment opportunities. In other words we should not be surprised to see socio-economic disparities creep in to allocations, as the potential market activity available through good health will be weighted more firmly in favour of certain classes rather than others. This may be only partly off-set by the opportunity cost of taking up health care, especially where there is an outlet for certain health care demands in private medicine alongside the state provision. However, these patterns of consumer choice within health care are not unproblematic. For health care may be a derived demand (Grossman 1972) and we do not always have choice in relation to health as such -as evidenced by my thinning thatch. Moreover, the derivation of demand in relation to health care means that we constantly have information needs concerning which of the health care available will meet our eventual requirements of health. Just as I repeatedly place my faith in the new forms of shampoo or hair oils.

Problems of information

I have similar problems with barbers. I never know how to answer: 'how would you like your hair, sir?' I would simply like more of it. Never having been trained as a hairdresser I have no idea how they might make a little go a long way. This is a problem which economists might label informational asymmetry. The problem is not only that of consumer sovereignty - that consumers have the available means to best judge their own welfare. Even if consumers of health care did have such means - and generally they do not - some utility may be derived from delegating difficult decisions - even about oneself. There may be advantage in allowing another actor to shoulder the risks inherent in the choice of regimes of treatment. This derogation of choice may be affected by the cost and availability of information, for clearly the required information might be bought - in the form of second opinions or more specialist advice. Again, we might expect to see socio-economic patterns emerge with certain groups gaining access to specialist advice rather than or in advance of others. Certainly it seems to be the pattern in the USA that stronger doctrines of informed consent have increased patient participation in decision-making (Miller, 1991).

It may be difficult to resist the force of such participatory mechanisms as evidence grows stronger that patterns of disease are more complex than previously imagined and medical solutions prepounded with certainty are now overshadowed by doubt (Cooper 1975). The current debate concerning cholesterol provides a ready example of this. Thus whatever attempts are made to overcome information deficiencies there may be flaws in the delivery of health care. This pattern is further complicated by the complex and perplexingly different make-ups of patients: anatomically, functionally, psychologically, and hirsutely.

It is immediately obvious that these types of information problems may lead to market failure and hinder the operation of those systems which seek to use the market as the primary process of allocation. Yet all of these difficulties will present problems in state allocation systems too. Both systems can seek to remedy

173

problems arising from informational asymmetry on consumer preference. The common method of doing so might be by utilising merit good frameworks of allocation. The merit good concept involves the acceptance (or imposition) that certain groups within society are allowed to form judgments as to what society's preferences ought to be, or would be if better informed (Musgrave 1959; Besley 1988). It is a concept which is treated with scepticism by some economists, one of whom offers an alternative definition of 'any item of public expenditure that seems socially reasonable, but cannot be accounted for within the ordinary theory of demand' (Margolis, 1982).

Need

Within a 'market' system of allocation, an example of the merit good approach might include the legal requirement that everyone purchases health insurance. However, it is in the state systems of allocation that we grasp this concept most strongly, in the rejection of market systems with their emphasis upon evaluations of individual utility in the light of full consumer sovereignty. Rather than meet all demand, however capricious or ill-informed, there will be some form of elite judgment made concerning access to the commodity, health care. I am well aware of this, since, quite remarkably, the NHS pay scant regard to my continual requests for more and thicker hair. Not uncommonly, I am fobbed off with excuses that no cure is available. I am refused consultations to discuss the problem further. There is no cure for the common cold, but this does not prevent some twenty per cent of my fellow patients consulting my GP with just this problem. Equally, doctors are consulted by a variety of patients whose health improvements might be better (perhaps, only) achieved by dietary improvement, adequate housing or improved working environment. But this comes close to what my doctor says about my baldness. She accepts that I may have a legitimate interest in research into premature hair loss, and she does what she can to boost my ego (telling me how well I look) because she feels I require this. But she insists that I should not have health care resources diverted to me in the absence of obviously effective treatment. In short, I am not in what others define as 'need'.

Doctors, within the NHS system, are continually seeking to isolate need from the competing demands with which they are faced. The need in question is the need for health care resources (as opposed to health) and valuations, indeed value judgments will have to be made. This may worry us, since there are many such judgments which we might regard as morally unacceptable if used as the basis for health care allocation - let us suppose race, or social class, or hairstyle, and what about wealth? Doubtless doctors insist that allocations are based primarily upon medical criteria. As is indicated above, this assumes that objective medical criteria is available. More than this, it implies that medical indicators will assist in reaching hard choices in situations of comparative need.

This can be demonstrated by the illustration of two patients in competition for a single organ which both require for transplant. Where tissue incompatibility indicates that the organ would be rejected by one patient, but not the other, then we are unlikely to be uncomfortable in allowing the transplant to the compatible patient - even where the other patient is likely to die. We could also classify the basis of this decision as 'medical'. Where both patients show compatibility, but the prognosis is that one will die within a year and the other in a week, we may be prepared to offer the organ to the latter patient - in the hope, though not the certainty, that another compatible organ will become available in the next year. Assuming that we are satisfied with the accuracy of the prognosis, we might accept the decision as objective on the basis of more urgent clinical need while agreeing that both patients are ethically equally entitled. In this instance, however, we may feel less comfortable about denying the other patient the treatment, since (s)he clearly falls within the net of 'need'. None of this assists, however, if both patients competing for the organ have an equally tragic prognosis.

Yet decisions in such instances have been made upon the basis of the lifestyle of the patient. Equally organs have been allocated to those with the capacity to pay a price (Scott, 1981). (We might add that persons also donate organs (or blood) as part of one of the many altruistic actions which market theorists can at best cope with by reference to externalities). A range of other criteria, such as age, or dependants have also been invoked to justify allocative decisions. it is hard to see on what basis they might. By this stage, the value judgments which are brought to bear discriminate unacceptably (Harris, 1985). They are ageist, or they discriminate against whole groups of people who cannot claim the necessary dependants. Indeed the very suggestion of such criteria may lead us to question the role of doctors as allocators.

Clinical freedom

The role of allocator is not easy. There is a great comfort in passing it to doctors and freeing ourselves from responsibiliy. It is altogether easier to allow doctors to make decisions, the criteria for which we do not question, than to expose the nature of the tragic choices which re-occur as 'available' resources for health care fail to cope with need. This is a point which health care economists recognise and articulate

> the consumption of health care - especially for life threatening conditions - may also include the characteristic of being able to pass the burden of decision-making to the clinician. In other words, the demand for health care may include a demand to avoid having to make difficult decisions and bear the responsibility of such decision-making (Macquire, Henderson & Mooney, 1988).

It is suggested that this is true not simply of individual preferences but for societal choices as a whole. Doctors, for their part, have tended not only to accept this role, but even to guard it, jealously asserting clinical freedom to treat as a bulwark against both governmental intervention and, sometimes, the caprice of patient choice (Lee & Miller, 1990).

Clinical freedom attracts two immediate problems relating to allocation. First, it was gained, in part, by other guarantees - especially professionalism and ethical conduct. In view of the inadequacy of the consumer's information, these guarantees are accepted even though in market terms they implicitly restrict supplies, and hence supply. Only certain people can provide medical services and only certain things may be done. Secondly, decisions protected as they are by clinical freedom tend to go unchallenged. Certainly this is the evidence in relation to legal challenges. Yet what quality does the doctor's decision possess? We should hope that it is technically correct; that it accurately assesses the efficacy of a prescribed treatment. But this does not get us very far, since we run up against the problem of comparative need. Thus if tomorrow an outright cure for baldness was found (oh joy!) the doctor's assessment based on readings of technical literature does not resolve whether or not I should actually be prescribed this (doubtless costly) product. When it comes to ranking my desire for this treatment alongside the host of other simultaneous demands for other courses of treatment, what is it that allows a doctor the right to rank such demands in terms of need?

Yet within the state system of allocation ranking need assumes considerable import beyond that of market based systems. This is because such market provision can pretend that allocative decisions are made easier by granting a resource to those who are willing to spend what it takes to produce it. In reality, as Calebresi and Bobbit have written, 'this test of relative desire - a single dollar for example - has a different importance for different choosers' (Calebresi and Bobbitt, 1978). Nonetheless, proponents of such systems have asserted the ability to pay as a prefered method to that of 'queuing by waiting' which, they allege, is the predominant mode of rationing operated by the NHS. Such appeals are not without point. The way things are going, if I have to wait two years for treatment to arrest hair loss, it will be a futile exercise. This does not produce a conclusion that we should deny state allocations, merely to question whether such allocations can ration by queues. If we wish to defend non-market systems on the basis that they do not allocate on the basis of ability to pay, then we must show that they operate a system of allocations which is not similarly unfair.

Queuing by waiting might be taken to be unfair unless we assess the comparative need of those in the queue. Thus central to the claim of fairness in state allocation is some neutral assessment of need, which Daniels asserts has to be considered as objective and not determined by subjective preferences. This poses an enormous problem, however, for supporters of the NHS. All of the evidence shows that there exists massive inequalities in states of health. Shocking though this sounds, it is no worse than saying that not everyone is equally endowed with hair. However, as the Black Report showed, inequalities in health are systematic, class-based and rooted in the socio-economic structure. This is not necessarily an indictment of the quality of health care provision, although it may call into question its scope and indeed its very nature. As Black emphasised: 'improvement in health is likely to come in the future, as in the past, from the modification of the conditions which led to disease after it has occurred' (Black, 1980).

We may have legitimate complaints that the NHS has always concentrated too much upon curing, and then caring, rather than preventing. Certainly we have made greater investments in what has been described as halfway technology (aftermath efforts to compensate for disability) than a more decisive technology which might prevent the disability outright (Mehlman, 1985). The higher cost of the halfway technology may restrict its availability and allow inequalities to persist in or to be created by health care provision. Illich (1981) has pointed to the class specific origins of the medical profession and all the evidence shows that class affects the length of consultations with working class groups persistently receiving less lengthy attention. Le Grand (1982) has argued that equitable use of NHS facilities has never been achieved, although Collins and Klein (1980) suggest a broad equity in access to primary health care. Whichever view is accepted, there is a legitimate concern with equity in health care which concentrates upon the role of the physician as gatekeeper of medical services. Such an inquiry is informed by Foucault's observations upon panopticism and his interest in the relationship between the discourse of scientific knowledge and the exercise of professional power.

General Practitioners operate as arbiters of comparative need amongst the morass of apparent need which confronts them and which have filtered from the compelling demands which they face. Unenviable though this task may be, it is necessary to review their record in this regard. For doctors disagree. They follow courses of treatment later found to be, at best, ineffective but perhaps even iatrogenic. They prescribe placebos in the absence of cure or in the face of difficulty of diagnosis. Even I have picked up the odd prescription in respect of my hair loss. Cross-cultural comparisons show astonishing disparities between treatment of diseases reflected in length of stay (in hospital) rates, pharmaceutical dispensing, rates of surgical intervention and the like (Wemberg 1984). Historical comparisons demonstrate similar (or rather dissimilar) results.

This is not so surprising. Illness is not an unambiguous state and is to a large degree, socially constructed. I dream of a more caring society which offers sympathy and support to those losing their hair. My doctors argue, in their defence that they make choices against the backdrop of some notional harm which may befall me. This merely repeats what has been said. The demand for health care will be framed against some expectation and the conferring of the status of need upon that demand will award some degree of legitimacy upon the patient's claim. Within this process considerable social power is structured by relations with the doctor. It is they that will define the reality and in so doing will assume the power to isolate the deviant. This shift in illness from a state to a status is in the hands of the doctor. This power is intertwined with the claim of knowledge on the part of the doctor, notwithstanding the problems labelled informational asymmetry and of technical uncertainty considered above. Yet there is a partiality in such knowledge. Significantly all of the male doctors within the group practice which I attend have full heads of hair - even Dr Senior who is almost sixty. In his younger days Dr Senior used to greet the prostrate problems of his male patients with scepticism regarding surgical intervention as almost cosmetic. Now, I am told, he regularly refers patients for prostatectomy.

Accountability

Given the significant role of the doctor in allocating scarce medical resources and the broad problems of equity considered above, it is appropriate to investigate the processes by which the doctor is held accountable for decisions which involve access to those resources for some, and denial to others. The lack of formal accountability is striking and is rooted in the bargaining power of the medical lobby at the formation of the NHS (Forsyth, 1966). The insistence by doctors on answerability only in terms of their contract with the state rather than their duties to the patient left providers protected and consumers voiceless. Submission to this pressure by the Government may be forgiven in view of the genuine if misguided belief that health care provision would be universal. Once it became clear, however, that tough rationing decisions would need to be made, accountability ought to have been imperative. The freedom to make decisions which offer the possibility of life to some, but not to others, implies answerability for decisions made. Yet mechanisms for accountability remain absent outside of complaints procedures and common law actions which dissatisfied consumers of service have utilised in order to challenge the current process of allocations (Klein, 1971). In addition to these, of late, various modes of financial control have been imposed in order to confer greater rights on certain patients or classes of patient.

Complaints

Many providers of medical and paramedical services are governed by ethical principles expressed in the conduct rules of their professional organisations. These processes of self-regulation can lead to the practitioner being found guilty of a breach of professional conduct leading in the extreme to suspension or withdrawal of the licence to practice. Problems arise from such processes of self-regulation especially in an arena in which the providers of the service have some monopoly right to control it. In such contexts, self-regulation may bolster the pre-eminent position of the professional rather than protect the consumer. In the case of doctors, the General Medical Council (GMC) has a statutory disciplinary jurisdiction over the professional conduct of doctors. The Medical Act 1983 permits the GMC to lay down standards of professional conduct and other ethical guidelines. Generally the GMC regulates serious professional misconduct such as gross neglect of the patient, breaches of duty of confidence, sexual liaisons with patients, and the like. Complaints regarding such matters are often patient initiated, and can lead to an inquiry by the GMC. It can immediately be seen however that although the conduct of a doctor may be challenged where (s)he fails completely to offer medical services to a patient within her care, it is virtually impossible to challenge the clinical decisions once these are made by the doctor in good faith. This may explain why, notwithstanding my doctor's impatience with my persistent complaints about hair loss, she always makes a perfunctory perusal of the rate of its development.

Restrictions on questioning the exercise of clinical freedom occur again and again with the multi-tiered complaints procedures of the NHS. Thus bodies such as the Family Health Services Committee and the Health Service Ombudsman are constrained in relation to their investigation of matters of diagnosis and quality of treatment. Yet of all of the 180 bodies providing evidence to the Davies Committee (1973), the only bodies supporting the retention of an exclusion from the investigation of clinical matters were those representing the medical profession. The limited scope of such complaints procedures renders objections to allocation processes difficult to maintain and probably maintain an artificially low level of formal complaints. Klein has pointed to the 'iceberg' effect of the system, with formal objections providing the tip of what is a more fundamental underlying problem. By measuring dissatisfaction in terms of less formal 'grumbles' or requests to change doctors (without a change of patient or doctor address) Klein found that for every one formal complaint registered there were four hundred expressions of patient dissatisfaction (Klein, 1973).

Civil litigation

In view then of the jurisdictional difficulties, procedural hurdles and problems of representation within the complaints system, many aggrieved patients choose the more appropriate, or even only available, means of redress - civil litigation. Any entrant to this process with a complaint of medical injury risks a long tradition of judges upholding clinical freedom, sometimes to the point of shielding doctors against negligence actions, and of judges sanctioning the non-disclosure of risks to the patient. In relation to health care allocations, however, there are particular problems to be faced. These stem from the refusal of the judges to enter the political minefield surrounding resource issues. Surprisingly, this policy of non-interference is not always to the disadvantage of the patient as plaintiff, but much will depend on how the action is pursued.

Where plaintiffs denied medical interventions on the basis of a lack of available resources have sought to compel health authorities to act, they have been singularly unsuccessful. Such cases have often been brought with the knowledge and perhaps even the connivance of the doctors involved in the care, and they may have achieved the pragmatic, political victory of ensuring that the requisite treatment was provided, but legal redress has always been denied. In the first such case, *R v Secretary of State for Social Services ex p Hincks*,[1] when planned improvements to orthopaedic services in the Birmingham area were shelved due to expenditure cuts, patients on the orthopaedic waiting list sought a declaration that the Secretary of State had failed to meet the statutory duty imposed by the National Health Services Act 1977 sec 3(1) to provide a comprehensive health service for the area. On appeal against the first instance decision not to interfere with the exercise of ministerial discretion conferred by the statute, the arguments of the appellant received little sympathy. In the view of Lord Denning MR the assurance of the Minister that he was doing what he could to meet NHS needs could not be faulted. It was not the role of the court to attempt to redress the problems of resource allocations in the health care system.

This judgment has been upheld just as forcefully by another Master of the Rolls in two cases also involving hospital provision in Birmingham - albeit in the rather different context of emergency treatment for particular patients. *R v Central Birmingham Health Authority ex p Walker*[2] concerned the decision of Birmingham Children's Hospital to place a moratorium upon heart surgery due to a shortage of intensive care nursing facilities. The infant plaintiff was very likely to die from denial of this care but Lord

Donaldson MR in the Court of Appeal stated a preparedness to intervene only on grounds of *Wednesbury* principles (*Associated Provincial Picture Houses v Wednesbury Corporation*[3] - manifest unreasonableness in allocative decisions. In the second case *R v Central Birmingham Health Authority ex p Collier*[4] only a few weeks later this principle was applied in even stronger terms when the same solicitor as in *Walker* pursued a case on identical facts to appeal. It was said that, 'the courts of this country cannot arrange the lists in the hospital ...'

The difficulty with the notion of intervention on the limited grounds of unreasonableness is that it will prove impossible for a plaintiff to sustain in practice given the problems which establishing arbitrary administrative behaviour ordinarily pose. Birmingham has the highest level of infant mortality in the UK. That it should further be forced into taking action destined to worsen its own grim record in this regard seems little short of a disgrace. Yet *Walker* and *Collier* permitted little investigation into such epidemiological evidence. It was never likely to, however, for to allow enquiry into the sufficiency of provision in Birmingham demands implicit scrutiny of the adequacy of the level of facility nationwide, and not merely in open heart surgery but across medical specialisms generally. One wonders, therefore, what element of alleged unreasonable behaviour would be sufficient to cause the courts to lift the lid upon this particular can of worms. The reality may be, that whatever formal grounds the court may reserve for themselves, the truth is that allocative decisions denying access to treatment will never be challenged.

Yet, oddly, the stance that the courts adopt in refusing to enquire into health care resourcing decisions may assist the plaintiff in another context - litigation concerning medical accidents. Consistently with general tort law, a duty to treat a patient probably will not arise until there has been some process of admission of that patient into the regime of care. In relation to general practice this will be the listing of the patient - hence my own GPs readiness to see me on the off-chance that my problem is not hair loss; (it always is). In hospitals care begins with the admission of the patient. This assumption of care gives rise to a duty to treat which would not otherwise arise. This duty must be then discharged in

183

accordance with *Bolam* principles; (*Bolam v Friern HMC*)[5] the standard is that of the ordinarily competent practitioner acting in accordance with a practice accepted as proper by a responsible body of practitioners. Two particular problems arise regarding this formulation in relation to difficulties in providing adequate resources: (i) what happens if inadequate resources makes it impossible to meet standards set by approved practice? and (ii) can we expect the inexperienced practitioner to meet the standard of the ordinarily competent counterpart? These are variants of the same question but it will further an analysis of the case-law if they can be separated.

As regards the first of these questions, there is little new in the claim that constraints make it impossible to guard against a particular event. Indeed the whole of the law of negligence in relation to the question of breach concerns issues of balancing the practicability of precautions in relation to risks of a particular magnitude, having in mind the importance of the object which is to be attained. There are a series of cases in relation to nursing supervision which seek to explain a failure in procedures by pointing to staffing difficulties. Thus in *Selfe v Ilford and District HMC*[6] a 17 year old patient, having been admitted as a suicide-risk, escaped from the ward by a ground floor window, and climbing up to the roof of the building threw himself to the ground. In awarding damages in respect of his subsequent injuries, Hincliffe J stated that whilst he was sympathetic to the staffing difficulties, the question was whether the accident could have been avoided by the provision of an adequate level of supervision. In finding that this was so, the Judge quoted from the case of *Thorne v Northern Group Hospital Management Committee*[7] which expresses the objective nature of the requisite standard of care in the following way:

> The duty owed by hospital authorities and staff to a patient is that of reasonable care and skill in the given circumstances. Whether a breach of duty has been established depends on the proven facts including what was known or should have been known about a particular patient and the fact that the defendants impliedly undertook to exhibit professional skill

and administrative care of reasonable competence and adequacy towards their patient. They must take reasonable care to avoid acts or omissions which they can reasonably foresee would be likely to harm the patient entrusted to their charge; but they need not guard against merely possible (as distinct from reasonably probable) harm. On the other hand the degree of care which will be regarded as reasonable is proportionate both to the degree or risk involved and the magnitude of the mischief which may be occasioned to the particular patient in the absence of due care.

The important qualification expressed by Edmund Davies J in *Thorne* is that the standard will vary in the circumstances according to the risk. This is well expressed in the later case of *Wilsher v Essex AHA*[8] where it was said that 'in what may be called "battle conditions" ... if an individual is forced by circumstances to do many things at once, the fact that he does one of them incorrectly should not lightly be taken as negligence. *Wilsher* is an importance case in its own right, since it supports the notion of direct liability of a health authority rather than its mere vicarious liability for the actions of its staff. This view stemmed from the judgment of the Court of Appeal in that case, and particularly the judgment of Browne-Wilkinson V-C. In his judgment he raised the question of whether 'the authority (should) be liable if it demonstrates that, due to the financial stringency under which it operates, it cannot afford to fill the post with those possessing the necessary experience?'. In answering his own question he said 'the law should not be distorted by making findings of personal fault against individual doctors who are, in truth, not at fault ...'. This line of argument seems to indicate quite strongly that once a health authority assumes a duty towards a particular patient, it is committed to administer care without negligence, and cannot be seen to evade that duty by delegating its duty absolutely to its staff. Where the breach arises, in truth, from the organisation of the regime of care, which fails to meet the objective requirements of modern day medicine, then a plea that resources fell short of requirements will not absolve a hospital from a breach of duty. To a large degree, this analysis is supported by the more recent case of *Bull v Devon*

AHA^9 in which the Court of Appeal applied the doctrine of *res ipsa loquitur* in a situation in which the hospital had failed to offer necessary specialist care to deal with an emergency within what the court considered a reasonable time. This involved a finding that, in effect, the system for ensuring the attendance of a requisite specialist was unreliable and unsatisfactory. In that case, Mustill LJ pointed to the danger in assuming that 'it is necessarily a complete answer to say that even if the system in any hospital is unsatisfactory, it was no more unsatisfactory than those in force elsewhere'. Nonetheless, Mustill LJ expresses a real fear; as was said in *Sidaway v Board of Governors of Bethlem Royal Hospital*[10] the *Bolam* standard upholds 'practice accepted at the time as proper by a responsible body of medical opinion even though other doctors adopt a different practice'. There is a danger that, if public expenditure cuts lead to a decline in care, then the standards demanded by law will fall as doctors begin to work under a more limited regime. This downward boot strapping should be the subject of the courts' vigilance for 'neglect of duty does not cease by repetition to be neglect of duty'.

Because the standard of care in the law of negligence is objective, it may well be that the law demands a requisite standard which subjectively the tortfeasor cannot meet. The prime example of this is the case of *Nettleship v Weston*[11]. In that case the standard of a reasonably competent motorist was attributed to a learner driver. This bears directly upon the second question of the standard to be expected from less experienced staff. We have seen that in the medical context the problems of an objective standard arising most commonly in relation to problems resulting from lack of funding and staffing. In an early case *Jones v Manchester Corporation*[12] Lord Denning argued that it would be

> unjust that the hospital board by getting inexperienced doctors to perform their duties for them, without adequate supervision, should be able to throw all the responsibility onto those doctors as if they were fully experienced practitioners.

Most recently the issues were raised in the case of *Wilsher*. Essentially, in this case, the defendants argued that they had made considerable use of recently qualified staff, and whilst it was necessary for them to learn within the hospital, it was inevitable that they could not operate with the similar degree of competence as experienced staff, with the result that the standard of care would be lower. However, it was argued that this would be in the best long-term interests of the patients whatever the short-term difficulties.

The judgment of Mustill LJ addressed these points at greatest length. His view was that the standard of care should be defined according to the requirements of the post, so that, for example, someone occupying the post of Registrar should act with a sufficient degree of expertise as might be shown by a reasonably competent person occupying that sort of post. However, Browne-Wilkinson V-C dissented from this view and expressed a preference for a law of negligence based on the concept of personal fault. The merit of this line is that someone of experience occupying a relatively junior post would be judged by a standard of actual knowledge, this might accord with general legal principle. The third Judge, Glidewell LJ, adopted a similar approach to Mustill LJ and stated that

> [t]he law requires the trainee or learner to be judged by the same standard as his more experienced colleagues. If it did not, inexperience would frequently be urged as a defence to an action for professional negligence.

In the end, the answer to this dilemma must lie in supervision. If a doctor occupying a particular post lacks the overall competence to carry out a particular procedure, then it is necessary for the health authority to provide an adequate degree of supervision from a person of greater experience.

Allocation and quality assurance

Although this line of case law limits the excuse of resources in the event of medical accident it does little to resolve pressing problems of access to care. Mechanisms have been suggested to ensure considered processes of allocation other than adjudication, however, these usually proceed in the name of efficiency, but argue that in so far as they analyse costs and utility they inform decision-making and allow social justice. This approach is exemplified by the development of the QALY (quality-adjusted life year) (Williams, 1985). There is now extensive literature and heated debate on the whole issue of the QALY which within the confines of this essay cannot be addressed (but see Jenkinson and Wilkinson, infra, and the literature discussed therein). The following criticisms may be made. The notion of measuring outputs in terms of quality and quantity of life achieved by a particular medical procedure is not in itself unwelcome. Providing a normative stance in relation to such information is avoided, we ought to be better informed as a result. Yet what is left is broad information on health maximisation of the type which, however useful on the macro level in reviewing allocations as between specialisms, can never help at the micro level of individual, (hard-case) decision-making. In addition, it is the health output only which is measured, and actually wider questions of equity are problematic. The truth is that benefits other than improved health status may be derived from the health care system - so that I still value my visits to complain to my GP even though she never cures my baldness. Economists could argue that mine is the very case which should be rooted out by cost/utility analysis, but in wider terms they have the problem that the QALY pays insufficient regard to patient wishes which will be so varied as to cast doubt upon their measure of output since the patient may derive utility from making autonomous choices (Mooney and Olsen, 1991).

Thus in relation to both the legal and economic regulation of health care allocation the standing of the patient to participate in the making of decisions counts for little. It was this problem that the present Government's reform of the NHS claimed to redress. The white paper, *Working for Patients* (1989) announced that reform would enhance patient choice by introducing market forces into the NHS. At the same time, such competition would promote efficiency without cost to the patient. The key lay in separating the purchaser and provider functions allowing both District Health Authorities and fundholder GPs to negotiate deals for specialist hospital care. Competition between groups of purchasers seeking to attract patients for capitation fees and providers seeking to sell services would produce efficiencies within a newly created internal market. NHS hospitals would be allowed to elect for trust status bringing the ability to manage themselves in order to respond to the competitive challenge quickly and flexibly. Cost effective performance from the NHS Trusts would place them ahead of competitor providers.

There are some gains here. Providers of treatment will be forced to evaluate the cost of it more carefully than ever before - if only to be able to contract successfully. It may well be that some cost savings may result. The reform is also likely to see greater accountability on the part of doctors who will face pressures to justify clinical processes. It is also likely that there will be a greater flow of information as part of the general marketing endeavour of selling medical services. It is not obvious, however, that all of the advantages will accrue to the patient notwithstanding the sentiments of *Working for Patients*. Any increase in the accountability of doctors is primarily financial accountability and largely to health administrators within the system rather than to the patient. Even assuming a greater flow of information to patients, in the final analysis the GP will continue to act as gate-keeper to specialist and hospital services and whatever incentive the GP fundholder has to contract with the cheapest provider, such a choice is neither necessarily that of the patient nor, perhaps, in the patient's best interests (McBride, infra).

Of course, I feel sure that if my present GP finally loses her patience with my persistent complaint I shall have little difficulty in placing myself elsewhere. As a healthy, well-to-do and relatively young (if prematurely balding) non-smoker, I must seem an attractive catch for a GP not wishing for too great a burden on the practice budget. Equally it might make sense for me to choose a GP provider who has been sufficiently risk averse to choose patients unlikely to make considerable demands for health care. Since a GP cannot charge patients for care once the practice budget is exhausted it seems apparent that GPs finding themselves stretched financially will ration care. All the incentives are there for GPs to select young healthy patients and for young healthy patients to select GPs who have already made such choices. Age and morbidity related capitation weightings, similar to RAWP, may limit, but will not eliminate this trend.

While supporting the thesis of an emerging two-tier system within the NHS, all of this indicates the importance of patient choice of GP. Yet this is the only choice which can effectively be made. Thereafter, for all purposes, the GP acts as agent for the patient. So rather than patient choice, choice is exercised on behalf of the patient. One must assume that the overriding factor will be cost. However, this will not necessarily be cost to the patient, rather it may reflect cost to the practice budget. The patient may set store by certain qualities, such as convenience, which may not be reflected in the GP's assessment of cost, although the costs in terms of travel, time etc are real enough to the patient. Moreover the GP's assessment of cost may or may not reflect quality of care. Providers will often contract to provide, in blocks, a certain number of medical interventions. They will quote a price for this some time ahead. The difficulty for the purchaser is how to recognise whether, intentionally or as a result of bad planning, a particular provider is substituting price for quality? Already, since the reforms, we have seen allegations that costs have been shifted by making additional charges for facilities or pharmaceuticals outside the contract price.

Thus informational asymmetry may remain to derogate from the force of the supposed internal market. If informed choices cannot be made between competing providers then the very underpinning of the revised system collapses. If quality issues are ignored in a relentless drive to curtail price, and if price is the only basis on which purchasers choose, then the self-regulation of the internal market has achieved nothing. Of course, it could be the case that purchasers would be prepared to pay higher costs to providers of a higher quality service, but it is not clear on what basis such assessments of quality can be made by the purchasers, particularly when offered prospective block contracts. Nor is it clear that the patient will be able to direct the agent purchaser towards quality provision in the even more unlikely instance that (s)he had sufficient information to assess the quality.

Conclusion

Major problems arise when we seek to isolate need from the many competing demands within the health care system. In practice, in many parts of our system we are content to allow doctors to act as the arbiters of need and comparative need. While this places a heavy and unenviable responsibility upon doctors, the fact remains that they nonetheless exercise a power which may be either life-saving or life-denying. In view of this, it might be anticipated that there would be sophisticated processes whereby both doctors could be held accountable for decisions made, and the wider community would participate in the allocation system in order to ensure social justice. In fact such processes do not exist leaving patients to resort to legal intervention. This has achieved little in terms of establishing the accountability of decision-makers or of enhancing participation in their decisions. It is impossible to challenge outright decisions made on allocations, and although it may be possible to found an action in the aftermath of medical injury resulting from inadequate resourcing of health care, this provides little comfort to the patient and does little to remedy future inequity.

It is in the context of this legal lacuna that economists have attempted to suggest other allocative mechanisms. These do little to enhance patient participation within the system, and although they do tend to increase the accountability of medical staff, they do so in a limited way, without handing any autonomy back to the patient. Oddly enough, most problems which face market-based allocation, including those of the new internal market within the NHS revolve around informational asymmetries. Ironically, the law has always taken a very limited view of information which needs to be disclosed to patients. The lack of development of a doctrine of the informed consent and limited traditional rights for patients to see information about themselves has restricted the flow of information on medical services. Until we can inject into the system an openness about how resources are allocated, it is idle to think that economic or legal regulatory mechanisms can better enhance the rationing of health care. It is enough to make you tear your hair out.

* Director of Education at Wilde Sapte Solicitors.
1. 1980 March 18, unreported.

2. 1987, The Times, 26 November.

3. [1948] 1 KB 233.

4. 1988, 6 January, unreported.

5. [1957] 2 All ER 118.

6. 1970, The Times, 26 November.

7. (1964) 108 SJ 115.

8. [1987] QB 730, CA.

9. 1989, 2 February, unreported.

10. [1985] 1 All ER 643.

11. [1971] 2 QB 691.

12. [1951] 2 QB 852, 871.

Medical Audit: A Critical Review

Anne McBride*

Introduction

From 1st April 1991, every doctor is required to participate in regular Medical Audit. Medical Audit is defined in the White Paper as the 'systematic analysis of the quality of medical care, including the procedures used for diagnosis and treatment, the use of resources and the resulting outcome and quality of life for the patient' (Department of Health, 1989a). The quality of medical care has been assessed for a number of years in the United Kingdom. However, this analysis has tended to be self-orientated in nature and sporadic in use enabling it to fall within the category of 'voluntary self-regulation'. In contrast, although not written into the National Health Service (NHS) and Community Care Act 1990, the introduction of medical audit within the new environment of the NHS 'internal market', coupled with the open support of the Royal Colleges to its implementation, arguably changes its status to that of mandatory self-regulation and thereby increases its capacity to encourage high quality medical care.

This essay discusses the nature of medical audit and explores its potential impact on the quality of medical care. Reference is made initially to the nature of quality assessment pre-White Paper. The paper then reviews the methodology of medical audit and sets this within the context of its current introduction. It then looks at the variety of pressures which arguably exist to give medical audit its de facto mandatory status and which could contribute to its wholesale adoption within the NHS. These emanate from within the medical profession itself; from the fact that medical care is now the subject of contracts with purchasing Health Authorities; and from the potential for the legal profession to use medical audit in medical negligence claims. Taken to their fullest potential, these pressures could lead to doctors becoming subject to increased regulation both from within and without the profession which, in turn, could lead to a dramatic reduction in the clinical autonomy they currently 'enjoy'.

The essay concludes by discussing the critical assumptions which underpin - and may undermine - such a regulatory scenario - the assumption, for example, that agreed standards of quality already exist for the provision of medical care; or that in their absence 'new' standards can be determined in isolation from value judgements or behaviourial instincts of clinicians. In the endeavour to improve quality through regulating doctors and reducing their clinical autonomy, it is to be noted that medical audit itself cannot provide answers to such important questions. Medical audit can only provide a means for monitoring and improving upon standards of care which have already been agreed as indicators of quality. In some specialties, for certain conditions, standards of practice exist which are unequivocal and appropriate for widespread adoption and regulation. In other settings, however, more research and discussion is required in order to determine explicit standards of practice to be adopted by all.

Pre-White Paper quality assessment

Quality assessment describes 'the monitoring and appraisal of care against pre-determined standards' (Irvine, 1990, p.19). Prior to the introduction of medical audit, the quality of clinical practice was mainly assessed on an informal and voluntary basis by the medical profession itself. This 'freedom' to regulate oneself is often justified on the grounds that only clinicians have the requisite expertise required for determining and monitoring their own standards of practice. As noted by Shaw (1989, p.12) it also reflects the high degree of clinical autonomy which clinicians in Britain have compared to those countries such as North America, Australia and Canada where standards of practice are monitored by external bodies.

Within this self-regulatory framework, the method of quality assessment used most frequently was that of peer review. Peer review is the evaluation or review of one's 'work' by one's equals. In the medical profession, this takes a variety of forms ranging from an informal peer group discussion of case note presentations by colleagues through to the more systematic and formal review which exists in the confidential enquiries into Maternal Deaths, and Perioperative Deaths (Buck et al 1987; Department of Health, 1991).

However, its status as a voluntary exercise may well have led to its usage being haphazard and less than comprehensive. The *Confidential Enquiry into Perioperative Deaths* (CEPOD) noted that many surgeons and anaesthetists did not hold regular audits of their operation results (traditionally known as mortality and morbidity meetings) (Buck et al 1987a,p.vii). Moreover, despite the enquiry itself being the first of its kind to enable collaborative review between surgeons and anaesthetists and despite its protocol stating that 'the Medical profession has a responsibility to the public and to itself to assess its own standards..', participation could not be other than voluntary. Although, 95 per cent co-operation with the survey was achieved, the actions of the 79 consultants who declined to participate determined that approximately 500 cases could not be investigated.

Quality assurance is an extension of quality assessment, and requires that action be taken regarding any deficiencies of quality which are revealed through quality assessment (Irvine, 1990, p.19). However, if participation in peer review is only conducted on a voluntary basis, then changing one's practice as a result of this review tends also to be only of a voluntary nature. Although clinicians may participate in peer review, the review group has no means of ensuring that evaluative expressions by colleagues are acknowledged or appreciated, or that recommendations for a change in clinical practice are effected. CEPOD illustrates how this phenomena relates both to individuals and the specialty group as a whole. Despite the high degree of co-operation with CEPOD, very few anaesthetists and surgeons telephoned the CEPOD office for personal feedback on their cases. In fact there were only five cases where both the surgeon and anaesthetic received feedback on the same case, contrasting with the collaborative nature of the study. In addition, CEPOD arranged for feedback to be given on a regional basis, but invitations to over 1,300 participating consultants to attend such meetings were accepted by only ten per cent, with attendance on the day being only five per cent. If feedback is not received, there is no avenue for exploring where deficiencies in care may exist and therefore no impetus for changing any clinical practice where this appears necessary.

CEPOD further illustrates the difference between quality assessment and quality assurance. Although the cases reviewed in CEPOD were not self-selected - encompassing all deaths occurring within 30 days of an operation - and they revealed a number of practices which were not considered to be of an appropriate standard, the report itself was only able to make recommendations as to appropriate changes in practice. It was not able to effect any change. Arguably, however, the methodology of medical audit does enable change to be effected and represents a significant move away from quality assessment to quality assurance.

Medical Audit

In America during the 1950s and 1960s, Lembcke endeavoured to develop a more scientific approach to the quality assessment of health care which, whilst maximising objectivity and minimising subjectivity, would also enable the assessment of routine practice on a wider scale than was possible with individual peer review. As a result, Lembcke developed the explicit criteria approach to quality assessment, using criteria and standards. This enabled a more objective and systematic quality assessment which could be repeatable at any time (Lembcke, 1967, p.117). This systematic form of quality assessment became known as 'medical audit'.

In explanation, criteria are things to be measured which, when measured, give an indication of quality. Standards are those measurement levels which it has been agreed represent quality. An illustration of this two-pronged identification of quality is given by Black who suggests that a criterion for the care of patients with acute abdominal pain could be 'that appendicectomies should be performed only when appendicitis is present'. The standard to be set would then relate to the number of inflamed appendices which were removed in total. If the standard were set at 75 per cent, then the removal of appendices of which only 65 per cent were inflamed would indicate a need to improve the care of patients with acute abdominal pain - which in this instance might require an improvement of the diagnostic practice of the clinicians (Black, 1990, p.100).

The contribution such explicit standard setting gives to quality assurance lies in the relationship between the standards which have been set and the quality of care which the definers of the standards believe should be provided. By agreeing that a certain set of criteria and standards represents the quality of care which the peer group should be achieving, the peer group is also acknowledging that where these standards are not achieved, corrective action will, prima facie, be required. Shaw noted that effective audit could be regarded as a three-part cycle of 'setting standards, evaluating care, and modifying practice in the light of the evaluation' and graphically illustrated the process with 'The Cycle of Audit' (1980,1444). Using the 'cycle' to represent the process of medical audit has now become established practice within the literature with the general acknowledgement of activities being as follows:-

STAGE 1
Setting of
standards

STAGE 2
Comparison of
standards with
observed practice

STAGE 3
Implementation of
appropriate change

In stage 1 of the cycle, the peer group defines the quality of care it believes should be provided for a particular condition, or particular set of patients, and expresses this in terms of criteria and standards. It is the establishment of this benchmark of quality which enables the identification of any shortfall of standards when current practice is observed in stage 2 of the cycle. Stage 3 of the cycle refers to the implementation of change which may be necessary if the pre-defined standards are to be met by the peer group in current practice. Obviously if standards are easily achieved, then the standards may need re-assessment and amended. The setting of standards in an explicit manner in stage 1 of the cycle, and the systematic comparison with practice in stage 2, provides a benchmark against which practice can be re-audited at a later date thus enabling the identification of changes in practice and the assurance of an agreed quality of care on a regular basis.

It might be useful at this stage to provide an example of how this methodology can be translated into practice. An audit of the hospital care of acute asthma was able to set its standards of care in accordance with those standards recognised by the British Thoracic Society (Bell et al 1991, p.1440). Similarly, an audit concerning the care of diabetes in general practice, took as its standards, the eight clinical interventions identified by the British Diabetic Association as being critical to the effective care of diabetes in the community (Hill, 1991). Using nationally recognised guidelines as the basis for their explicit criteria, enabled both audit groups to compare their current local practice with national standards and determine where they were not being met. Having previously agreed that achievement of the guidelines was an appropriate objective, in the absence of this achievement, both groups are in a stronger position to take remedial action.

Government implementation of Medical Audit

Medical Audit was introduced in 1st April 1991 as part of the reforms proposed in the White Paper *Working for Patients* which followed the Prime Minister's Review of the NHS in 1988. Although not given legal force in the NHS and Community Care Act 1990, the government's prescriptions for its introduction determine that it contrasts significantly with the government's previous requirements for the quality assessment of medical care. For example, *Working Paper No. 6* indicates that Medical Audit is to be (i) undertaken by every doctor; (ii) regular and systematic; (iii) central to quality programmes; (iv) conducted within a clearly defined organisational framework; (v) agreed locally between the profession and management (vi) the responsibility of local Medical Audit committees; and (vii) include the patient's perspective (Department of Health, 1989b).

Post-White Paper a number of government directives have been issued which seek to determine the purpose and proposed operation of medical audit with precise responsibilities being given to Regional and District Health Authorities, local management and clinicians. In return, the introduction has been underpinned with considerable funding from central Government. The government has officially acknowledged the investment required by the development of medical audit and stated that any costs arising will be assessed and considered in future Public Expenditure Surveys. In 1991/92, funds to the value of £48.8 million have been allocated to support the implementation of medical audit. However, this financial support has not been committed beyond March 1993. The extent of the bureaucratic framework developed to support and facilitate the implementation is indicated in the following brief summary of Health Authority responsibilities.

The Regional Health Authorities have a dual role. They are required to facilitate the introduction of medical audit within their region: distributing monies and advice to Health Districts and specifically supporting audit in certain defined areas of health care. They are also required to monitor the organisation and implementation of medical audit in Health Districts - ensuring that it is both adequately organised and effectively implemented. Regional Health Authorities receive medical audit monies from the Department of Health and are obliged to ensure that District Health Authorities are making appropriate arrangements to facilitate medical audit. At the year-end, they report to the Department of Health with regard to progress made during the previous year and on plans for proposed future developments. Under the 1991/92 allocation of funds for medical audit, the 'carrot' dangled in front of the Regional Health Authorities to encourage their support of medical audit, was the awarding of approximately 30 per cent of funds upon the production of a satisfactory report of developments to date.

At a local level, District Health Authorities are required to ensure that appropriate committees are in place to oversee audit activities in all units. In turn, these District Committees are obliged to plan and monitor a comprehensive programme of medical audit within their locality, whilst securing and distributing appropriate resources to support audit programmes. The local committee principally consists of medical personnel, with most major specialties being represented on the committee.

However, despite the extent to which a bureaucratic framework has been developed to monitor the implementation of medical audit, the requirement for every doctor to regularly participate in medical audit is still not mandatory. As such, it is arguably doubtful whether these mechanisms in themselves will manage to achieve a more widespread and vigorous form of self-regulation than that previously established. It is the existence of additional external pressures which provide the de facto mandatory framework to 'encourage' the implementation of medical audit. These are reviewed below and emanate from within the medical profession itself; from the fact that medical care is now the subject of contracts with purchasing Health Authorities Service; and from the potential of the legal profession to use medical audit in medical negligence claims.

The medical profession

In contrast to their earlier reluctance to embrace the concept of medical audit, practical support for the recent introduction and implementation of medical audit has come from the medical profession itself. In their submission to the Secretary of State, the Standing Medical Advisory Committee noted that the quality of medical care was the responsibility of doctors and should be 'subject to monitoring and revision' (Department of Health, 1990a, p.1). The Working Party felt that taking part in medical audit was such an important component of medical practice that a failure to take part should be regarded very seriously. These sentiments are increasingly becoming a feature of Royal College pronouncements on Medical Audit. For example, in their initial report on Medical Audit, the Royal College of Physicians comment that medical audit should quickly become established practice for all physicians, noting that some form of medical audit will become a requirement for accreditation purposes (Royal College of Physicians, 1989, p.8).

This overt support from the Royal Colleges complements the government stance which, whilst requiring the participation of all doctors in medical audit also notes that the detailed practice of medical audit is a matter for the medical profession. The Department of Health has indicated that medical audit will evolve as experience is gained and noted that guidance was being prepared for the profession by the Conference of Royal Colleges.

The Royal Colleges have also noted their commitment to developing adequate and meaningful indicators of quality which could be used on a national basis. For instance, the British Paediatric Association has prepared a number of outcome measurements for child health which it regards as a minimum data set and which it believes will enable Districts to monitor their own performance and compare their performance with others. The set includes categories for care of the newborn; screening, immunisation, acute and chronic illness and facilities for hospital care (British Paediatric Association, 1990).

However, the setting of nationally recognised standards is a relatively new development and the pressure to implement effective medical audit, for the moment, may rely on pressures within the medical profession at a local level. As a result of the comparatively recent introduction of doctors into local management, via such organisational structures as 'Clinical Directorates', the pressure to both participate in medical audit, and change one's practice where this is shown to be necessary, is likely to be greatly increased.

A Clinical Directorate is an organisational structure which holds devolved power and autonomy at the level of the clinical team. The principle behind the Clinical Directorate is that the clinical team which directly uses resources is best placed to hold the budget for those resources and allocate their usage accordingly. In many Clinical Directorates, it will be the clinician (known as Clinical Director) who makes the final decisions regarding resource management, supported by a Nurse Director and Business Manager. In others, decisions will be made on a consensus basis.

To gain a greater understanding of the full potential of the effect such local devolvement of power and budgetary control to Clinical Directors may have on 'encouraging' colleagues to participate in effective medical audit, it is necessary to view the process within the context of the post-White Paper NHS environment.

Contracts for medical care

As aforementioned, the reforms proposed in the White Paper *Working for Patients* followed the then-Prime Minister's review of the NHS in 1988. The purpose of the reforms was to introduce market forces into the NHS by separating the funding and provision functions and creating the roles of 'purchasers' and 'providers' of health care. As a purchaser, the Director of Public Health of a District Health Authority is responsible for assessing the needs of the community - purchasing the requisite services from provider units under contracts drawn up between the two parties. This arguably encourages NHS provision to be driven by the needs of the community as opposed to the desires and prejudices of those providing the services. Furthermore, the split between the purchasing and provider elements of the District Health Authorities arguably enables purchasers to buy services from any provider unit - not necessarily from those located in the District. This is intended to encourage competition between provider units whose income can no longer be guaranteed by their local District Health Authorities.

A further competitive element has been introduced into the NHS with the development of a variety of purchasers and providers. Hospitals, or 'provider units', can make an application to the Secretary of State for Health to become 'Self Governing Trusts'. By opting for self-governance, providers are arguably able to break-away from traditional centralised control over decision making and increase their operational flexibility and general responsiveness to 'the market'. Likewise, in the primary health care sector, General Practices can make an application to become 'GP fundholding practices'. Whilst remaining in effect providers of primary health care, by becoming their own budgetholders, General Practices can become purchasers of health care from both the secondary and primary sector.

As a result of the purchaser/ provider split within the NHS, and the competitive element which now conceivably exists between providers, purchasing authorities are arguably in a stronger position from which to negotiate quality into their contracts with provider organisations. Before the splitting of the functions, it is argued that there was a strong tendency for service delivery to be dictated by the quantity and nature of the services which currently existed in the locality - as opposed to matching the needs of the community. In the new environment where purchasing organisations are able to purchase health care from any provider organisation, the purchaser is arguably able to determine what services are required, both in terms of quantity and quality, and require provider organisations to compete for those services. Within this environment, Bowden and Walshe argue that the purchasers of health care will be establishing progressively more advanced quality standards and outcome measures in the contracts they agree between themselves and the service providers - forcing providers to demonstrate the existence of formalised audit programmes and meet jointly agreed standards (Bowden, Walshe, 1991, p.103).

To illustrate his 'new-found' negotiating powers, the Director of Public Health for North East Essex Health Authority, recently outlined his expectations as a purchaser and stressed the importance quality would play in the new market environment. Jessop argues that obtaining information about the quality of health care which could be provided by competing provider organisations will enable him to make a genuine choice between them in his role as a securer of 'high quality value for money services' for his community (Jessop, 1990, p.13).

If the Royal Colleges and the medical profession generally are reaching consensus about national standards of practice to be achieved, then these too could inform the content of purchaser/provider contracts. So, for example, a purchaser could conceivably require its provider to provide respiratory medicine for the treatment of asthma in accordance with the British Thoracic Society Guidelines (British Thoracic Society, 1990, p.797-800). If the contract for those services was placed on that basis, the respiratory physicians in the provider unit would be obliged to work in accordance with these Guidelines with the possible added incentives that (i) the purchasing authority might require evidence from time to time that these Guidelines were being adhered to; and (ii) if the purchaser were not satisfied that the Guidelines were being adopted on a regular basis, the contract could be placed elsewhere the following year.

It is within this competitive scenario that the aforementioned 'Clinical Directors' may begin to bring pressure to bear on their colleagues where they are not providing their medical care to agreed standards. Across the nation, this has the potential to make a considerable impact on the delivery of high quality medical care. Ham, Dingwall et al (1988, p.26-34) noted that there were three main options for deterring doctors from acting negligently - one of which was the process of self-regulation. In the absence of any legal liability, Ham, Dingwall argued that a market situation might provide powerful incentives for providers to maintain standards, 'simply as a way of ensuring commercial viability'. However, they noted the nature of current incentives - at that time these were the protection and improvement of reputations - which did not always operate effectively. As described above, the development of medical managers with 'contracts' to pursue and retain for their specialty, may indeed lead to a more effective form of self-regulation than previously envisaged by Ham, Dingwall et al.

The legal profession

Although hitherto the use of litigation has not been significant in deterring clinicians from acting negligently, the formal introduction of medical audit may provide the legal profession with a new and enhanced regulatory role. The existence of medical audit in its current form could conceivably enable the legal profession to provide two means of external pressure - (i) the use of medical audit standards to better determine the 'appropriate standard of care imposed by law'; and (ii) the use of medical audit findings to prove that a clinician was (or was not) in breach of the appropriate standard of care imposed by law.

No contractual relationship exists between the clinician and the patient, so if a patient feels they have been the subject of medical malpractice, their recourse to compensation is sought through the law of tort. In the UK, only those clinicians whose standard of care is found to be inadequate by the Courts are held liable for the adverse consequences of their action. Although in theory the law exists to deter clinicians from acting negligently, Ham and Dingwall argue that in practice it is an ineffective deterrent (1988, p.26-34). The volume of cases coming to Court is restricted and once at Court, the success of a claim rests on the establishment of four factors - outlined concisely by Kennedy & Grubb as

1. That a duty of care was owed by the doctor to the patient.

2. That the doctor was in breach of the appropriate standard of care imposed by the law.

3. That the breach of duty caused the patient harm or injury recognised by law as meriting compensation.

4. That the extent and *quantum* of the loss that has flowed from the breach of duty is recoverable in law. (Kennedy & Grubb, 1989, p.143).

Use of Medical Audit standards

The formal introduction of medical audit into medical practice may provide evidence which facilitates the establishment of the second element of a successful negligence claim: 'that the doctor was in breach of the appropriate standard of care imposed by law'. John Evans, the Legal Advisor of Trent Regional Health Authority, draws attention to the possibility that medical audit materials could be used to prove what is an appropriate standard of care. Evans believes that agreed protocols and standards developed for the purposes of Medical Audit could be used when giving evidence about acceptable practice within a particular speciality (Evans, 1991, p.6). This could obviously be used either for the benefit of a clinician or to their detriment. He also stresses the unlikelihood of such documents being protected from the Court's discovery process - and believes that even the documents leading to the formation of standards could be liable to access.

Kennedy and Grubb note that English judges rarely challenge the accepted views of the medical profession, though establishing what that view is may cause the court some difficulty (1989, p.368). However, in the wake of Medical Audit the development of nationally recognised standards is being requested and encouraged. Although judges may still be reluctant to decide between contrasting local definitions of quality, they will be more likely to accept those defined by Royal Colleges or consensus conferences thus placing a burden on clinicians to adopt nationally recognised standards for their practice. So, for example, the use of standards in this manner may encourage all respiratory physicians to act in accordance with the British Thoracic Society guidelines for the emergency treatment of asthma, knowing that failure to do so in an incidence of mortality may make the existence of at least one of the four factors of a successful claim easier to prove.

Disclosure of Medical Audit findings

Turning to the use of medical audit findings in Court to establish the actions of a clinician, Evans notes that, at the moment, the findings are not in any special position with regard to their disclosure in Court (1991, p.6). A lawyer arguing for their disclosure will argue on the basis that disclosure of such documents would give substantial support to the claimant and that without the documents, the claimant would be deprived of important evidence. The only ground for non-disclosure of medical audit findings would seem to be that of the public interest. The defendant would have to argue that disclosure would be injurious to the public interest because it would deter and undermine the useful application of medical audit. So, for example, with regard to CEPOD, it was argued that the assessment of work by both Anaesthetists and Surgeons - which proved a significant contribution to quality assessment in this field of work and was therefore conceivably in the public interest - would have been impossible to pursue without the protection of immunity from disclosure.

To date no such call for the disclosure of Medical Audit findings has been made and Blyth notes that the Department of Health is waiting for an opportunity to invoke public interest immunity and thereby enable a test case to set the precedent for the future (1990, p.31). Blyth indicates the courts should decide the question of public interest and declines to second guess their decision. Evans however notes that the trend in litigation is towards greater openness and questions whether it is in fact either in the public interest - or the long-term interests of the medical profession - to call upon the defence of public immunity (1991, p.6).

Certainly, if external pressures are required to ensure the full participation of all clinicians in Medical Audit, the disclosure of Medical Audit findings for negligence claims may well provide an adequate sanction, with clinicians encouraged to improve their practice in order to improve their audit results.

Potential of existing external pressures

Given that external pressures arguably exist to ensure medical audit is introduced and implemented in a de facto mandatory framework, it is worth considering which approach is likely to be used to greatest effect. In many respects the legal profession is ready to take on this role, with there being, as yet, no restrictions on the disclosure of Medical Audit materials - particularly when the Department of Health has made it clear that it has no intention at present to seek a wider application of public interest immunity to all medical audit information collected by Health Authorities (Walshe, Bennett, 1991, p.12). However, from the American experience, the implications of the Government sitting back and watching the law become more and more involved in the regulation of Medical Audit are two-fold. Irrespective of the adverse effect it may have on the willing participation of clinicians, and the restriction of pertinent feedback on current practice which may arise through a desire to anonymise all results, it could also lead to an explosion of defensive medicine. Widespread patient litigation against doctors in the United States has prompted the use of 'defensive medicine' whereby to cover themselves against possible liability, doctors ensure that all tests and procedures which might conceivably help patients are performed. The financial implications of this practice in the National Health Service could be catastrophic and would clearly work against the then-Prime Minster's original intention of the Review to provide a value for money service.

Given the organisational issues, and cost implications, which arise from using the legal profession as a means of externally regulating the use of medical audit, it is likely that the present Tory Government will rely on the new internal market to improve the quality of medical care. However, the potential of this means of regulation rests on several important assumptions: (i) that competition exists within the new internal market - a factor questioned by some commentators (Paton, 1991); (ii) that competition, if it exists, guarantees that providers will compete on the basis of quality; (iii) that a Labour government would pursue the same policies for organising the funding and provision of the health service as the Tory Government.

If the aforementioned pressures were inadequate to encourage the adoption of medical audit in a more than voluntary and sporadic manner - on either political or practical grounds - it may well be that attention would be paid to other forms of regulation. For example, in countries such as North America, standards of medical care are monitored by bodies which are external to the local peer group.

External review

In the United States, external review has increasingly been the method of monitoring the quality of care provided by clinicians and hospitals. An accreditation programme for hospitals was originally established in the 1920s, and it evolved into the Joint Commission on Accreditation of Hospitals in the 1950s. An additional form of external review - by other doctors - was provided by the Professional Standards Review Organisations (PSROs) set up in 1972. These were for the Medicare programme (for over 65s) and were concerned to relate quality and cost-control. In 1982, they were replaced by Peer Review Organisations (PROs) which did not have to be composed of other doctors.

Supporters of medical audit often argue that its wholesale adoption and implementation by clinicians will ensure that external review will not be introduced as a means of quality control in the United Kingdom - in other words 'physician, heal thyself'!

However, the King's Fund Centre is currently piloting a scheme of accreditation which may have more currency in the light of the new competitive environment. In addition, the Royal College of Pathologists have just piloted their accreditation scheme for national use. Although not to every pathologist's liking, it cannot be ignored and those either not applying or not finding accreditation may well find themselves uncompetitive in the new market - which in itself may be enough to ensure later conformance with accrediting standards.

Despite the piloting of external review bodies, as a means of comprehensively regulating the effective use of medical audit, this is likely to be viewed as being too bureaucratic and too expensive for the National Health Service. It also has the disadvantage that unless its standards are sensitive to local conditions, it does not encourage an ownership and commitment to desired standards on a regular basis. For example, when reviewing the experience of the PSRO medical-care evaluation studies, Nelson noted that physicians who did not participate in the development of the peer review criteria challenged the validity of the criteria when the data suggested an unacceptable level of compliance with the criteria (Nelson, 1976). This is particularly pertinent when regular visits by review bodies or accrediting agencies will not be feasible - raising the question as to what degree quality can be assured on a regular basis using this methodology.

The paradox is that without external intervention in the process of medical audit, the assessment, and assurance, of the quality of medical care may well remain an exercise solely for those least likely to require it. With external regulation, however, it could lead to a personal disassociation from the management of quality, to the long term detriment of medical care. Ideally a balance needs to be made between the provision of 'teeth' for those clinicians needing to take more responsibility for the quality of their care and the development of a supportive environment which encourages rather than imposes the management of quality as part of clinical practice.

Such a balance also needs to take account of the fragility of the scientific base of medicine. This may undermine the assumption that standards can easily be determined and agreed. When discussing the importance of criteria and standard setting to quality assurance, it was noted that the exercise enabled the identification of corrective action to be taken by the peer group determining the criteria and standards. In turn, it has been noted that the establishment of such explicit criteria and standards could enable colleagues, purchasers of health care, and the legal profession, to 'regulate' the practice of doctors to a certain standard of medical care. However, the complexity of determining and agreeing standards for the purposes of medical audit should also be appreciated - a few considerations of which are briefly discussed below.

Validity of standards

In encouraging the setting of standards for the purposes of medical audit, the assumption is made that a degree of knowledge exists as to causal relationships between clinical interventions and their effectiveness in achieving desired results. Yet, as Eddy notes, only about 15 per cent of medical interventions are supported by solid scientific evidence. Eddy illustrates this poverty of medical evidence with his initial research on the standard treatment of glaucoma: despite searching published medical reports back to 1906, no evidence was found of one randomised controlled trial of the standard treatment. Rather, the confident statements on treating glaucoma had been handed down from generation to generation (Smith, 1991, p.798). In the absence of scientific-based medicine, standard setting will be more susceptible to the vagaries of local practice and prejudice.

Patient perspective

The patient ideally should have a key role to play in the definition of the quality of the care to be provided. Jennett, for example, notes that surgery often incurs burdens as well as benefits and that it is therefore important that the patient be consulted as to their validation of the burdens and benefits involved and the quality of the resultant outcome (Jennett, 1988). However, when consulting patients, at least two considerations arise. First, the classic inequality of the doctor/ patient relationship - the doctor has more knowledge than the patient - tends to prohibit an open and equal dialogue (Steffen, 1988). Secondly, the use of patient satisfaction surveys to assess patient perceptions of the benefits of medical treatment are only just developing (Fitzpatrick, 1990). The vast majority of patient satisfaction surveys seeking to measure the quality of services provided have shown that most patients - more than 85 per cent in many surveys - are satisfied, highlighting the difficulty of drawing conclusions from small variations. This is possibly also attributable to the traditionally passive role played by the patient and this would need to be addressed if one wanted to measure quality in this domain. Furthermore, patients' comments on quality in surveys tend to focus on hotel services rather than clinical services. Thus the role for patient perceptions in medical audit raises a number of difficult questions.

Behaviourial aspects of practicing medicine

When outlining the methodology of medical audit, it was noted that peer group agreement to standards of quality enabled the assurance of that quality by the peer group at a later date. However, this assumption of group compliance perhaps oversimplifies the process and ignores important behaviourial considerations of the individual doctor. For instance, although 90 per cent of all obstetricians in Ontario agreed with guidelines for the indications for caesarean section, two years after the dissemination of the guidelines, the rate had changed very little (Hopkins, 1991, p.2). Eisenberg reviewed various approaches to changing physician's practices and noted that there were a variety of influences which impacted on the individual clinical decision making process. He concluded that no one approach to changing behaviour could be expected to be comprehensively effective and suggested the use of an orchestrated combination of approaches as opposed to the use of one particular methodology (Eisenberg, 1986, p.125-142).

Hard choices

Peer review is recognised as an important determinant in the maintenance of professional standards within medicine and the government's implementation of medical audit is encouraging its use by all clinicians on a systematic, regular basis. This essay has shown that within a de facto mandatory framework, medical audit has the capacity to encourage the attainment of high quality medical care at a national level. However, the development of nationally laid-down and de facto enforceable standards may well lead to the loss of clinical autonomy and judgement on a far wider scale than ever anticipated which may be ethically unacceptable for the individual clinician. The effect of this is best illustrated by a scenario in which there are two alternative care regimes. The outcome of Regime A is that 98 per cent of patients are restored to 'perfect' health but 2 per cent of patients die as a result of the clinical intervention. The outcome of Regime B is that 70 per cent of patients are restored to 'perfect' health, 30 per cent are totally unaffected by the clinical intervention, and there are no post-intervention deaths. If the criteria of clinical success was determined at a national level as 'low mortality', then Regime B would be the chosen standard by which all clinicians would be bound, but would it be right for such a decision to be made on a national basis? If an individual clinician was particulary perceptive as to which patients were more likely to die as a result of Regime A, they may well be able to apply Regime A to all but those identified patients. Conversely if the criteria of clinical success was determined as restoration to perfect health, Regime B would be chosen - which clinicians would use knowing it could lead to mortality.

It is important for all parties wishing to encourage and regulate the effective implementation of medical audit to recognise that medical audit is not able to facilitate the making of such a choice. At best medical audit can only be expected to ensure that where there is a known causal relationship between process and outcome, this is assessed and improved where necessary; and where there is uncertainty about the process to be adopted and outcome to be expected, this is considered on the basis of detailed research.

Conclusion

Given the methodology of medical audit and its introduction within an environment which encourages its regular usage, its potential to make a significant impact on the quality of medical care delivered in the NHS is quite substantial: voluntary and sporadic quality assessment, which rarely resulted in significant alterations in patterns of clinical care, could be replaced by systematic and informed discussions which enable the development and assurance of agreed standards of care on a regular basis.

However, given the complexity of determining standards of care, the success of medical audit in encouraging the delivery of high quality care relies heavily on the continued development of concise, meaningful and appropriate standards of practice by the medical profession. Paradoxically, the pressures which may ensure the regular participation of doctors in medical audit, may also be the pressures which, if not handled sensitively, result in a lack of commitment to its widespread adoption. If the medical profession perceive medical audit standards as tools which will lead to greater regulation, by either their colleagues, management, or the legal profession, in the absence of compensatory factors or an acknowledgement of the behavioural aspects of practicing medicine, they may be loath to participate in such developments. In these circumstances, at worst the impact of medical audit on maintaining and improving the quality of medical care will be negligible and at best it will be marginal.

* Research Fellow, Centre for Health Planning and Management, Keele University.

Personal Injuries Compensation and Quality of Life

The lawyer seeking damages for his client on the basis of mental and emotional disturbances (mental 'pain and suffering') finds proof difficult. Until the sciences can supply an accurate measure of mental and emotional disturbances due to stress, the legal profession will drift upon the stormy seas of judicial indecision (Wasmuth, 1957).

Crispin Jenkinson* and Brian Wilkinson**

Introduction

Historically, the aims of the law of tort have been described as appeasement, deterrence, justice, punishment, compensation and loss spreading (Dias and Markesinis, 1984; Harris et al; 1984). However, it seems reasonable, in the light of widespread insurance, to argue that the primary purpose of current negligence law is the provision of compensation for loss caused by injury. This objective is only satisfied where the compensation provided is adequate. In personal injuries cases, one of the areas where the adequacy of compensation is most contentious is in relation to non-pecuniary loss, such as loss of amenitiy and pain and suffering. While adequacy may be deemed a subjective concept, a working definition which is proposed in the context of this essay is that compensation should come as close as possible to providing monetary solace for the reduction in quality of life suffered. In order to do this, it is necessary to put forward a method of assessing the extent and effect of the reduction.

The efficacy of the tort system as a source of compensation has been the subject of considerable critical commentary (Ison, 1967, 1980). The problems created by lengthy and expensive procedures, which tend to result in only those with independent means or those who qualify for legal aid pursuing claims, and the adversarial nature of the system with its emphasis on demonstrating fault, injury and loss, 'turns the tort system into a lottery' (Ham et al; 1988).

A number of studies have been undertaken which inquire into or advocate the replacement of the current fault-based tort system with a system based on 'no-fault' compensation (Pearson Commission, 1978; Ison, 1980; BMA, 1987). However, given that such proposals have not been accepted to date in this country, this essay is not concerned with alternative methods of injury compensation. Nor is it overly concerned with the methods of payment available in personal injury cases. While one of the important criticisms made of the tort system is in relation to the delay in recovery of damages, it has to be recognised that the available forms of payment are considerably underused (Pritchard, 1989). However, in relation to either structured settlements or lump sum awards, it is the finality of the sum awarded which is striking. Ultimately, the final award ends the plaintiff's claim; there is little opportunity for the claim to be re-opened at a later date. This makes the need for an accurate assessment of the effect and extent of reduction in quality of life all the more significant, as the sum finally invested or awarded will depend on an appreciation of the true extent of the injury on the date of settlement or award. The focus of this essay is to consider current methods of assessment of injury and their effect as applied by the courts, and how such methods of assessment could be improved so as to reflect better the needs of the plaintiff.

In concentrating on the area of legal assessment of reduction in quality of life, we are conscious that only a small proportion of personal injury cases are ever heard in court, the majority being either settled out of court or abandoned (Harris et al, 1984; Genn, 1987).[1] However, given that research has shown that claims inspectors, barristers and solicitors have difficulties in assessing the effect, extent and value of injury, whether in the context of actual trials or settlement negotiations (Genn, 1987)[2], to focus on alternative methods of assessment of the extent and effect of injury on quality of life is to engage in a project which has implications for cases other than those which end with formal legal adjudication. As the methods by which the court currently assesses the extent and effect of injury on quality of life have an effect on decisions as to whether a case should be settled, abandoned or continued in court,[3] it is proposed that some of the problems involved in assessing the central element of non-pecuniary loss, viz. the reduction in quality of life, be examined.

In this essay the approach taken in negligence cases to the assessment of the effect of injuries on health and quality of life will be outlined. We will argue that whereas the tort system is better able to evaluate the pecuniary effect of physical injuries, such as the effect on loss of earnings, by using broadly accepted approaches, difficulty remains in assessing the non-physical manifestations of injury such as the psychological impact and effect on quality of life. Consequently, an alternative, or perhaps additional, method of assessment is necessary. Subjective health indicators are a method of health assessment which may prove useful in such cases. An outline will be given of the current uses of such questionnaires and an explanation of their development, testing, and refinement. Finally, we will put forward a case for the possible use of such instruments as providing additional data for courts to determine the effect of illness or injury. In describing the operation of this method, the case is made that subjective health assessment questionnaires are sufficiently reliable to satisfy legal requirements of certainty and accuracy. Recognising that lawyers have exhibited scepticism about psychological measures in the past, we will further discuss how appropriate it is to apply the subjective health assessment methodology to personal injury claims and indicate a variety of uses to which such methods can be put.

Compensation and Tort Law

The purpose of awarding damages in negligence cases is to attempt to restore the plaintiff to the position occupied before the injury occurred. Restoring the plaintiff to this position is to implement the principle of restitutio in integrum. According to Atiyah, 'it is the simple principle that the plaintiff is entitled to a full indemnity

216

for his losses; that he is to be made "whole" so far as money can do this' (Atiyah, 1980; Cane, 1987; Goodin, 1989). Usually, assessment of damages under this heading is not difficult. However, while in the case of pecuniary loss an award of damages will often result in the plaintiff being placed in the same financial position as was occupied before the injury occurred, awards of damages in cases of non-pecuniary loss cannot perform the same task as money can not reverse the occurrence of an injury. The area of personal injury litigation which gives rise to the greatest problems and the most controversy is that of compensating the plaintiff for non-pecuniary loss, that is, pain and suffering, loss of amenity and loss of expectation of life. In the following discussion we shall refer to these headings of non-pecuniary loss as cases concerning reduction in the plaintiff's quality of life (Somerville, 1986).

Despite the inability of monetary compensation to restore the plaintiff to his or her pre-injury position, such awards are made with a purpose. On one level, they are intended to provide the plaintiff with some form of solace for the reduction in quality of life. Consequently, the amount of damages to be awarded in any case depends on the theoretical approach taken to compensation.

Approaches to compensation

Currently, the law of negligence in England follows an objective approach to compensating the plaintiff for non-pecuniary loss by applying a type of tariff system under which the damage to or loss of a limb or other organ is objectively valued in monetary terms (Kemp and Kemp, 1989). Because the objective approach does not require the plaintiff to be aware of the loss suffered, the application of the tariff system resulted in cases such as *Wise v Kaye*[4] and *West v Shephard*,[5] where plaintiffs who were largely unaware of their injuries received compensation for non-pecuniary loss on the basis of an approach which objectively quantified in monetary terms the value of the injury. Justifications for this objective approach included that it should not be cheaper to kill than to injure,[6] and that the plaintiff was entitled to compensation for the injury done on a basis analogous to recovery for injury to property.[7] However, the results of *Wise* and of *West* raised queries as to who really benefited from such awards and whether a different approach to compensation should be implemented (Pearson Commission, 1978, para 393-8).

In 1972, in an article calling for changes in the system of compensation for non-pecuniary loss, Ogus identified three approaches used to measure the compensation to be awarded. The first, which is currently used by the courts, he called the 'conceptual approach', in which each limb or organ bears an objective monetary value. Under this approach, the plaintiff's own use or enjoyment of the affected limb or organ is an irrelevant consideration. Instead, a tariff system operates for each part of the body. Ogus argued that making awards on this basis was unjustified as the expression 'loss of amenities of life', 'as a head of damages in personal injuries cases... is intended to denote a loss of the capacity of the injured person to enjoy life to the full as, apart from his injury, he might have done'. Furthermore, he argued that by adopting the view that damages increased according to the nature of the injury, the assessment is based on the original injury rather than the consequent losses. Such an approach was erroneous, being contrary to the principle of compensation which is aimed at compensating not for injury per se but for loss suffered due to the injury. Using damage to chattel property as an example, Ogus pointed out that if the conceptual approach were applied, a court would award £x for a broken axle and £y for a shattered windscreen, rather than awarding for costs of the repairs. In addition, he argued that the award of damages in personal injuries cases is not intended to be punitive, despite the view expressed by members of the court in *Wise v Kaye*. Rather, the duty of the court is to award such damages as will compensate the plaintiff for the losses actually sustained; the court was not required to nominate a sum which it thought the defendant ought to pay.

Finally, Ogus argued that the conceptual approach leads to situations where very large sums of money are awarded to persons who cannot enjoy them, the true beneficiaries being the plaintiff's dependants or relatives. Ogus argued that if the concern of the law is to compensate such individuals for the loss suffered by the injury to the plaintiff, then compensation for the dependants should reflect their actual losses and not be based on a figure which would be awarded to the plaintiff per se. Having critically analysed the conceptual approach to compensation, he proceeded to outline two alternative approaches, which he termed the 'personal' and the 'functional' approach, respectively.

Under the 'personal approach', measurement of loss can only be conceived of in terms of the subjective happiness of the plaintiff. It follows that under this approach no attempt should be made to place an 'objective value' on the disability suffered by the plaintiff. Rather, an attempt should be made to assess in monetary terms the plaintiff's past, present and future deprivation of pleasure and happiness as a result of the loss of the use of the limb rather than the injury to the limb. Under the 'functional approach', while concern is expressed for the plaintiff's subjective happiness, damages are awarded only if justified through the provision of some consolation to the plaintiff in the form of compensation, requiring the plaintiff to be suffiently aware of the loss and the award of damages.

In summary the conceptual approach measures the award by the extent of the physical injury, the personal approach measures the award by the extent of the subjective loss of happiness, and the functional approach measures it by the extent to which monetary compensation can provide reasonable solace. In the context of the unaware plaintiff, quite different results are achieved where either the functional or conceptual approach is adopted. Under the conceptual approach, a plaintiff would theoretically receive similar damages to a fully aware plaintiff. Under the functional approach, however, since subjective awareness of loss is the central criteria, and this is minimal, the plaintiff would receive much less.[8] Having regard to decisions in other jurisdictions, notably the Australian case of *Skelton v Collins*,[9] Ogus advocated a change to the functional approach when awarding compensation for non-pecuniary loss.[10]

Whether to award damages on the basis of a functional or conceptual approach is an issue over which commentators and judges are divided (McLachlin, 1981).[11] However, some sympathy must lie with the view that as compensation under all heads of non-pecuniary loss is intended to provide solace for mental distress, no such compensation should be paid where no distress is evident, ie in the case of the unaware plaintiff (Cooper-Stephenson & Saunders, 1981). It should be remembered that this is not to deny the unaware plaintiff all compensation: damages for the costs of care and other pecuniary loss would still be made. It is only in relation to reduction in quality of life that the award would not be made unless it could be shown both that the plaintiff is aware of the loss and that the award would provide the plaintiff with some form of consolation for that loss. The issue which arises from the adoption of a functional approach is how to assess the effect of the injury on the plaintiff. As the award is only to be made to the extent that it provides solace, the determination of the degree to which the plaintiff has been affected is crucial.

Legal and evidentiary problems in the assessment of the effect of injury on quality of life.

While a plaintiff is entitled to recover for past, present and future reductions in quality of life resulting from the injury, such recovery is dependent on the plaintiff adducing sufficient evidence to show the deleterious effect of the injury on quality of life over the period. While a plaintiff may seek to claim for pain and suffering or loss of amenities which are not supported by medical evidence, a court will be reluctant to award damages, however honest the plaintiff may appear to be. To succeed in such pain and suffering claims, and to succeed generally for reduction in quality of life where the functional approach has been adopted, a plaintiff must produce evidence to confirm the change in quality of life. Assessing changes in quality of life necessarily invites evidentiary problems. Since issues of pain and quality of life are subjective, particular difficulties of proof confront the plaintiff and the courts (Cantor, 1951). For example, in relation to pain and suffering, considerable difficulty confronts the courts in distinguishing between real distress on the one hand and injury to feelings on the other. Similarly, in relation to loss of amenities, evaluation and assessment of the degree of loss is difficult.

In personal injury cases a plaintiff will usually rely on certain traditional forms of evidence to show the extent of the injury suffered. Thus in cases of physical injury, problems of proof are resolved mainly by the use of medical testimony, 'X-rays' and other objective data from the medical profession. It has been increasingly recognised by the medical profession that often such objective data is neither a full nor accurate picture of the health of the patient, as it does not include a measure of the needs of the patient (Patrick, Peach and Gregg, 1982), therefore it cannot adequately fulfil the needs of all aspects of personal injuries cases.

As the compensation awarded in personal injury cases is intended to be a final settlement, accurately assessing the effect of an injury on the plaintiff is of crucial importance.[12] The plaintiff has to recover for all losses, whether past, present or future, at the same time. This is of significance to the issue of compensating the plaintiff for reduction in quality of life as it is only in the unusual circumstances covered by the Supreme Court Act 1981 sec. 32A when a court may allow a case to be reopened where the plaintiff's condition deteriorates subsequent to the trial being concluded.

Consequently, only at the trial does the plaintiff have an opportunity to demonstrate to the court the effect of the injury on quality of life. This is unsatisfactory as judicial decisions as to the extent of the effect of the injury on the plaintiff are determined often on the basis of a short period of testimony by the plaintiff, albeit supported by medical evidence in some cases. We have already noted that the medical profession is not always aware of the true extent or effect of illness or injury on patients. Thus this period of testimony by the plaintiff is of considerable importance as is demonstrated in cases where the judiciary has refused to award compensation where the plaintiff is unaware of the extent and effect of the injury,[13] and in cases where the judiciary has refused to award damages because they have not been convinced by the plaintiff's testimony as to the degree of change which the injury has brought to the plaintiff's life.

It may be immediately argued that if the plaintiff cannot prove a deterioration in quality of life, then no compensation should be paid. Initially, one would tend to agree. Yet such agreement is premised on the supposition that it is possible for the tort system, as it operates at present, to discover the true effect of the injury on the plaintiff's quality of life. This must be doubted given the adversarial nature of the process and the stress on the average plaintiff of testifying about psychological and emotional issues in court.

A distinct problem exists with the current method of awarding compensation for reductions in quality of life. Either the plaintiff must adopt a demeanour of constant complaint in testimony, or risk not having the true effect of the injury on quality of life recognised. Such a requirement on the plaintiff is objectionable for two reasons: first, if the law of negligence is really to work on the basis of compensating the plaintiff for loss, the most which should be required of the plaintiff is to adduce evidence of the reduction in quality of life, not to engage in dramatic performances; secondly, some plaintiffs will be sufficiently subdued by legal procedures so as to be incapable of expressing the true effect of the injury on quality of life, resulting in a reduced award of damages. In a number of cases, judges have declared that the compensation due to a plaintiff should not be dependent on the plaintiff adopting a 'long face' in the witness box.[14] However, current evidentiary problems of demonstrating reduction in quality of life would, if anything, encourage a plaintiff to exaggerate the extent of the change in quality of life in order to be assured of some measure of adequate compensation. The question to be asked is whether the law of negligence is to operate as a lottery (Ison, 1967) awarding damages to good actors, or whether some other method of assessment can be found to rationalise the system somewhat more.

The new method which we seek to import into compensation cases is a process developed to measure changes in individuals' health and quality of life. The subjective health assessment system, if administered in the way we propose, could yield benefits to both courts and plaintiffs in clarifying one difficulty encountered by the law in the area of personal injuries compensation.

Perceived health measurement: What it is and why it is important

The term measurement as used in the physical sciences conveys an impression of a procedure based on well established criteria (Kind

1988). The situation in the social sciences is somewhat different. There are numerous methods suggested for measuring areas such as intelligence, personality, attitudes, and mental state. For the most part lawyers have remained largely unconvinced by such methods, preferring more traditional methods as employed by the medical profession. However, whilst it may be tempting for the lawyer to resort to the (seemingly) more objective measures of health which medical practitioners can furnish, such an approach overlooks research which suggests that medical practitioners often have quite a different view of the state of their patients' health than the patients themselves do. For example, it has been estimated that general practitioners are unaware of almost half of the disabilities of patients in their care, despite the fact such ailments may have pervasive effects upon the patients' lives (Patrick, Peach & Gregg 1982; Brody 1980; Fitzpatrick & Hopkins 1981). This research is of obvious importance to personal injuries litigation where reliance is placed on medical testimony as the means of measuring the effect of injury on quality of life.

A result of this research has been the development of instruments to measure quality of life and perceived health status. Perceived health status refers to individuals' own subjective evaluation of the impact of illness on their daily lives. As Hunt et al (1986) remark, it has sometimes been suggested that perceived health status may simply be no more than a subjective assessment determined more by social and psychological factors than by any basis in actual illness state. However, they also remark that belief about illness is an intervening variable between objective health (ie health status as measured clinically by the medical profession) and the adoption of what Parsons (1951) calls the sick role. Thus, subjective assessments of health are important to those making them. It is through subjective assessments of health that individuals refer themselves to the medical profession.

Measures of quality of life have not historically been part of medical assessment. However, quality of life has historically been inferred indirectly from more traditional measures. Thus, quality of life assessments made by clinicians are based upon data gained from traditional measures of health. The advances of scientific medicine have caused doctors to develop a substantial distrust of information which does not come from laboratories (Leighton Reed, 1988). However, increasing realisation of the importance of the patient's perspective has caused attention to shift from purely medical measures gained from laboratory, clinical and radiological assessment, to include subjective health assessment.

How can we measure quality of life?

Methods and techniques of subjective health measurement are continuously being refined and developed. A great deal has been written concerning difficulties in measurement of subjective assessments of health. There are some, such as those who seek to develop Quality Adjusted Life Years (QALY's),[15] who wish to measure health in a global sense (Sackett et al; 1977) and gain a single score or 'index' of well being; others argue that health is a multidimensional concept and that profiles, covering numerous areas which ill health can affect, should be used to measure subjective well being (Ware, 1987). However, a number of questionnaires have become established and are increasingly used in the assessment of quality of life and subjective health for the purposes of providing improved care through a better understanding of the subjective effect of ill health on the patient, and for evaluation in clinical drug trials, discussed further below.

Health status measures can be constructed as specific measures for use with a single patient group, or as generic indicators of health, which permit for comparison of perceived health across illness groups. Thus, for example, the Arthritis Impact Measurement Scales and the Stanford Health Assessment Questionnaire (Meenhan et al; 1980) were both designed to assess subjective health in rheumatoid arthritis patients. On the other hand, the Sickness Impact Profile (SIP) (Bergner, 1988), the Nottingham Health Profile (Hunt et al; 1986) (NHP) and the RAND Medical Outcomes Study Questionnaires[16] were all designed with the intention that they could be used upon different groups and results could be compared. At the time of writing the most frequently used measures are the SIP (and the English derivative of the SIP the Functional Limitations Profile (FLP)), and the NHP. This section of the essay will outline how these questionnaires were designed and validated, and to what uses they have been put so far.

Design and validity of the questionnaires

Both the SIP/FLP and the NHP were developed in similar ways. Broadly speaking, the designers of these questionnaires wished to tap aspects of health that were of importance to lay people rather than to clinicians. For example the designers of the NHP remark,

> Traditional psychological measurement items or statements have generally been written by the person developing the measure. A large pool of statements is produced and each is then tested out in a number of ways, checking for such requisites as lack of ambiguity, meaningfulness, relevance... Such an approach may well provide a test which is psychometrically good but which may reflect the understanding and attitude of the test constructor (Hunt et al; 1986, p.76).

To overcome the problem of questionnaire constructors imposing their own understandings and attitudes onto the questionnaires they develop it is possible to sample from an appropriate population, and request them to invent statements tapping the area under study. Both the NHP and SIP/FLP were developed by asking lay people to create statements describing undesirable aspects of ill health. From the statements given, repetitions and statements that could not be understood were removed. The remaining statements were then rated for severity. The statements were thus scaled and appropriate weights were attached. The method of weighting used for these questionnaires is beyond the scope of this chapter, but is summarised elsewhere.[17] Each statement carries a specific value assigned to it on these basis of a ranking technique. The value reflects the severity of the statement as ranked by the lay respondents.

The administration of the questionnaire required individuals to respond 'yes' or 'no'. The final scores in such questionnaires depend on the number and severity of items that respondents affirm. The questionnaires all contain a number of sections, on, for example, mobility, emotional reactions, pain, sleep disturbances, etc. Individual scores are calculated for every dimension. The table below gives a sample of the sort of questions asked on the NHP and SIP. Respondents reply either 'yes' or 'no' to questions.

NHP Items:

I find it painful to change positions
I'm unable to walk at all
I have trouble getting up and downs stairs and steps
I'm in pain when I walk
I lie awake for most of the night
I'm in pain when I'm standing
I wake up feeling depressed

FLP Items:

I do not walk up or down hills
I get about in a wheelchair
I am in a restricted position all the time
I go out less often to enjoy myself
I stay in bed most of the time
I spend much of the day lying down to rest

There have been a number of trials on the validity and reliability of the NHP and SIP/FLP. Validity refers to the extent to which a questionnaire measures that which it purports to measure and reliability refers to the extent to which a questionnaire can be administered to individuals in the same state and gain similar scores. Clearly a questionnaire that fails these tests would be of little use to lawyers, clinicians or social scientists. Trials have been undertaken on subjective health indicators to determine their validity by administering the questionnaires to different groups and comparing scores. Whilst the very nature of subjective health assessment begins with the assumption that individuals are best placed to assess their own well being, it seems reasonable to assume that certain illness will be associated with higher scores on the questionnaires. If, for example, it was found that respondents at a minor procedures clinic scored higher than a chronically ill group this would cast doubt upon the validity of the questionnaire.

Similarly the questionnaires have been checked for their reliability over time.

The use of health assessment questionnaires

So far the ground has been prepared for the possible use of health assessment questionnaires in assessing awards of damages for personal injuries. Two important issues still remain to be addressed; where such questionnaires are currently used, and how they may be used in personal injury cases. This section will address both of these issues.

Subjective health assessment is a relatively recent phenomena. However, in the past decade interest in the area has grown substantially and use of health assessment questionnaires has moved beyond the realm of academic research into health care. There is evidence to suggest that health assessment questionnaires can uncover symptoms of which clinicians have been unaware in the patients under their care (Patrick et al; 1982). Further, the systematic collection of quality of life data in primary care medicine has begun to increase (Nelson et al; 1983). As has been noted elsewhere, health care professionals are becoming increasingly conscious of the fact that enhancing quality of life is one of the major goals of medical care and, subsequently, interest in subjective measurement of well being has grown. This interest has spread to drug companies who now include quality of life measures in clinical trials (Fletcher et al; 1987). For example, the NHP was administered in a drug trial study on rheumatoid arthritis patients, with scores on all the dimensions of the NHP being lower (and therefore indicating improvement) after treatment than before (Parr et al; 1989). Such use of a health assessment questionnaire is not isolated. The NHP was administered to patients who had undergone heart transplants in order to determine whether this major operation caused an improvement in the quality of life of those who had survived this risky procedure. Results indicated an overall improvement in the quality of life, as measured on the dimensions in the NHP (Buxton et al; 1985). Similarly the SIP has been shown to indicate change in patients undergoing treatment for hypothyroidism (Rockey et al; 1980). Such studies indicate that quality of life measurement, whilst still a field that is developing, is one in which there has been growing interest and belief. This interest is not simply confined to social scientists, but also to those working in applied medical and pharmaceutical environments.

Application of subjective health assessment methods to personal injury cases

Having outlined how the subjective health assessment questionnaire operates, it is necessary to explain how it is envisaged that the system would operate in personal injuries litigation.

Subjective health assessments would be of help in assessing reductions in quality of life where the assessment is given to a plaintiff on a repeated basis over a period of time, such as between the commission of the tort/discovery of the injury and the date of trial or the date of assessment of the claim in cases which do not proceed to trial. This would enable an assessment of the effect of the injury on the life of the person over the time span to be made, and also allow a better assessments to be made as to the long-term reduction in quality of life. This result would occur because the subjective health assessment questionnaire is specifically designed to show such information, through a measurement of how well the plaintiff responds to changes in quality of life.

Secondly, it may be possible to establish a general data set of the effect of certain injuries or events on people's lives. This could be used to provide courts and other assessors of claims with an initial benchmark against which to judge the extent of change in the individual plaintiff's life and thus award appropriate compensation. The existence of such information by supplementing the results of the individual questionnaire, could help avoid erroneous under/over estimation of the effect of an injury on the plaintiff's quality of life. Such data sets already exist for certain illnesses, and there is an increasing wealth of data on health status and various illness states, as well as data on scores from general populations currently being generated.

One problem which may cause courts to be wary of such data is its subjective nature. A perceived problem of using subjective health assessment questionnaires in legal cases may be the danger of plaintiffs providing false information in the hope of increasing compensation awards. As against this objection, it is necessary to point out that the inducement to fabricate is not exclusive to the use of questionnaires. Rather, it is a problem faced by the medical and legal profession generally where reliance is placed on the results of even 'objective' medical testimony based on clinical observation as to pain and suffering. Moreover, the current method of the plaintiff testifying as to the effect of an injury on quality of life is no less subjective an inquiry. It is the failure of that system to provide sufficiently accurate information which has prompted this call for the use of additional and alternative assessment methods.

Certainly the possibility of respondents completing questionnaires with an eye to the potential rewards of compensation may cause them to over-report their symptoms. However, we are not advocating the use of such questionnaires alone, but also with standard clinical assessments, and other data furnished from the medical profession. Hopefully, this will provide a fuller view of the state of health of the plaintiff. There has been little in the way of attempts to quantify health status in personal injury cases, and the system suggested here may go some way towards assisting this calculation by courts. Certainly such questionnaires will provide a basis for further exploration. The respondent who gains high scores on health status questionnaires can be further examined in a court. Similarly, the NHP designers have suggested that their questionnaire can be useful in the clinical interview (Hunt et al; 1986). It may tap into areas of concern for patients that doctors may not cover, and patients may simply fail to report.

A second objection which may be raised is that in assessing reductions in quality of life, the yardstick used may be seen as too qualitative. Quantitative determination is far more preferable for assessment purposes. Writing in the context of ascertaining the extent of the plaintiff's pain and suffering. Pound stated

> [t]here are obvious difficulties of proof in such cases, so that false testimony as to mental suffering may be adduced easily and is very hard to detect. Hence this individual interest has to be balanced carefully with a social interest against the use of the law to further imposture (Pound 1924).

Again, such an argument has little application to subjective health assessment questionnaires as the assessment method used in these has a distinct quantitative result. In advocating the use of subjective health assessment questionnaires, it must be emphasised that we are not advocating a complete change from the present system of primarily objective assessment of damages. Rather, we wish to argue that by supplementing existing methods of assessment with information derived from subjective health assessment questionnaires, the system of personal injuries compensation can be improved.

Conclusion

It is not the contention of this essay that compensation for reduction in quality of life should be determined by the evidence of medical sociologists, or other experts, whether social scientists or not (Kenny 1983). Moreover, nothing in our suggestion for reform seeks to remove the ability of lawyers on either side to cross-examine the expert witness in relation to the result of the subjective health assessment questionnaire and the weight that should be given to the witness's testimony generally.

The introduction of information which measures the effect of changes in quality of life and health is not intended to determine the outcome of a claim for compensation. The mere fact that an expert states that data is statistically significant does not determine the case (Kaye 1983). Rather than seeking to pre-empt the judicial role of decision making, the justification advanced for the introduction of subjective health assessment information is more modest: the current system of reliance on objective information from the medical profession and, where possible, testimony by the plaintiff, cannot adequately respond to the needs of the courts or of plaintiffs in cases concerning reduction of quality of life. On the other hand, subjective health assessment questionnaires can provide sufficient reliable information for the courts to award adequate compensation while maintaining vigilance against the fraudulent plaintiff. They provide information which can assist in a quantitative assessment of reduction of 'quality of life'.

* Jenkinson, Research Fellow Nuffield College Oxford.
** Wilkinson Barrister at Law, D.Phil student Nuffield College Oxford.

1. According to Hazel Genn, (1987)

(Harris et al) showed that only a small proportion of those people injured in accidents each year actually initiate claims for damages; that only 80 per cent of those claims initiated achieve any kind of settlement..; that the settlements reached are generally for relatively small amounts... and that in two thirds of cases settlement is concluded on the basis of the first offer from the defendant's insurers.

2. At pp. 75-81.

In general, evidence from interviews suggested that some of the greatest difficulties in constructing claims were encountered when attempting to estimate the quantum of damages. This seemed to present more of a problem in general than deciding whether or not the defendant was guilty of any negligence in the first place. Both claims inspectors and solicitors talked of the imprecision involved in estimating quantum, especially in relation to future losses of earnings and general damages for pain and suffering ...Overall 75 per cent of solicitors said that it was 'difficult' to estimate general damages and 13 per cent said it was 'very difficult' to estimate general damages. ..All solicitors, barristers and claims inspectors were asked how they approached the estimation of quantum, especially general damages. Some claims inspectors adopted a rough formula based on the number of weeks of hospitalisation, incapacity, and difficulty in functioning multiplied by a notional sum...Most of those interviewed, however, could not express the way in which they arrived at an assessment of quantum, generally saying that it was a matter of 'feel'...The quality of the information collected by the parties to a large degree determines the outcome of settlement negotiations. The substance of face-to-face negotiations turns on the 'facts' which the parties have to hand and which they can call to give substance to their demands.

3. Genn, notes at page 78 that

.... imprecision of the process and uncertainty about how a judge would view any particular combination of injuries on any given plaintiff has at least two important effects on the settlement process. First it makes it difficult for a plaintiff to argue convincingly against a claims inspector making a low offer of settlement while being confident that a judge would agree. Second, imprecision provides the conditions in which almost any settlement can ultimately be justified.

4. [1962] 1 Q.B. 638.

5. [1964] A.C. 326.

6. According to Upjohn L.J. in *Wise v Kaye* 'it would be a slur upon the law, if the complete doctrine is that it is cheapest to kill but if you cannot kill then reduce the damages by injuring him so severely that it is most improbable that he can personally use the damages'.

7. 'The fact of unconsciousness does not .... eliminate the actuality of the deprivation of the ordinary experiences and amenities of life which may be the inevitable result of some physical injury' (per Lord Morris in *West v Shephard*).

8. Note that while the House of Lords adopted the conceptual approach in *Wise v Kaye* [1962] 1 Q.B. 638, and confirmed this in *West v Shephard* [1964] A.C. 326 and *Lim Poh Choo v Camden and Islington Area Health Authority* [1979] 2 All ER 910, it appears that the amount of any award will be increased where the plaintiff shows awareness of the loss suffered. Note also that the Administration of Justice Act 1982 sec. 1(1)(a) requires the plaintiff to be conscious of loss of expectation of life before compensation

can be awarded.

9. *Skelton v Collins* (1966) 39 A.L.J.R. 480.

10. Ogus characterised the personal approach as having the following benefits

> .... anomalies arising from the conceptual approach would disappear: compensation would be based on the loss rather than the injury; there would be no question of any punitive considerations applying; the dependants would receive no windfall; and the victim would recover compensation only to the extent that he appreciated his conditions.

However, he saw the adoption of the functional approach as having a further advantage: 'by requiring the plaintiff to show that the money awarded would serve a useful function, the doctrine is drawing near to the fundamental notion in the law of damages of *restitutio in integrum*'.

11. For example, Denning M.R. in *Lim Poh Choo v Camden and Islington Area Health Authority* [1979] 1 All ER 332 favoured the functional approach, but this preference was not adopted by the House of Lords [1979] 2 All ER 910.

12. While a court can make an award conditional on the plaintiff's health deteriorating in the future, most cases are resolved on the basis of a once-off judgment. The problems inherent in the finality of the method of making awards were commented upon by Lord Scarman in *Lim Poh Choo v Camden and Islington Area Health Authority* as follows

> [t]he course of the litigation illustrates with devastating clarity, the insuperable problems implicit in a system of compensation for personal injuries which (unless the parties agree otherwise) can yield only a lump sum assessed by the court at the time of judgment.. the award is final; it is not susceptible to review as the future unfolds, substituting fact for estimate. Knowledge of the future being denied to mankind, so much of the award is to be attributed to future loss and suffering..(and)..will almost certainly be wrong. There is really only one certainty: the future will prove the award to be either too high or too low.

13. Compare *H. West & Son Ltd. v Shephard* and *Lim Poh Choo v Camden and Islington Area Health Authority* where damages were awarded using the conceptual approach, with the Australian case of *Skelton v Collins* where the functional approach was adopted; similarly, see the Canadian trilogy of cases *Andrews v Grand & Toy Albert Ltd.* (1978) 83 D.L.R. (3d) 452; *Arnold v Teno* (1973) 83 D.L.R. (3d) 609; *Thornton v Board of School Trustees of School District No.52 (Prince George)* (1978) 1 W.W.R. 607; and the Irish case of *Cooke v Walsh* [1984] I.L.R.M. 208, where the difference in approaches affected compensation awarded.

14. 'It would be lamentable if the trial of a personal injury claim put a premium on protestations of misery and if a long face was the only safe passport to a large award' (per Lord Pearce, in *West v Shephard*). Although written in the context of support for the conceptual approach, the quotation seems nonetheless appropriate.

15. This area of research is predominantly undertaken by health economists who argue that the demand for health care is unlimited, yet resources available for health care are limited. Thus when assessing a patient for a possible medical intervention clinicians should not only concern themselves with how long an individual may live if treatment is successful, but should also consider the quality of life of an individual. If an intervention will prolong life, but the quality of life is poor, then those advocating the use of QALY data would suggest an intervention may be inappropriate. Much of the debate centres on the paper of Rosser, and Kind, (1978) 'A scale of valuations for states of illness: is there a social concensus?', *International Journal of Epidemiology*, vol. 7, p.347-358, in which they report results of how much better or worse than death were varying states of ill health. The states of health have two dimensions of disability and distress. In their study they asked subjects to rank in order six cards with typed descriptions of health states incorporating a wide range of distress/disability combinations. Subjects were asked to specify how many more times better off an individual in one state of health was than another person with ostensibly higher levels of disability and/or distress. This work forms the basis of much British QALY research with all states of health supposedly falling into one of Rosser and Kind's categories. Whilst using such a matrix to allocate resources may in itself seem questionable, it is perhaps even more so when one considers that

only 70 people were interviewed in the original exercise. Further, ill health is a multi-dimensional concept and reducing a state of health to a single figure seems both optimistic and misleading.

16. The RAND Medical Outcomes Study was a large scale survey undertaken in the United States of America with the intention of determining whether variations in patient outcomes could be explained by differences in systems of care, clinician speciality and skills. It was intended that for this research practical tools would be developed for use in routine monitoring of patient outcomes in medical practice. Work from this study is summarised in Wells, K.B. et al (1989) and also in Tarlov, A.R. et al (1989).

17. The method of weighting the SIP is fully explained in Bergner et al, (1988) and the re-weighting of this questionnaire for use in Britain is outlined in Patrick, D. and Peach H. (1989). The method of scaling used to weight the NHP is summarised in Hunt, S., McEwen, J., and McKenna, S. (1986).

Bibliography

Advisory Council on the Misuse of Drugs Report (1989), *AIDS and Drug Misuse*, HMSO, London.

Almond, B. (1990), (ed.) *AIDS: A Moral Issue*, Macmillan, London.

Armstrong, D. (1976), 'The decline of the medical hegemony: a review of government reports during the NHS', *Social Science and Medicine*, vol. 10, pp.157-63.

Armstrong, D. (1983), *Political Anatomy of the Body*, Cambridge University Press, Cambridge.

Armstrong, D. (1986), 'The patient's view', *Social Science and Medicine*, vol. 18, p.737.

Atiyah, P. (1980), *Accidents, Compensation and the Law*, Weidenfeld and Nicolson, London.

Bainham, A. (1987), 'Handicapped Girls and Judicial Parents,' *Law Quarterly Review* vol. 103, p.334.

Barthes, R. (1972), *Myth Today*, Hill & Wang, New York.

Bell, D., Layton, A.J., Gabbey, J. (1991), 'Use of a guideline based questionnaire to audit hospital care of acute asthma', *British Medical Journal*, vol. 302, pp.1440-3.

Benjamin, W. (1986), *Reflections, Essays, Aphorisms and Autobiographical Writings*, Schoken Books, New York.

Benn, S. & Peters, R. (1975), *Social Principles and the Democratic State*, George Allen & Unwin, London.

Bennett, C. (1990), 'A life sentence cut short', *The Correspondent Magazine*, 18 March.

Bennington, G. (1988), *Lyotard, Writing the event*, Manchester University Press, Manchester.

Bennington, G. (1990), 'Postal politics and the institution of the nation', in Bhabha, H. (ed), *Nation and Narration*, Routledge, London.

Bergner, M. (1988), 'The Development, Testing and Use of the Sickness Impact Profile', in Walker, S. & Rosser, R. (eds), *Quality of Life: Assessment and Application*, MTP/Kluwer, Lancaster.

Besley, T. (1988), 'A simple argument for merit good arguments', *Journal of Public Economics*, p.35.

Besley, T. (1991), 'The Demand for Health Care and Health Insurance', in McGuire, Fenn, and Mayhew (eds), *Providing Health Care: The Economics of Alternative Systems of Finance and Delivery*, Oxford University Press, Oxford.

Bettle, J. (1987), 'Suing Hospitals Direct: Whose Tort is it Anyhow ?', *New Law Journal*, vol. 137, pp.537-77.

Bhabha, H. (1990), 'DissemiNation: time, narrative, and the margins of the modern nation', in H. Bhabha (ed.), *Nation and Narration*, Routledge, London.

Black, (1980), *Inequalities in Health: Report of a Research Working Group*, DHSS, London.

Black, N. (1990), 'Quality Assurance of Medical Care', *Journal of Public Health Medicine*, vol. 12, no. 2, pp.97-104.

Blanchot, M. (1986), *The Writing of the Disaster*, University of Nebraska Press, Lincoln.

Bloom, H. (1991), *The Book of J*, Faber, London.

Bluglass, R. (1990), 'Recruitment and Training of Prison Doctors', *British Medical Journal*, vol. 301, p. 249.

Blythe, T. (1990), 'The legal issues arising out of the implementation of Medical Audit', *Action on Audit*, pp28-36, Healthcare Independent, Colchester.

Bowden, D., Walshe. K. (1991), 'When medical audit starts to count', *British Medical Journal*, vol. 303, pp.101-3.

Bowden, P. (1976) 'Medical Practice: Defendants and Prisoners', *J. of Medical Ethics*, vol. 12, p. 163.

Brazier, M. (1990), 'Sterilisation: Down the Slippery Slope', *Professional Negligence*, vol. 6, p.25.

British Medical Association, (1987), *No-Fault Compensation Working Party Report*, British Medical Association, London.

British Paediatric Association, (1990), *Outcome Measurements for Child Health*, British Paediatric Association, London.

British Thoracic Society, (1990), 'Guidelines for Management of Severe Asthma in Adults: II -Acute Severe Asthma', *British Medical Journal*, vol. 301, pp797-800.

Brody, D. (1980), 'Physician recognition of behavioral, psychological and social aspects of medical care', *Archives of Internal Medicine*, vol. 140, pp.1286-89.

Brown, B. (1986), 'I read the metaphysic of morals and the

categorical imperative and it doesn't help me a bit', *Oxford Literary Review*, vol. 8, p.155.

Buck, N., Devlin, H.B., Lunn, J.N. (1987), *The Report of a Confidential Enquiry into Perioperative Deaths*, The Nuffield Provincial Hospitals Trust, London.

Bundesvereinigung Lebenshilfe, *Stellungnahme zur Sterilisation einwilligungsunfähiger Menschen*, Marburg.

Buxton, M., Acheson, R., Caine, N., Gibson., & O'Brien, B. (1985), *Cost and benefits of the heart transplant programmes at Harefield and Papworth Hospitals*, HMSO, London.

Calebresi & Bobbitt, (1978), *Tragic Choices*, Norton, New York.

Camus, A. (1962), *The Plague*, Penguin, Harmondsworth.

Cane, P. (1987), *Accidents, Compensation and the Law*, Weidenfeld and Nicolson, London.

Canguihelm, M. (1949, 1987 ed), *The Normal and the Pathlogical*, Dordecht, The Hague.

Carlen, P. (1983), 'On rights and powers: some notes on penal politics' in D. Garland and P. Young (eds.), *The Power to Punish*, Heinemann, London.

Carroll, D. (1987), *Paraesthetics*, Methuen, London.

Carson, D. (1989), 'The Sexuality of People with Learning Difficulties', *Journal of Social Welfare Law*, p.355.

Carvel, A.L.M. & Hart, G.J. (1990), 'Risk behaviours for HIV infection among drug users in prison', *British Medical Journal*, vol. 300, pp.1383-4.

Casale S. (1984), *Minimum Standards for Prison Establishments*, NACRO, London.

Coester, M. (1991), 'Von anonymer Verwaltung zu persönlicher Betreuung - Zur Reform des Vormunds- und Pflegschaftsrechts für Volljährige', *Juristische Ausbildung*, 1.

Collins, E & Klein, R. (1980), 'Equity and the NHS: Self-reported mobility, access, and primary care', *British Medical Journal*, vol. 281.

Collins, H. (1991), 'Methods and Aims of Comparative Contract Law', *Oxford Journal of Legal Studies*, vol. 11, p.396.

Committee on a National Strategy for AIDS (1986), *Confronting AIDS*, National Academic Press, Washington.

Conrad, J.P. (1982), 'What do the undeserving deserve?', in

Johnson, R. and Toch, H. (eds.), *The Pains of Imprisonment*, Sage, London and Beverley Hills.

Cooper, M. (1975), *Rationing Health Care*, Croom Helm, London.

Cooper-Stephenson, K. & Saunders, I. (1981), *Personal Injury Damages in Canada*, Carswell, Toronto.

Corea, G. (1985), 'The Reproductive Battle', in Corea et al (eds), *Man Made Woman; How the new Reproductive Technologies Affect Women*, Hutchinson, London.

Cornell, D. (1989), 'Post-structuralism, the ethical relation and the law', *Cardozo Law Review*, vol. 9, p.1587.

Council of Europe, (1988), *Human Rights in Prisons*, Council of Europe, Strasbourg.

Coward, R. (1989), *The Whole Truth*, Faber and Faber, London.

Curran, L. (1990), 'HIV in Prisons: Psychological Issues', *Prison Service Journal*, p.14.

Curran, L. (1990), 'HIV in prisons: psychological issues', *Prison Service Journal*, Spring, pp.14-16.

Dalton H.L. & Buris, S. (1987), (eds.) *AIDS and the Law*, Yale University Press, New Haven.

D'Eca, C. (1990), 'Medico-legal aspects of AIDS', in Harris, D. & Haigh, R. (eds), *Aids: A Guide to the Law*, Routledge, London.

De Certeau, M. (1986), *Heterologies: Discourse on the Other*, Manchester University Press, Manchester.

De Cruz, P. (1988), 'Sterilisation, Wardship and Human Rights', *Family Law*, vol. 18, p.6.

P. De Cruz (1990), 'Sterilisation of mentally handicapped persons: In Re C', *Journal of Child Law*, vol. 2, p.130.

Deleuze, G., Guattari, F. (1988), *A Thousand Plateaus: Capitalism and Schizophrenia*, Athlone: London.

De Man, P. (1979), *Allegories of Reading*, Yale University Press, New Haven.

Department of Health (DoH) (1989a), *Working for Patients*, HMSO, London.

DoH (1989b), *Working for Patients*, Working Paper 6 - Medical Audit, HMSO London.

DoH (1989c), *Claims of medical negligence against NHS hospital and community doctors and dentists*, circular HC(89)34.

DoH (1990a), *The Quality of Medical Care - Report of the*

239

Standing Medical Advisory Committee, HMSO, London.

DoH (1990b), *Report of the Advisory Group on Nurse Prescribing*, HMSO London.

DoH, Welsh Office, Scottish Home and Health Department, DHSS (1972), *Management Arrangements for the Reorganised Health Service*, HMSO, London.

DHSS (1986), *Report of the Review of Community Nursing*, HMSO, London.

DHSS Northern Ireland (1991), *Report on Confidential Enquiries into Maternal Deaths in the United Kingdom 1985-87*, HMSO, London.

Derrida, J. (1978), *Writing and Difference*, Routledge, London.

Derrida, J. (1982), *Margins of Philosophy*, Harvester Press, Brighton.

Derrida, J. (1986a), 'Declarations of independence', *New Political Science*, vol. 15, p.7.

Derrida, J. (1986b), *Memoires: for Paul de Man*, Columbia University Press, New York.

Derrida, J. (1989a), 'Psyche: inventions of the Other', in L. Waters, W. Godzich (eds), *Reading de Man Reading*, University of Minnesota Press, Minneapolis.

Derrida, J. (1989b), 'Devant la loi', in A. Udoff (ed.), *Kafka and the Contemporary Critical Performance*, Indiana University Press, Bloomington.

Derrida, J. (1990), 'The force of law: the "mystical foundation of authority"', *Cardozo Law Review*, vol.11, p.919.

De Saint Exupery, A. (1939, 1975 ed), *Wind, Stars and Sand*, Pan, London and Sydney.

Dias, R. & Markesinis, B. (1984), *Tort Law*, Clarendon Press, Oxford.

Doanne, M.A. (1990), 'Technophelia: technology, representation and the feminine', in M. Jacobus, E. Fox Keller, S. Shuttleworth (eds.), *Body/Politics*, Routledge, London.

Donzelot, (1979), *The Policing of Families*, Hutchinson, London.

Douzinas, C., Warrington, R., McVeigh, S. (1991a), *Postmodern Jurisprudence*, Routledge, London.

Douzinas, C., Warrington, R. (1991b), 'Posting the law; social contracts and the postal rule's grammatology', *International Journal of the Semiotics of Law*, vol. 4, p.115.

Douzinas, C., Warrington, R. (1991c), 'A well founded fear of justice', *Law and Critique*, vol.2, p.115.

Doyal, L. (1981), *The Political Economy of Health*, Pluto, London.

Duff, R.A. (1990), *Intention, Agency and Criminal Liability*, Blackwell, Oxford.

Dworkin, A. (1984), *Pornography: Men Possessing Women*, The Womens Press, London.

Dyer, C. (1987), 'Decisions from the House of Lords', *British Medical Journal*, vol. 294, p.1219.

Edelman, B. (1979), *Ownership of the Image*, RKP, London.

Eisenberg, J.M. (1986), *Doctors' Decisions and the Cost of Medical Care*, Health Administration Press Perspectives, Ann Arbor, Michigan.

Elston, M.A. (1991), 'The politics of professional power: medicine in a changing health service', in Gabe, J., Calnan, M., & Bury, M., (eds), *The Sociology of the Health Service*, Routledge, London.

Eser, A. (1986), 'Reform of German Abortion Law: First Experiences', *American Journal of Comparative Law*, vol. 34, p.369.

Eser, A. (1989), *Legal Aspects of Bioethics*, Proceedings of the 1st Symposium of the Council of Europe on Bioethics, Strasbourg.

Evans, J.D. (1991), 'A Lawyers Perspective', *Medical Audit News*, vol. 1, no. 1, January.

Faden, R., Beauchamp, T. (1986), *A History and Theory of Informed Consent*, Oxford University Press, Oxford.

Faulder, C. (1985), *Whose Body Is It? The Problem Of Informed Consent*, Virago, London.

Fennell, P. (1990), 'Inscribing Paternalism in the Law: Consent to Treatment and Mental Disorder', *Journal of Law and Society*, vol. 17, p.29.

Finch, J. (1982), 'A costly oversight' *New Law Journal*, vol. 132, pp. 176-77.

Finger, P. (1988), 'Zulässigkeit einer Sterilisation geistig Behinderter aus eugenischer oder sozialer Indikation', *Medizinrecht*, p.231.

Fitzpatrick, R. & Hopkins, A. (1981), 'Patients' satisfaction with communication in neurological outpatient clinics', *Journal of*

Psychosomatic Research, vol. 25, pp.329-34.

Fitzpatrick, R. (1990), Measurement of Patient Satisfaction, in Hopkins, A. and Costain, D. (eds) *Measuring the Outcomes of Medical Care*, The Royal College of Physicians of London, London.

Fletcher, A., Hunt, S., & Bulpitt, C. (1987), 'Evaluation of Quality of Life in Clinical Trials of Cardiovascular Disease', *Journal of Chronic Diseases*, vol. 40, pp.557-566.

Foot, M. (1973), *Aneurin Bevan*, Davis Poynter, London.

Forsyth, G. (1966), *Doctors and State Medicine*, PHMAN, Hamburg.

Fortin, J. (1988), 'Sterilisation, the Mentally Ill and Consent to Treatment', *Modern Law Review*, vol. 51, p.634.

Foucault, M. (1976), *The Birth of the Clinic*, Tavistock, London.

Foucault, M. (1977), *Discipline and Punish*, Pantheon Books, New York.

Foucault, M. (1988), 'The ethic of care for the self as a practice of freedom: an interview with M. Foucault on January 20th, 1984', in J.Bernauer, D. Rasmussen (eds.), *The Final Foucault*, MIT Press, Cambridge, MA.

Freeman, M. (1988), 'Sterilising the Mentally Handicapped', in M. Freeman (ed.), *Medicine, Ethics and the Law*, Sweet & Maxwell, London.

Freidson, E. (1970a), *Professional Dominance*, Atherton Press, New York.

Freidson, E.(1970b), *Profession of Medicine*, Dodd, Mead & Co., New York.

Freidson, E.(1977), 'The futures of professionalism' in Stacey, M., Reid, M., Heath, C., & Dingwall, R. (eds), *Health and the Division of Labour*, Croom Helm, London.

Freud, S. (1913), *Totem and Taboo*, Standard Edition vol. 13, Hogarth Press, London.

Freud, S. (1986), *The Essentials of Psychoanalysis*, Penguin, Harmondsworth.

Fox Keller, E. (1990), 'From secrets of life to secrets of death', in M.Jacobus, E. Fox Keller, & S. Shuttleworth (eds.), *Body/Politics*, Routledge, London.

Garcia, J., Garforth, S. (1991), 'Midwifery policies and policy-making', in Robinson, S., & Thomson, A.M., (eds) *Midwives, Research and Childbirth Volume II*, Chapman & Hall, London.

Gardner, S. (1991), 'Necessity's Newest Inventions', *Oxford Journal of Legal Studies*, vol. 11, p.125.

Genn, H. (1987), *Hard Bargaining*, Clarendon Press, Oxford.

General Medical Council, (1987), Professional Conduct and Fitness to Practice, British Medical Association, London.

Gewirth, A. (1978), *Reason and Morality*, University of Chicago Press, Chicago.

Gibson, S. (1989), 'The anatomy of autonomy', *Journal of Law and Society*, vol.16, p.373.

Gibson, S. (1990), 'Continental Drift: The Question of context in Feminist Jurisprudence', *Law and Critique*, vol. 1, no. 2, Autumn 1990.

Gillett, G. (1989), 'Informed consent and moral integrity', *Journal of Medical Ethics*, vol. 15, p.117.

Goldstein, R. (1989), 'AIDS and the social contract', in Carter and Watney (eds), *Taking Liberties*, Serpent's Tail, London.

Goodhart, A.L. (1938), 'Hospitals and Trained Nurses', *Law Quarterly Review*, vol. 54, pp553-575.

Goodin, R. (1989), 'Theories of Compensation', *Oxford Journal of Legal Studies*, vol. 9, p.55.

Goodrich, P. (1990), *Languages of Law*, Weidenfeld and Nicholson, London.

Grant, R. (1987), *John Locke's Liberalism*, University of Chicago Press, Chicago.

Greens, (1988), Die Grünen im Bundestag (eds.), *Sterilisation Behinderter - Hilfe statt Zwang*, Bonn.

Griffiths, J. (1979), 'Is Law Important', New York University Law Review, vol. 54, p.339.

Grimshaw, J. (1989), in Carter, E. and Watney, S. (eds.), *Taking Liberties*, Serpent's Tail, London.

Grimshaw, J. (1990), 'Inmates with HIV, A Double Sentence', *Prison Service Journal*, p. 22.

Grossman, M. (1972), 'On the concept of health capital and the demand for health', *Journal of Political Economy*, p.80.

Grunfeld, C.(1954), 'Recent Developments in the Hospital Cases' *Modern Law Review*, vol. 17, pp.547-556.

Guttmacher, S. (1990), 'HIV infection: individual rights v disease control', *Journal of Law and Society*, vol.17, no.1, pp.66-76.

Habermas, J. (1984), *The Theory of Communicative Action*, Beacon, Boston.

Ham, Dingwall et al (1988), *Medical Negligence, Compensation and Accountability*, King's Fund Publishing and Press Office, London.

Hanfling, O. (1987), *Life, a reader*, Basil Blackwell/Oxford University Press, Oxford.

Harding, T.M. (1987), 'AIDS in prison', *The Lancet*, p. 1260.

Harris, D. (1984), *Compensation and Support for Illness and Injury*, Clarendon Press, Oxford.

Harris, J. (1985), *The Value of Life*, RKP, London.

Harris, J. (1987), 'QALYfying the value of life', *Journal of Medical Ethics*, p.13

Hegel, G.W.F. (1969), *The Difference between Fichte's and Schelling's system of Philosophy*, S.U.N.Y. Press, Albany.

Hegel, G.W.F. (1969), *The Science of Logic*, Allen and Unwin, London.

Heidegger, M. (1962), *Being and Time*, Harper and Row, New York.

Heidegger, M. (1976), *The Question Concerning Technology*, Harper and Row, New York.

Heidegger, M. (1984), *Metaphysical Foundations of Logic*, Indiana University Press, Bloomington.

Hill, R.D. (1991), Paper delivered to Royal College of Physicians Conference on 4th July 1991, London.

Hirsch, G. & Hiersche, H. (1987), 'Sterilisation geistig Behinderter', *Medizinrecht*, p.135.

Hopkins, A. (1991), 'Approaches to Medical Audit', *Journal of Epidemiology and Community Health*, vol. 45, pp.1-3.

Horn, E. (1983), 'Strafbarkeit der Zwangssterilistion', *Zeitschrift für Rechtspolitik*, p.265.

Hornblum, A.M. (1990), 'The Condom Wars - Should America's Jails/Prisons Distribute Condoms?', *Prison Service Journal*, p. 20.

Hunt, S., McEwen, J. & McKenna, S. (1986), *Measuring Health Status*, Croom Helm, London.

Husser, E. (1964), *The Paris Lectures*, Nijhoff, The Hague.

Illich, (1981), *Limits to Medicine*, Penguin, Harmondsworth.

Illingworth, P. (1990), *AIDS and the Good Society*, Routledge, London.

Irvine, D. (1990), *Managing for Quality in General Practice*, King's Fund Centre, London.

Ison, T. (1967), *The Forensic Lottery*, Staples Press, London.

Ison, T. (1980), *Accident Compensation*, Croom Helm, London.

Jacobs, J.B. (1980), 'The prisoners' rights movement and its impacts, 1960-1980', in Morris & Tonry (eds.), *Crime and Justice: An Annual Review of Research, vol.2*, Chicago University Press, Chicago.

Jacob, J.M. (1988), *Doctors and Rules*, Routledge, London.

Jennett, B. (1988), 'Balancing Benefits and Burdens in Surgery', *British Medical Journal*, vol. 44, no. 2, pp499-513.

Jessop, E.G. (1990), 'Medical Audit: What the Purchaser Expects', *Action on Audit*, pp.13-22, Health Care Independent, Colchester.

Jolliffe, D. (1990), 'HIV/AIDS - the prison medical officer's perspective', *Prison Service Journal*, Spring, pp. 32-33.

Jones, M. (1989), 'Justifying medical treatment without consent', *Professional Negligence*, vol. 5, p.178.

Jonson, E. (1988), *AIDS. Myths, Facts and Ethics*, Pergamon Press, Sydney.

Kafka, F. (1971), 'Before the Law', in *Franz Kafka: The Complete Stories*, Schoken Books, New York.

Kafka, F. (1976a), *The Trial*, Martin Secker and Warburg, London.

Kafka, F. (1976b), *In the Penal Settlement*, Martin Secker and Warburg, London.

Kahn-Freund, O. (1951), 'Servants and Independent Contractors' *Modern Law Review*, vol.14, pp.504-9.

Kant, I. (1956a), *Critique of Practical Reason*, Bobbs-Merrill, Indianapolis.

Kant, I. (1956b), *Foundations of the Metaphysics of Morals*, Bobbs-Merrill, Indianapolis.

Kant, I. (1964), *Critique of Pure Reason*, MacMillan, London.

Kant, I. (1965), *On History*, Bobbs Merril, Indianapolis.

Kant, I. (1973), *Critique of Judgement*, Oxford University Press, Oxford.

Kaye, D. (1983), 'Statistical significance and the burden of persuasion', *Law and Contemporary Problems*, vol. 46, p.13.

Kennedy & Grubb, (1989), *Medical Law - Text and Materials*, Butterworths, London.

Kenny, A. (1983), 'The Expert in Court', *Law Quarterly Review*, vol. 99, p.197.

Kern, B. (1991), 'Die Bedeutung des Betreuungsgesetzes für das Arztrecht', *Medizinrecht*, p.66.

Kilgour, J. (1988), *Prison Service News*, vol.6, no. 54, July.

Kilgour, J. (1989), *Prison Service News*, vol. 7, no. 60, February.

Kilgour, J. (1989), *Prison Service News*, vol. 7, no. 65, July.

Kitzinger, J., Green, J., Coupland, V. (1990), 'Labour relations: midwives and doctors on the labour ward', in Garcia, J. Kilpatrick, R., & Richards, M., (eds), *The Politics of Maternity Care*, Oxford University Press, Oxford.

Klein, R. (1971), 'Accountability in the NHS', *Political Quarterly*, vol. 42.

Klein, R. (1973), *Complaints against Doctors*, Charles Knight, London.

Klein, R. (1989), *The Politics of the NHS*, Longman, Harlow.

Kind, P. (1988), 'The Development of Health Indices', in Teeling Smith (ed), *Measuring Health: A Practical Approach*, Wiley, Chichester.

Köttgen, D. (1988), *Deutscher Arzteblatt*, vol. 85, B51.

Kottow, M. (1986) 'Medical Confidentiality: an intransigent and absolute obligation', *J. of Medical Ethics*, vol. 22, p. 117.

Lachwitz, K. (1990), 'Das neue Betreuungsrecht. Perspektiven für Menschen mit geistiger Behinderung', *Familie und Recht*, p.266.

Lalumiere, C. (1989), *Allocations D'Ouvertare*, Proceedings of the 1st Symposium of the Council of Europe on Bioethics, Strasbourg.

Larkin, G. (1983), *Occupational Monopoly and Modern Medicine*, Tavistock, London.

Laufs, A. (1984), *Arztrecht*, C.H. Beck, Munich.

Lawler, J. (1991), *Behind the Screens*, Churchill Livingstone, London.

Lee, R. (1986), *Legal Control of Health Care Allocation*, Sonderruck.

Lee, R. & Miller, (1990), 'The Doctor's Changing Role in Allocating US and British Medical Services', *Law, Medicine and*

Health Care, vol. 18, no. 1.

Lee, R & Morgan, D. (1988), 'Sterilisation and Mental Handicap: Sapping the Strength of the State', *Journal of Law and Society*, vol. 15, p.229.

Lee, S. (1987), 'Towards a jurisprudence of consent', in J. Eekelaar and J. Bell (eds), *Oxford Essays in Jurisprudence, third series*, Oxford University Press, Oxford.

Le Grand, J. (1982), *The Strategy of Equality*, Allen Unwin, London.

Leighton Reed, J. (1988), 'The new era of quality of life assessment', in Walker, S. & Rosser, R., *Quality of Life: Assessment and Application*, MTP/Kluwer, Lancaster.

Lembcke, P.A. (1967), 'Evolution of the Medical Audit', *Journal of American Medical Association*, vol. 199, no. 8, February 20.

Lesser, H. & Pickup, Z. (1990), 'Law, ethics and confidentiality', *Journal of Law and Society*, vol.17, no.1, pp.17-28.

Levin, D.M. (1987), 'Psychopathology in the epoch of nihilism', in Levin (ed) *Psychopathologies of the Modern Self*, New York University Press, New York.

Levinas, E. (1986), *Totality and Infinity*, Nijhoff, The Hague.

Locke, J. (1963), *Two Treatises of Government*, ed. P Laslett, Cambridge University Press, Cambridge.

Lucas, J. (1985), *The Principles of Politics*, Clarendon Press, Oxford.

Lyotard, J-F. (1988a), *The Differend: Phrases in Dispute*, Manchester University Press, Manchester.

Lyotard, J-F. (1988b), *Peregrinations*, Columbia University Press, New York.

MacIntyre, A. (1981), *After Virtue*, Duckworth, London.

MacIntyre, A. (1988), *Whose Justice? Which Rationality?*, Duckworth, London.

McLachlin, B. (1981), 'What Price Disability? A Perspective on the Law of Damages for Personal Injury, *Canadian Bar Review*, vol. 59, p.1

McGuire, Fenn, and Mayhew, (1991), *Providing Health Care: The Economics of Alternative Systems of Finance and Delivery*, Oxford University Press, Oxford.

Maguire, Henderson & Mooney, (1988), *The Economics of Health*

Care, RKP, London.

Maguire, M. Vagg, J. and Morgan, R. (1985) (eds.) *Accountability in Prisons*, Tavistock, London.

Mahnkopf, A. & Spengler-Sadowski, K (1984), *Recht und Psychiatrie*, p.132.

Margolis, H. (1982), *Selfishness, Altruism and Rationality*, Cambridge University Press, Cambridge.

Martin, E. (1989), *The Woman in the Body*, Open University Press, Milton Keynes.

Mason, J. & McCall Smith, A. (1991), *Law and Medical Ethics*, Butterworths, London.

Masters, W.H., Johnson, V.E. & Kolodny, R.C. (1988), *Crisis: Heterosexual Behaviour in the Age of AIDS*, Weidenfeld and Nicolson, London.

Meenhan, R., Gertman, P., & Mason, J. (1980), 'Measuring Health Status in Arthritis: the Arthritis Impact Measurement Scales' *Arthritis and Rheumatism*, vol. 23, pp.146-52.

Mehlman, (1985), 'Rationing Expensive Lifesaving Medical Treatments', *Wisconsin Law Review*, p.239.

Miller, (1991), *Denial of Health Care and Informed Consent in Anglo-American Law*.

Ministry of Health (1954), *Legal proceedings*, Circular HM(54)32.

Ministry of Justice (1987), *Explanatory Memorandum on the preliminary draft of a law on guardianship*, November 1987, reprinted in *Der Frauenarzt* 1988, p.533.

Minson, G. (1985), *Genealogies of Morals*, MacMillan, London.

Montgomery, J. (1987), 'Suing Hospitals Direct: What Tort ?' *New Law Journal*, vol. 137, pp.703-05.

Montgomery, J. (1988), 'Power/Knowledge/Consent: Medical decision making', *Modern Law Review*, vol. 51, pp.245-251.

Montgomery, J. (1989), 'Medicine, Accountability and Professionalism', *Journal of Law and Society*, vol. 16, pp.319-339.

Montgomery, J. (1989b), 'Rhetoric and "Welfare"', *Oxford Journal of Legal Studies*, vol. 9, p.397.

Montgomery, J. (1990), 'Victims or threats? The framing of HIV', *Liverpool Law Review*, vol. xxi, 1, p.26.

Montgomery, J. (1991), 'Rights, Restraints and Pragmatism' (1991) *Modern Law Review*, vol. 54, pp.524-534.

Mooney & Olsen, (1991), 'QUALYs: Where Next?' in McGuire, Fenn & Mayhew (eds), *Providing Health Care: the Economics of Alternative Systems of Finance and Delivery*, Oxford University Press, Oxford.

Moran, L.J. (1988), 'Illness: a more onerous citizenship?', *The Modern Law Review*, pp.343-354.

Moran, L.J. (1990), 'HIV, AIDS and human rights', *The Liverpool Law Review*, vol. xxi, 1, pp.3-23.

Mordaunt, J. (1989), *Facing Up To Aids*, O'Brien Press, Dublin.

Morgan, D. (1990), Case note on Re F, *Journal of Social Welfare Law*, p.204.

Morgan, D. & Lee, R. (1991), *Abortion and Embryo Research, The New Law*, Blackstone, London.

Musgrave, R. (1959), *The Economics of Public Finance*, McGraw Hill, New York.

Nagel, T. (1970), *The Possibility of Altruism*, Princeton University Press, Princeton.

National Institute of Justice, (1989), *Aids in Correctional Facilities*, US Department of Justice, Washington.

Nelson, A.R. (1976), 'Orphan Data and the Unclosed Loop: A dilemma in PSRO and Medical Audit', *The New England Journal of Medicine*, vol. 295, no. 11, 9th September.

Nelson, E. (1983), 'Functional Health Status Levels of Primary Care Patients', *Journal of the American Medical Association*, vol. 239, pp.3331-3338.

Nielson, L. (1991), *The Right to a Child v The Right of a Child*, V11 World Conference of the International Congress of Family Law, Opatija.

Ogbourne, D. & Ward, R. (1989), 'Sterilisation, the Mentally Incompetent and the Courts', *Anglo-American Law Review*, vol. 18, p.230.

Ogus, A. (1972), 'Damages for lost amenities: for a foot, a feeling or a function', *Modern Law Review*, vol. 35, p.1.

Ovretveite, J. (1985), 'Medical dominance and the development of professional autonomy in physiotherapy', *Sociology of Health and Illness*, vol.7, pp.76-93.

Parr, G., Darekar, B., Fletcher, A., Bulpitt, C. (1989), 'Joint pain and Quality of Life', *British Journal of Clinical Pharmacology*, vol.

27, pp.235-243.

Parsons, T. (1951), *The Social System*, Free Press, New York.

Patrick, D., Peach, H., & Gregg, I. (1982), 'Disablement and Care: A comparison of patient views and general practitioner knowledge', *Journal of the Royal College of General Practitioners*, vol. 32, pp.429-434.

Paton, C. (1991), 'The Myths of Competition', *Health Services Journal*, 30th May, pp.22-23.

Pearson Commission (1978) *Civil Liability and Compensation for Personal Injury*, HMSO, London.

Pellegrino, E., Thomasma, D. (1981), *A Philosophical Basis of Medical Practice*, Columbia University Press, New York.

Petchesky, R. (1987), Foetal Images: The Power of Visual Culture, in Stanworth (ed), *Reproductive Technologies: Gender, Motherhood and Medicine*, Polity Press, Cambridge.

Pieroth, B. (1989), 'Verfassungsrechtliche Aspekte des para. 1905 Betreuungsgesetz-Entwurf', in Bundesvereinigung Lebenshilfe (ed.), *Regelungen zur Sterilisation einwilligungsunfähiger Personen im Betreuungsgesetz*, Report of an Interdisciplinary Colloquium held on May 10-11 1989.

Pieroth, B. (1990), 'Die Verfassungsmässigkeit der Sterilisation Einwilligungsunfähiger gemäss dem Entwurf für ein Betreuungsgesetz', *Zeitschrift für das gesamte Familienrecht*, p.117.

Pigou, A. (1928), *A Study in Public Finance*, Macmillan, London.

Porter, S. (1991), 'A participant observation study of power relations between nurses and doctors in a general hospital' *J. Advanced Nursing*, vol. 16, pp.728-735.

Pound, R. (1924), *Selected Essays on the Law of Torts*, Harvard Law Review Association, Cambridge, Mass.

Pritchard, J. (1989), *Personal Injury Litigation*, Longman, London.

Protocol (1990), *Deutscher Bundestag - Rechtsausschuss, Anlage zum Protokoll der 61. Sitzung vom 15./16. November 1989 zum Entwurf eines Betreuungsgesetzes*, January 3 1990.

Rawls, J. (1971), *A Theory of Justice*, Harvard University Press, Cambridge, MA.

Redfield, R. & Tramont, E. (1989), 'Toward a better classification system for HIV infection', *New England Journal of Medicine*, pp.144-6.

Reis, H. (1988), 'Sterilisation bei mangelnder Einwillingungsfähigkeit', *Zeitschrift für Rechtspolitik*, p.318.

Richardson, G. (1984), 'Time to take prisoners' rights seriously', *Journal of Law and Society*, vol.11, pp.1-32.

Richardson, G. (1985), 'Judicial intervention in prison life', in Maguire, Vagg and Morgan, (eds.), *Accountability in Prisons*, Tavistock, London.

Richardson, R. (1988), *Death, Dissection and the Destitute*, Penguin, Harmondsworth.

Rivet, J. (1990), 'Sterilization and Medical Treatment of the Mentally Disabled: Some Legal and Ethical Reflections', *Med. Law* vol. 9, p.1150.

Robinson, S. (1989), 'Caring for childbearing women: the interrelationship between midwifery and medical responsibilities', in Robinson, S. & Thomson, A.M., (eds), *Midwives, Research and Childbirth Volume I*, Chapman & Hall, London.

Rockey, P. & Griep, J. (1980), 'Behavioural dysfunction in hyperthyroidism. Improvement with Treatment', *Archives of Internal Medicine*, vol. 140, pp.1194-1197.

Rose, G. (1984), *Dialectic of Nihilism*, Blackwell, Oxford.

Rose, N. (1988), *Governing the Soul*, Routledge, London.

Rousseau, J-J. (1953), *The Social Contract*, Nelson, London.

Rousseau, J. (1968), *Discourse on the Origins of Social Inequality*, ed. M. Cranston, Penguin, Harmondsworth.

Royal College of Physicians of London (1989), *Medical Audit: A First Report - What, why and how?*, Royal College of Physicians of London, London.

Sackett, D. (1977), 'The development and application of indices of health: general methods and summary of results', *American Journal of Public Health*, vol. 67, pp.423-428.

Schönke/Schröder (1986), *Strafgesetzbuch Kommentar*, 22nd Edition.

Schiterman, (1983), *Feminity: The Politics of the Personal*, Polity Press, Cambridge.

Schumacher, U. & Jürgens, A. (1988), 'Anmerkungen zum Betreuungsgesetzentwurf', *Recht und Politik*, no. 2, 2.

Schwab, D. (1990), 'Das neue Betreuungsrecht', *Zeitschrift für das gesamte Familienrecht*, p.681.

Scott, (1981), *The Body as Property*, Penguin, Harmondsworth.

Scroggie, F. (1990), 'Why do parents want their children sterilised? A broader approach to sterilisation requests', *Journal of Child Law*, vol. 2, p.25.

Seuss, (1957), *The Cat in The Hat*, Random House, New York.

Shaw, C.D. (1980), 'Acceptability of Audit', *British Medical Journal*, 14th June 1980, pp.1443 -1446.

Shaw, C.D. (1989) *Medical Audit - A Hospital Handbook*, The King's Fund Centre, London.

Shaw, J. (1986), 'Informed Consent: A German Lesson', *International and Comparative Law Quarterly*, vol. 35, p.864.

Shaw, J. (1990), 'Sterilisation of Mentally Handicapped People: Judges Rule OK?', *Modern Law Review*, vol. 53, p. 91.

Shaw, S. (1990), 'HIV and AIDS', *AMBoV Quarterly*, no.37, April.

Shelley, M. (1985), *Frankenstein*, Penguin, Harmondsworth.

Shilts, R. (1988), *And The Band Played On*, Penguin, Harmondsworth

Silverman, W.A. (1989), 'The myth of informed consent: in daily practice and in clinical trials', *Journal of Medical Ethics*, vol. 15, p.6.

Smith, R. (1991), 'Where is the Wisdom ..?', *British Medical Journal*, vol. 303, 5th October, pp.798-799.

Somervill, M. (1986), 'Pain and Suffering at the interfaces of Law and Medicine', *University of Toronto Law Journal*, vol. 36, p.286.

Sontag, S. (1978), *Illness as Metaphor*, Farrar, Strauss and Giroux, New York.

Sontag, S. (1989), *Aids and its Metaphors*, Farrar, Strauss and Giroux, New York.

Spivak, G. (1987), *In Other Worlds*, Routledge, London.

Stacey, M. (1988a), 'Regulating the Professions in the UK: Nurses, Doctors and Others', Lucile P. Leone Lecture, University of California, San Francisco.

Stacey, M. (1988b), *The Sociology of Health and Healing*, Unwin, London.

Standing Committee On Postgraduate Medical Education (1989) *Medical Audit - The Educational Implications*.

Steffen, G.E. (1988), 'Quality Medical Care', *Journal of American Medical Association*, vol. 260, no. 1.

Stewart, G. 'Allocation of Resources to Health', *Journal of Human Resources*, p.103.

Stoddard, T. (1989), 'Paradox and paralysis: an overview of the American response to AIDS', in Carter and Watney (eds), *Taking Liberties*, Serpent's Tail, London.

Swanwick, S.J. (1989), 'Point of View: A vote for no confidence' *J. of Medical Ethics*, vol. 25, p. 183.

Thomas, P.A. (1990), 'HIV/AIDS in Prison', *Howard Journal*, vol. 17, no. 1.

Treichler, P. (1990), 'Feminism, medicine, and the meaning of childbirth', in M.Jacobus, E. Fox Keller, S. Shuttleworth (eds.), *Body/Politics*, Routledge, London.

Turner, B.S. (1987), *Medical Power and Social Knowledge*, Sage, London.

UKCC (1984), *Code of Professional Conduct for the Nurse, Midwife and Health Visitor*, UKCC, London.

UKCC (1986), *Administration of Medicines*, UKCC, London.

UKCC (1989), *Exercising Accountability*, UKCC, London.

Unsworth, C. (1987), *The Politics of Mental Health Legislation*, Oxford University Press, Oxford.

Vaid, U. (1987), 'Prisons' in Dalton and Buris (eds.), *Aids and the Law*, Yale University Press, New Haven.

Vernant, D., Vidal-Naquet, P. (1990), *Myth and Tragedy in Ancient Greece*, Zone Books, New York.

Walshe, K., Bennett, J. (1991), *Guidelines on Medical Audit and Confidentiality*, Brighton Health Authority.

Ware, J. (1987), 'Standards for Validating health Measures: Definition and Content', *Journal of Chronic Diseases*, vol. 40, pp.481-489.

Wasmuth, C. (1957), 'Medical Evaluation of Mental Pain and Suffering', *Cleveland Marshall Law Review*, vol. 6, p.1

Watney, S. (1987), *Policing Desire*, Comedia, London.

Wedderburn, K. (1991), 'The Social Charter in Britain - Labour Law and Labour Courts?', *Modern Law Review*, vol. 54, p.1.

Weeks, J. (1981), *Sex, Politics and Society*, Longman, London.

Wemberg, J. (1984), 'Dealing with Medical Practice Variations, *Health Affairs*.

Willcocks, A. (1967), *The Creation of the NHS*, RKP, London.

Williams, A. (1985), 'Economics of coronary artery bypass grafting', *British Medical Journal*, vol. 291.

Wolf, N. (1990), *The Beauty Myth*, Vintage, London.

Wool, R.J. (1990), 'HIV/AIDS in Prison', *Prison Service Journal*, p.13.

Wunder, K. (1988), 'Die Sterilisation Behinderter und der Schatten der Geschichte,' *Kritische Justiz*, p.318.

Wunder, M. (1990), 'Betreuungsgesetz verabschiedet - Sterilisation ohne Einwilligung legalisiert', *Recht und Psychiatrie*, p.197.

Wyschogrod, E. (1990), *Saints and Postmodernism*, Chicago University Press, Chicago.

Young, R. (1990), *White Mythologies*, Routledge, London.

Zimmermann, W. & Damrau, J. (1991), 'Das neue Betreuungs- und Unterbringungsrecht', *Neue Juristische Wochenschrift*, p.538.